D1543665

Pro Full-Text Search in SQL Server 2008

Michael Coles with
Hilary Cotter

Apress®

Pro Full-Text Search in SQL Server 2008

Copyright © 2009 by Michael Coles and Hilary Cotter

ISBN-13 (pbk): 978-1-4302-1594-3

ISBN-13 (electronic): 978-1-4302-1595-0

Printed and bound in the United States of America 9 8 7 6 5 4 3 2 1

Lead Editor: Jonathan Gennick
Technical Reviewer: Steve Jones
Editorial Board: Clay Andres, Steve Anglin, Mark Beckner, Ewan Buckingham, Tony Campbell,
    Gary Cornell, Jonathan Gennick, Michelle Lowman, Matthew Moodie, Jeffrey Pepper,
    Frank Pohlmann, Ben Renow-Clarke, Dominic Shakeshaft, Matt Wade, Tom Welsh
Project Manager: Denise Santoro Lincoln
Copy Editor: Benjamin Berg
Associate Production Director: Kari Brooks-Copony
Production Editor: Laura Esterman
Compositor/Artist: Octal Publishing, Inc.
Proofreader: Patrick Vincent
Indexer: Broccoli Information Management
Cover Designer: Kurt Krames
Manufacturing Director: Tom Debolski

Distributed to the book trade worldwide by Springer-Verlag New York, Inc., 233 Spring Street, 6th Floor, New York, NY 10013. Phone 1-800-SPRINGER, fax 201-348-4505, e-mail orders-ny@springer-sbm.com, or visit http://www.springeronline.com.

For information on translations, please contact Apress directly at 2855 Telegraph Avenue, Suite 600, Berkeley, CA 94705. Phone 510-549-5930, fax 510-549-5939, e-mail info@apress.com, or visit http://www.apress.com.

Apress and friends of ED books may be purchased in bulk for academic, corporate, or promotional use. eBook versions and licenses are also available for most titles. For more information, reference our Special Bulk Sales–eBook Licensing web page at http://www.apress.com/info/bulksales.

The source code for this book is available to readers at http://www.apress.com.

For Devoné and Rebecca
—Michael

Contents at a Glance

Contents

About the Authors

 **MICHAEL COLES** is a Microsoft MVP with nearly 15 years' experience in SQL database design, T-SQL development, and client-server application programming. He has consulted in a wide range of industries, including the insurance, financial, retail, and manufacturing sectors, among others. Michael's specialty is developing and performance-tuning high-profile SQL Server–based database solutions. He currently works as a consultant for a business intelligence consulting firm. He holds a degree in information technology and multiple Microsoft and other certifications.

Michael has published dozens of technical articles online and in print magazines, including *SQL Server Central*, *ASPToday*, and *SQL Server Standard*. Michael is the author of the books *Pro SQL Server 2008 XML* (Apress, 2008) and *Pro T-SQL 2008 Programmer's Guide* (Apress, 2008), and he is a contributor to *Accelerated SQL Server 2008* (Apress, 2008). His current projects include speaking engagements and researching new SQL Server 2008 encryption and security functionality.

 **HILARY COTTER** is a SQL Server MVP with more than 20 years' IT experience working for Fortune 500 clients. He graduated from University of Toronto in applied science and engineering. He is the author of a book on SQL Server replication and has written numerous white papers and articles on SQL Server and databases.

About the Technical Reviewer

STEVE JONES, a Microsoft MVP, is the founder and editor of SQLServer-Central, the largest SQL Server community on the Internet. He has been working with SQL Server since 1991 and has published numerous books and articles on all aspects of the platform. He lives in Denver with his wife, three kids, three dogs, three horses, and lots of chores.

Acknowledgments

There are several people without whom this book would not be a reality. We'd like to start by thanking our editor, Jonathan Gennick. Thanks to Steve Jones, our technical reviewer and fellow MVP, for keeping us honest. Thank you to project manager Denise Santoro Lincoln for managing this project and keeping the lines of communication open between the team members. Also thanks to Sofia Marchant for assisting with project management. We'd also like to thank Benjamin Berg and Laura Esterman for making this book print-ready.

Special thanks go to Roman Ivantsov, inventor of the Irony.NET compiler construction kit, for assisting us in the development of the Irony.NET code sample. And special thanks also to Jonathan de Halleux, creator of the .NET ternary search tree code that's the basis for our spelling suggestion code samples.

We'd also like to thank the good folks at Microsoft who provided answers to all our questions and additional guidance: Alison Brooks, Arun Krishnamoorthy, Denis Churin, Fernando Azpeitia Lopez, Jacky Chen, Jingwei Lu, Josh Teitelbaum, Margi Showman, Ramanathan Somasundaram, Somakala Jagannathan, and Venkatraman Parameswaran.

Michael Coles would also like to thank Gayle and Eric Richardson; Donna Meehan; Chris, Jennifer, Desmond, and Deja Coles; Linda Sadr and family; Rob and Laura Whitlock and family; Vitaliy Vorona; and Igor Yeliseyev. Most of all, I would like to thank my little angels, Devoné and Rebecca.

Introduction

Begin at the beginning and go on till you come to the end . . .

—Alice in Wonderland

Linguistic (language-based) searching has long been a staple of web search engines such as Google and high-end document management systems. Many developers have created custom utilities and third-party applications that implement complex search functionality similar to that provided by the most popular search engines. What many people don't realize immediately is that SQL Server provides this advanced linguistic search capability out-of-the-box. Full-Text Search (FTS) has been included with SQL Server since the SQL Server 7 release. FTS allows you to perform linguistic searches of documents and text content stored in SQL Server databases using standard T-SQL queries. FTS is a powerful tool that can be used to implement enterprise-class linguistic database searches.

SQL Server 2008 increases the power of FTS by adding a variety of new features that make it easier than ever to administer, troubleshoot, and generally use SQL Server's built-in linguistic search functionality in your own applications. In this book, we'll provide an in-depth tour of SQL Server 2008's FTS features and functionality, from both the server and client perspective.

Who This Book Is For

This book is intended for SQL Server developers and DBAs who want to get the most out of SQL Server 2008 Integrated Full-Text Search (iFTS). To get the most out of this book, you should have a working knowledge of T-SQL, as most of the sample code in the book is written in SQL Server 2008 T-SQL. Sample code is also provided in C# and C++, where appropriate. Although knowledge of these programming languages is not required, basic knowledge of procedural programming will help in understanding the code samples.

How This Book Is Structured

This book is designed to address the needs of T-SQL developers who develop SQL Server–based search applications and DBAs who support full-text search on SQL Server. For both types of readers, this book was written to act as a tutorial, describing basic full-text search functionality available through SQL Server, and as a reference to the new full-text search features and functionality available in SQL Server 2008. The following sections provide a chapter-by-chapter overview of the book's content.

Chapter 1

Chapter 1 begins by putting full-text search functionality in context. We discuss the history of SQL Server full-text search as well as the goals and purpose of full-text search, and provide an overview of SQL Server 2008 Integrated Full-Text Search (iFTS) architecture. We also define the concept of search quality and how it relates to iFTS.

Chapter 2

In Chapter 2, we discuss iFTS administration, setup, and configuration. In this chapter, we show how to set up and populate full-text indexes and full-text catalogs. We discuss full-text index change-tracking options and administration via SQL Server Management Studio (SSMS) wizards and T-SQL statements.

Chapter 3

Chapter 3 introduces iFTS basic and advanced query techniques. We use this chapter to demonstrate simple FREETEXT-style queries and more advanced CONTAINS-style query options. We look at the full range of iFTS query styles in this chapter, including Boolean search options, proximity search, prefix search, generational search, weighted search, phrase search, and other iFTS search options.

Chapter 4

Chapter 4 builds on the search techniques demonstrated in Chapter 3 and provides demonstrations of client interaction with the database via iFTS. This chapter will show you how to implement simple iFTS-based hit highlighting utilities and search engine–style search interfaces.

Chapter 5

SQL Server iFTS supports nearly 50 different languages right out of the box. In Chapter 5, we explore iFTS support for multilingual searching. We describe the factors that affect representation of international character sets and multilingual searches. We also provide best practices around multilingual searching.

Chapter 6

SQL Server 2008 provides greater flexibility and more options for storing large object (LOB) data in your databases. Chapter 6 discusses the options available for storing, managing, and indexing LOB data in your database. In this chapter, we take a look at how SQL Server indexes LOB data, including use of the new FILESTREAM option for efficient storage and streaming retrieval of documents from SQL Server and the NTFS file system.

Chapter 7

In Chapter 7, we discuss iFTS stoplists, which help you eliminate useless words from your searches. We discuss word frequency theory, system stoplists, and creating and managing custom stoplists.

Chapter 8

Chapter 8 provides insight into iFTS thesauruses, with examples of the types of functionality that can be built using thesaurus expansion and replacement sets, including "word bag" searches, translation, and error correction. We also discuss factors affecting thesaurus expansion and replacement, including diacritics sensitivity, nonrecursion, and overlapping rules.

Chapter 9

SQL Server 2008 iFTS provides greater transparency than any prior release of SQL Server FTS. Chapter 9 explores the new catalog views and dynamic management views and functions, all of which allow you to explore, manage, and troubleshoot your iFTS installations, full-text indexes, and full-text queries with greater insight, flexibility, and power than ever before.

Chapter 10

As with prior versions of SQL Server FTS, SQL Server 2008 iFTS depends on external components known as filters, word breakers, and stemmers. These components are critical to proper indexing and querying in iFTS. Chapter 10 discusses iFTS filters and other components, including custom filter creation. In this chapter, we explore creating a sample custom iFTS filter.

Chapter 11

SQL Server iFTS is a great tool for linguistic searches against documents and textual data, but it's not optimized for other types of common database searches, such as name-based searching. In Chapter 11, we explore the world beyond iFTS and introduce fuzzy search technologies, such as phonetic search and n-grams, which fill the void between exact matches and linguistic full-text search.

Appendix A

In this book, we introduce several iFTS-related terms that may be unfamiliar to the uninitiated. We define these words in the body of the text where appropriate, and have included a quick reference glossary of iFTS-related search terms in Appendix A.

Appendix B

To provide more interesting examples than would be possible using the standard Adventure-Works sample database, we've decided to implement our own database known as iFTS_Books. This sample database includes the full text of dozens of public domain books in several languages, and provides concrete examples of the best practices we introduce in this book. Appendix B describes the structure and design of the iFTS_Books sample database.

Appendix C

Appendix C includes additional information about the mathematics and theory behind vector-space search, which is implemented in iFTS via weighted full-text searches.

Conventions

To make reading this book an enjoyable experience, and to help readers get the most out of the text, we've adopted standardized formatting conventions throughout.

C# and C++ code is shown in code font. Note that these languages are case sensitive. Here's an example of a line of C# code:

```
while (i < 10)
```

T-SQL source code is also shown in code font. Though T-SQL is not case sensitive, we've consistently capitalized keywords for readability. Also note that, for readability purposes, we've lowercased data type names in T-SQL code. Finally, following Microsoft's best practices, we consistently use the semicolon T-SQL statement terminator. The following demonstrates a line of T-SQL code:

```
DECLARE @x xml;
```

XML code is shown in code font with attribute and element content shown in bold for readability. Note that some XML code samples and results may have been reformatted in this book for easier reading. Because XML ignores insignificant whitespace, the significant content of the XML has not been altered. Here's an example:

```
<book published = "Apress">Pro T-SQL 2008 Programmer&apos;s Guide</book>
```

■**Note** Notes, tips, and warnings are displayed like this, in a special font with solid bars placed over and under the content.

SIDEBARS

Sidebars include additional information relevant to the current discussion and other interesting facts. Sidebars are shown on a gray background.

Prerequisites

This book requires an installation of SQL Server 2008 in order to run the T-SQL code samples provided. Note that the code in this book has been designed specifically to take advantage of SQL Server 2008 features, and most of the code in the book will either not run on prior versions of SQL Server, or will require significant modification to work on prior releases. The code samples provided in the book are designed specifically to run against the iFTS_Books sample database, available for download from the Apress web site at www.apress.com (see the following section). We describe the iFTS_Books database and provide installation instructions in Appendix B.

Other code samples provided in the book were written in C# (and C++ where appropriate) using Visual Studio 2008. If you're interested in compiling and executing the SQL CLR, client code, and other sample code provided, we highly recommend an installation of Visual Studio 2008 (with Service Pack 1 installed). Although you can compile the code from the command line, we find that the Visual Studio IDE provides a much more enjoyable and productive experience.

Some of the code samples may have additional requirements specified in order to use them; we will identify these special requirements as the code is presented.

Downloading the Code

The iFTS_Books sample database and all of the code samples presented in this book are available in a single Zip file from the Downloads section of the Apress web site at www.apress.com. The Zip file is structured so that each subdirectory contains a set of installation scripts or code samples presented in the book. Installation instructions for the iFTS_Books database and code samples are provided in Appendix B.

Contacting the Authors

The Apress team and the authors have made every effort to ensure that this book is free from errors and defects. Unfortunately, the occasional error does slip past us, despite our best efforts. In the event that you find an error in the book, please let us know! You can submit errors directly to Apress by visiting www.apress.com, locating the page for this book, and clicking on Submit Errata. Alternatively, feel free to drop a line directly to the authors at michaelco@optonline.net.

CHAPTER 1

■■■

SQL Server Full-Text Search

. . . but I still haven't found what I'm looking for.

—Bono Vox, U2

Full-text search encompasses techniques for searching text-based data and documents. This is an increasingly important function of modern databases. SQL Server has had full-text search capability built into it since SQL Server 7.0. SQL Server 2008 integrated full-text search (iFTS) represents a significant improvement in full-text search functionality, a new level of full-text search integration into the database engine over prior releases. In this chapter, we'll discuss full-text search theory and then give a high-level overview of SQL Server 2008 iFTS functionality and architecture.

Welcome to Full-Text Search

Full-text search is designed to allow you to perform linguistic (language-based) searches against text and documents stored in your databases. With options such as word and phrase-based searches, language features, the ability to index documents in their native formats (for example, Office documents and PDFs stored in the database can be indexed), inflectional and thesaurus generational terms, ranking, and elimination of noise words, full-text search provides a powerful set of tools for searching your data. Full-text search functionality is an increasingly important function in modern databases. There are many reasons for this increase in popularity, including the following:

- Databases are increasingly being used as document repositories. In SQL Server 2000 and prior, storage and manipulation of large object (LOB) data (textual data and documents larger than 8,000 bytes) was difficult to say the least, leading to many interesting (and often complicated) alternatives for storing and manipulating LOB data outside the database while storing metadata within the database. With the release of SQL Server 2005, storage and manipulation of LOB text and documents was improved significantly. SQL Server 2008 provides additional performance enhancements for LOB data, making storage of all types of documents in the database much more palatable. We'll discuss these improvements in later chapters in this book.

- Many databases are *public facing*. In the not too distant past, computers were only used by a handful of technical professionals: computer scientists, engineers, and academics. Today, almost everyone owns a computer, and businesses, always conscious of the bottom dollar, have taken advantage of this fact to save money by providing self-service options to customers. As an example, instead of going to a brick-and-mortar store to make a purchase, you can shop online; instead of calling customer service, you check your orders online; instead of calling your broker to place a stock trade, you can research it and then make the trade online. Search functionality in public-facing databases is a key technology that makes online self-service work.

- Storage is cheap. Even as hard drive prices have dropped, the storage requirements of the average user have ballooned. It's not uncommon to find a half terabyte (or more) of storage on the average user's personal computer. According to the Enterprise Strategy Group Inc., worldwide total private storage capacity will reach 27,000 petabytes (27 billion gigabytes) of storage by 2010. Documents are born digitally, live digitally, and die digitally, many times never having a paper existence, or at most a short transient hard-copy life.

- New document types are constantly introduced, and there are increasing requirements to store documents in their native format. XML and formats based on or derived from XML have changed the way we store documents. XML-based documents include XHTML and Office Open XML (OOXML) documents. Businesses are increasingly abandoning paper in the normal course of transactions. Businesses send electronic documents such as purchase orders, invoices, contracts, and ship notices back and forth. Regulatory and legal requirements often necessitate storing exact copies of the business documents when no hard copies exist. For example, a pharmaceutical company assembles medications for drug trials. This involves sending purchase orders, change orders, requisition orders, and other business documents back and forth. The format for many of these documents is XML, and the documents are frequently stored in their native formats in the database. While all of this documentation has to be stored and archived, users need the ability to search for specific documents pertaining to certain transactions, vendors, and so on, quickly and easily. Full-text search provides this capability.

- Researching and analyzing documents and textual data requires data to be stored in a database with full-text search capabilities. Business analysts have two main issues to deal with during the course of research and analysis for business projects:

  - Incomplete or dirty data can cripple business analysis projects, resulting in inaccurate analyses and less than optimal decision making.

  - Too much data can result in information overload, causing "analysis paralysis," slowing business projects to a crawl.

- Full-text search helps by allowing analysts to perform contextual searches that allow relevant data to reveal itself to business users. Full-text search also serves as a solid foundation for more advanced analysis techniques, such as extending classic data mining to text mining.

- Developers want a single standardized interface for searching documents and textual data stored in their databases. Prior to the advent of full-text search in the database, it was not uncommon for developers to come up with a wide variety of inventive and sometimes kludgy methods of searching documents and textual data. These custom-built search routines achieved varying degrees of success. SQL Server full-text search was designed to meet developer demand for a standard toolset to search documents and textual data stored in any SQL Server database.

SQL Server iFTS represents the next generation of SQL Server-based full-text search. The iFTS functionality in SQL Server provides significant advantages over other alternatives, such as the LIKE predicate with wild cards or custom-built solutions. The tasks you can perform with iFTS include the following:

- You can perform linguistic searches of textual data and documents. A *linguistic search* is a word- or phrase-based search that accounts for various language-specific settings, such as the source language of the data being searched, inflectional word forms like verb conjugations, and diacritic mark handling, among others. Unlike the LIKE predicate, when used with wild cards, full-text search is optimized to take full advantage of an efficient specialized indexing structure to obtain results.

- You can automate removal of extraneous and unimportant words (stopwords) from your search criteria. Words that don't lend themselves well to search and don't add value to search results, such as *and*, *an*, and *the*, are automatically stripped from full-text indexes and ignored during full-text searches. The system predefines lists of stopwords (stoplists) in dozens of languages for you. Doing this on your own would require a significant amount of custom coding and knowledge of foreign languages.

- You can apply weight values to your search terms to indicate that some words or phrases should be treated as more important than others in the same full-text search query. This allows you to normalize your results or change the ranking values of your results to indicate that those matching certain terms are more relevant than others.

- You can rank full-text search results to allow your users to choose those documents that are most relevant to their search criteria. Again, it's not necessarily a trivial task to create custom code that ranks search results obtained through custom search algorithms.

- You can index and search an extremely wide array of document types with iFTS. SQL Server full-text search understands how to tokenize and extract text and properties from dozens of different document types, including word-processing documents, spreadsheets, ZIP files, image files, electronic documents, and more. SQL Server iFTS also provides an extensible model that allows you to create custom components to handle any document type in any language you choose. As examples, there are third-party components readily available for additional file formats such as AutoCAD drawings, PDF files, PostScript files, and more.

It's a good bet that a large amount of the data stored by your organization is unstructured—word processing documents, spreadsheets, presentations, electronic documents, and so on. Over the years, many companies have created lucrative business models based on managing unstructured content, including storing, searching, and retrieving this type of content. Some rely on SQL Server's native full-text search capabilities to help provide the back-end functionality for their products. The good news is that you can use this same functionality in your own applications.

The advantage of allowing efficient searches of unstructured content is that your users can create documents and content using the tools they know and love—Word, Acrobat, Excel—and you can manage and share the content they generate from a centralized repository on an enterprise-class database management system (DBMS).

History of SQL Server FTS

Full-text search has been a part of SQL Server since version 7.0. The initial design of SQL Server full-text search provided for reuse of Microsoft Indexing Service components. Indexing Service is Microsoft's core product for indexing and searching files and documents in the file system. The idea was that FTS could easily reuse systemwide components such as word breakers, stemmers, and filters. This legacy can be seen in FTS's dependence on components that implement Indexing Service's programming interfaces. For instance, in SQL Server, document-specific filters are tied to filename extensions.

Though powerful for its day, the initial implementations of FTS in SQL Server 7.0 and 2000 proved to have certain limitations, including the following:

- The DBMS itself made storing, manipulating, searching, and retrieving large object data particularly difficult.

- The fact that only systemwide shared components could be used for FTS indexing caused issues with component version control. This made side-by-side implementations with different component versions difficult.

- Because FTS was implemented as a completely separate service from the SQL Server query engine, efficiency and scalability were definite issues. As a matter of fact, SQL Server 7.0 FTS was at one point considered as an option for the eBay search engine; however, it was determined that it wasn't scalable enough for the job at that time.

- The fact that SQL Server had to store indexes, noise word lists, and other data outside of the database itself made even the most mundane administration tasks (such as backups and restores) tricky at best.

- Finally, prior versions of FTS provided no transparency into the process. Troubleshooting essentially involved a sometimes complicated guess-and-fail approach.

The new version of SQL Server integrated FTS provides much greater integration with the SQL query engine. SQL Server 2008 large object data storage, manipulation, and retrieval has been greatly simplified with the new large object max data types (varchar(max), varbinary(max)). Although you can still use systemwide FTS components, iFTS allows you to use instance-specific installations of FTS components to more easily create side-by-side implementations. FTS efficiency and scalability has been greatly improved by implementing the FTS query engine directly within the SQL Server service instead of as a separate service. Administration has been improved by storing most FTS data within the database instead of in the file system. Noise word lists (now stopword lists) and the full-text catalogs and indexes themselves are now stored directly in the database, easing the burden placed on administrators. In addition, the newest release of FTS provides several dynamic management views and functions to provide insight into the FTS process. This makes troubleshooting issues a much simpler exercise.

MORE ON TEXT-BASED SEARCHING

Text-based searching is not exclusively the domain of SQL Server iFTS. There are many common applications and systems that implement text-based searching algorithms to retrieve relevant documents and data. Consider MS Outlook—users commonly store documents in their Outlook Personal Storage Table (PST) files or in their MS Exchange folders. Frequently, Outlook users will email documents to themselves, adding relevant phrases to the email (*mushroom duxelles recipe* or *notes from accounting meeting*, for example) to make searching easier later. What we see here is users storing all sorts of data (email messages, images, MS Office documents, PDF files, and so on) somewhere on the network in a database, tagging it with information that will help them to find relevant documents later, and sometimes categorizing documents by putting them in subfolders. The key to this model is being able to find the data once it's been stored. Users may rely on MS Outlook Search, Windows Desktop Search, or a third-party search product (such as Google Desktop) to find relevant documents in the future.

Searching the Web requires the use of text-based search algorithms as well. Search engines such as Google go out and scrape tens of millions of web pages, indexing their textual content and attributes (like META tags) for efficient retrieval by users. These text-based search algorithms are often proprietary in nature and custom-built by the search provider, but the concepts are similar to those utilized by other full-text search products such as SQL Server iFTS.

Microsoft has being going back and forth for nearly two decades over the idea of hosting the entire file system in a SQL Server database or keeping it in the existing file system database structure (such as NTFS [New Technology File System]). Microsoft Exchange is an example of an application with its own file system (called *ESE*—pronounced "easy") that's able to store data in rectangular (table-like) structures and nonrectangular data (any file format which contains more properties than a simple file name, size, path, creation date, and so forth). In short, it can store anything that shows up when you view any documents using Windows Explorer. Microsoft has been trying to decide whether to port ESE to SQL Server. What's clear is that SQL Server is extensible enough to hold a file system such as NTFS or Exchange, and in the future might house these two file systems, allowing SQL FTS to index content for even more applications.

Microsoft has been working on other search technologies since the days of Windows NT 3.5. Many of their concepts essentially extend the Windows NT File System (NTFS) to include schemas. In a schema-based system, all document types stored in the file system would have an associated schema detailing the properties and metadata associated with the files. An MS Word document would have its own schema, while an Adobe PDF file would also have its own schema. Some of the technologies that Microsoft has worked on over the years promise to host the file system in a database. These technologies include OFS (Object File System), RFS (Relational File System, originally intended to ship with SQL 2000), and WinFS (Windows Future Storage, but also less frequently called Windows File System). All of these technologies hold great promise in the search space, but so far none have been delivered in Microsoft's flagship OS yet.

Goals of Search

As we mentioned, the primary function of full-text search is to optimize linguistic searches of unstructured content. This section is designed to get you thinking about search in general. We'll present some of the common problems faced by search engineers (or as they're more formally known, *information retrieval scientists*), some of the theory behind search engines, and some of the search algorithms used by Microsoft. The goals of search engines are (in order of importance):

1. To return a list of documents, or a list of links to documents, that match a given search phrase. The results returned are commonly referred to as a list of *hits* or *search results*.

2. To control the inputs and provide users with feedback as to the accuracy of their search. Normally this feedback takes the form of a ratio of the total number of hits out of the number of documents indexed. Another more subtle measure is how long the search engine churns away before returning a response. As Michael Berry points out in his book *Understanding Search Engines- Mathematical Models and Text Retrieval* (SIAM, ISBN 0-89871-437-0), an instantaneous response of "No documents matched your query" leaves the user wondering if the search engine did any searching at all.

3. To allow the users to refine the search, possibly to search within the results retrieved from the first search.

4. To present the users with a search interface that's intuitive and easy to navigate.

5. To provide users a measure of confidence to indicate that their search was both exhaustive and complete.

6. To provide snippets of document text from the search results (or document abstracts), allowing users to quickly determine whether the documents in the search results are relevant to their needs.

The overall goal of search is to maximize user experience in all domains. You must give your users accurate results as quickly as possible. This can be accomplished by not only giving users what they're looking for, but delivering it quickly and accurately, and by providing options to make searches as flexible as possible.

On one hand, you don't want to overwhelm them with search results, forcing them to wade through tens of thousands of results to find the handful of relevant documents they really need. On the other hand, you do want to present them with a flexible search interface so they can control their searching without sacrificing user experience.

There are many factors that affect your search solution: hardware, layout and design, search engine, bandwidth, competitors, and so on. You can control most of these to some extent, and with luck you can minimize their impact. But what about your users? How do you cater to them?

Search architects planning a search solution must consider their interface (or search page) and their users. No matter how sophisticated or powerful your search server, there may be environmental factors that can limit the success of your search solution. Fortunately, most of these factors are within your control. The following problems can make your users unhappy:

- Sometimes your users don't know what they're looking for and are making best guesses, hoping to get the right answers. In other words, unsophisticated searchers rely on a hit-or-miss approach, blind luck, or serendipity. You can help your users by offering training in corporate environments, providing online help, and instituting other methods of educating them. Good search engineers will institute some form of logging to determine what their users are searching for, create their own "best bets" pages, and tag content with keywords to help users find relevant content efficiently. User search requirements and results from the log can be further analyzed by research and development to improve search results, or those results can be directed to management as a guide in focusing development dollars on hot areas of interest.

- Sometimes users make spelling mistakes in their search phrases. There are several ingenious solutions for dealing with this. Google and the Amazon.com search engine run a spell check and make suggestions for other search terms when the number of hits is relatively low. In the case of Amazon.com, the search engine can recommend best-selling products that you might be interested in that are relevant to your search.

- Sometimes users are presented with results in an overwhelming format. This can quickly lead frustrated users to simply give up on continuing to search with your application. A cluttered interface (such as a poorly designed web page) can overwhelm even the most advanced user. A well-designed search page can overcome this. Take a tip from the most popular search engine in the world—Google provides a minimalist main page with lots of white space.

- Sometimes the user finds it too difficult to navigate a search interface and gives up. Again, a well designed web site with intuitive navigation helps alleviate this.

- Sometimes the user is searching for a topic and using incorrect terminology. This can be addressed on SQL Server, to some degree, through the use of inflectional forms and thesaurus searches.

   In this chapter, we're going to consider the search site `Google.com`. We'll contrast Google against some of Microsoft's search sites, and against `Microsoft.com`. We'll be surveying search solutions from across the spectrum of possible configurations.

GOOGLE

Google, started as a research project at Stanford University in California, is currently the world's most popular search engine. For years, `http://google.stanford.edu` used to redirect to `http://www.google.com`; it now redirects to their Google mini search appliance (`http://www.stanford.edu/services/websearch/Google/`). Google is powered by tens of thousands of Linux machines—termed *bricks*—that index pages, perform searches, and serve up cached pages. The Google ranking algorithm differs from most search algorithms in that it relies on inbound page links to rank pages and determine result relevance. For instance, if your web site is the world's ultimate resource for diabetes information, the odds are high that many other web sites would have links pointing to your site This in turn causes your site to be ranked higher when users search for diabetes-related topics. Sites that don't have as many links to them for the word *diabetes* would be ranked lower.

Mechanics of Search

Modern search solutions such as iFTS rely on precompiled indexes of words that were previously extracted from searchable content. If you're storing word processing documents, for instance, the precompiled index will contain all of the words in the documents and references back to the source documents themselves. The index produced is somewhat similar to an index at the back of most books. Imagine having to search a book page by page for a topic you're interested in. Having all key words in an index returns hits substantially faster than looking through every document you're storing to find the user's search phrase.

SQL Server uses an inverted index structure to store full-text index data. The inverted index structure is built by breaking searchable content into word-length tokens (a process known as *tokenizing*) and storing each word with relevant metadata in the index. An inverted index for a document containing the phrase *Now is the time for all good men to come to the aid of the party* would be similar to Figure 1-1.

Word	Document ID	Occurrence
Now	1	1
is	1	2
the	1	3
time	1	4
for	1	5
all	1	6
good	1	7
men	1	8

Figure 1-1. *Inverted index of sample phrase (partial)*

The key fields in the inverted index include the word being indexed, a reference back to the source document where the word is found, and an occurrence indicator, which gives a relative position for each word. SQL Server actually eliminates commonly used stopwords such as *the*, *and*, and *of* from the index, making it substantially smaller. With system-defined stopwords removed, the inverted index for the previously given sample phrase looks more like Figure 1-2.

■**Note** The sample inverted index fragments shown are simplified to include only key information. The actual inverted index structure SQL Server uses contains additional fields not shown.

Word	Document ID	Occurrence
time	1	4
good	1	7
men	1	8
aid	1	13
party	1	16
{End Of File}	1	17

Figure 1-2. *Inverted index with stopwords removed*

Whenever you perform a full-text search in SQL Server, the full-text query engine tokenizes your input string and consults the inverted index to locate relevant documents. We'll discuss indexing in detail in Chapter 2 and full-text search queries in Chapter 3.

iFTS Architecture

The iFTS architecture consists of several full-text search components working in cooperation with the SQL Server query engine to perform efficient linguistic searches. We've highlighted some of the more important components involved in iFTS in the simplified diagram shown in Figure 1-3.

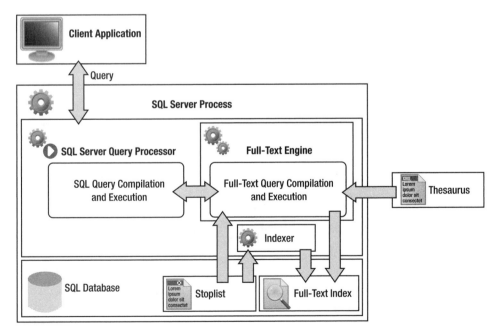

Figure 1-3. *iFTS architecture (simplified)*

The components we've highlighted in Figure 1-3 include the following:

- *Client application*: The client application composes full-text queries and submits them to the SQL Server query processor. It's the responsibility of the client application to ensure that full-text queries conform to the proper syntax. We'll cover full-text query syntax in detail in Chapter 3.

- *SQL Server process*: The SQL Server process contains both the SQL Server query processor, which compiles and executes SQL queries, and the full-text engine, which compiles and executes full-text queries. This tight integration of the SQL Server and full-text query processors in SQL Server 2008 is a significant improvement over prior versions of SQL Server full-text search, allowing SQL Server to generate far more efficient query plans than was previously possible.

- *SQL Server query processor*: The SQL Server query processor consists of several subcomponents that are responsible for validating SQL queries, compiling queries, generating query plans, and executing queries in the database.

- *Full-text query processor*: When the SQL Server query processor receives a full-text query request, it passes the request along to the full-text query processor. It's the responsibility of the full-text query processor to parse and validate the query request, consult the full-text index to fulfill the request, and work with the SQL Server query processor to return the necessary results.

- *Indexer*: The indexer works in conjunction with other components to retrieve streams of textual data from documents, tokenize the content, and populate the full-text indexes. Some of the components with which the indexer works (not shown in the diagram) include the gatherer, protocol handler, filters, and word breakers. We'll discuss these components in greater detail in Chapter 10.

- *Full-text index*: The full-text index is an inverted index structure associated with a given table. The indexer populates the full-text index and the full-text query processor consults the index to fulfill search requests. Unlike prior versions of SQL Server the full-text index in SQL Server 2008 is stored in the database instead of the file system. We will discuss setup, configuration, and population of full-text indexes in detail in Chapter 2.

- *Stoplist*: The stoplist is simply a list of stopwords, or words that are considered useless for the purposes of full-text search. The indexer consults the stoplist during the indexing and querying process in order to eliminate stopwords from the index and search phrase. Unlike prior versions of SQL Server, which stored their equivalent of stoplists (noise word lists) in the file system, SQL Server 2008 stores stopword lists in the database. We'll talk about stoplists in greater detail in Chapter 7.

- *Thesaurus*: The thesaurus is an XML file (stored in the file system) that defines full-text query word replacements and expansions. Replacements and expansions allow you to expand a search to include additional words or completely replace certain words at query time. As an example, you could use the thesaurus to expand a query for the word *run* to also include the words *jog* and *sprint*, or you could replace the word *maroon* with the word *red*. Thesauruses are language-specific, and the query processor consults the thesaurus at query time to perform expansions and replacements. We'll detail the mechanics and usage of thesauruses in Chapter 8.

Note Though the XML thesaurus files are currently stored as files in the file system, the iFTS team is considering the best way to incorporate the thesaurus files directly into the database, in much the same way that the stoplists and full-text indexes have been integrated.

Indexing Process

The full-text indexing process is based on the index population, or *crawl* process. The crawl can be initiated automatically, based on a schedule, or manually via T-SQL statements. When a crawl is started, an iFTS component known as the *protocol handler* connects to the data source (tables you're full-text indexing) and begins streaming data from the searchable content. The protocol handler provides the means for iFTS to communicate with the SQL storage engine. Another component, the *filter daemon host*, is a service that's external to the SQL Server service. This service controls and manages content-type-specific filters, which in turn invoke language-specific word breakers that tokenize the stream of content provided by the protocol handler.

The indexing process consults stoplists to eliminate stopwords from the tokenized content, normalizes the words (for case and accent sensitivity), and adds the indexable words to inverted index fragments. The last step of the indexing process is the *master merge*, which combines all of the index fragments into a single master full-text index. The indexing process in general and the master merge in particular can be resource- and I/O-intensive. Despite the intensity of the process, the indexing process doesn't block queries from occurring. Querying a full-text index during the indexing process, however, can result in partial and incomplete results being returned.

Query Process

The full-text query process uses the same language-specific word breakers that the indexer uses in the indexing process; however, it uses several additional components to fulfill query requests. The query processor accepts a full-text query predicate, which it tokenizes using word breakers. During the tokenization process, the query processor creates *generational forms*, or alternate forms of words, as follows:

- It uses *stemmers*, components that return language-based alternative word forms, to generate inflectional word forms. These inflectional word forms include verb conjugations and plural noun forms for search terms that require them. Stemmers help to maximize precision and recall, which we'll discuss later in this chapter. For instance, the English verb *eat* is stemmed to return the verb forms *eating, eaten, ate,* and *eats* in addition to the root form *eat*.

- It invokes language-specific *thesauruses* to perform thesaurus replacements and expansions when required. The thesaurus files contain user-defined rules that allow you to replace search words with other words or expand searches to automatically include additional words. You might create a rule that replaces the word *maroon* with the word *red*, for instance; or you might create a rule that automatically expands a search for *maroon* to also include *red, brick, ruby,* and *scarlet*.

■**Tip** Stemmer components are encapsulated in the word breaker DLL files, but are separate components (and implement a separate function) from the word breakers themselves. Different language rules are applied at index time by the word breakers than by the stemmers at query time. Many of the stemmers and word breakers have been completely rewritten for SQL 2008, which makes a full population necessary for many full-text indexes upgraded from SQL 2005. We'll discuss full-text index population in detail in Chapter 2.

After creating generational forms of words, the query processor provides input to the SQL Server query processor to help determine the most efficient query plan through which to retrieve the required results. The full-text query processor consults the full-text index to locate documents that qualify based on the search criteria, ranks the results, and works with the SQL Server query processor to return relevant results back to the user.

The new tighter integration between the full-text query processor and the SQL Server query processor (both are now hosted together within the SQL Server process) provides the ability to perform full-text searches that are more highly optimized than in previous versions of SQL Server. As an example, in SQL Server 2005 a full-text search predicate that returned one million matching documents had to return the full one-million-row result set to the SQL Server query processor. At that point, SQL Server could apply additional predicates to narrow down results as necessary. In SQL Server 2008, the search process has been optimized so that SQL Server can shortcut the process, limiting the total results that need to be returned by iFTS without all the overhead of passing around large result sets full of unnecessary data between separate full-text engine and SQL Server services.

Search Quality

For most intranet sites and other internal search solutions, the search phrases that will hit your search servers will be a small fraction or subset of the total number of words in the English language (or any other language for that matter). If you started searching for medical terms or philosophical terms on the Microsoft web site, for instance, you wouldn't expect to get many hits (although we do get hits for *existentialist*, *Plato*, and *anarchist*, we aren't sure how much significance, if any, we can apply to this).

Microsoft's web site deals primarily with technical information—it can be considered a subset of the total content that's indexed by Google. Amazon indexes book titles, book descriptions, and other product descriptions. They would cover a much larger range of subjects than the Microsoft web site, but wouldn't get into the level of detail that the Microsoft site does, as Amazon primarily indexes the publisher's blurb on the book or other sales-related literature for their products.

As you can see, Google probably contains many entries in its index for each word in the English language. In fact, for many words or phrases, Google has millions of entries; for example, the word *Internet* currently returns over 2.6 billion hits as of Fall 2008. Search engines with a relatively small volume of content to index, or that are specialized in nature, have fewer entries for each word and many more words having no entries.

BENEFITS OF INTEGRATION

As we mentioned previously, the new level of integration that SQL Server iFTS offers means that the SQL query optimizer has access to new options to make your queries more efficient than ever. As an example, the following illustration highlights the SQL Server 2005 *Remote Scan* query operator that FTS uses to retrieve results from the full-text engine service. This operator is expensive, and the cost estimates are often inaccurate because of the reliance on a separate service. In the example query plan, the operator accounts for 47% of the total cost of the example query plan.

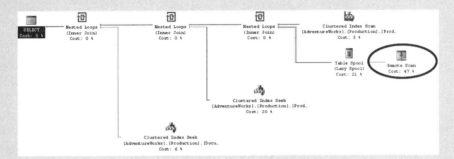

SQL Server 2008 iFTS provides the SQL query optimizer with a new and more efficient operator, the *Table Valued Function [FulltextMatch]* operator, shown in the following example query plan. This new query operator allows SQL Server to quickly retrieve results from the integrated full-text engine while providing a means for the SQL Server query engine to limit the amount of results returned by the full-text engine.

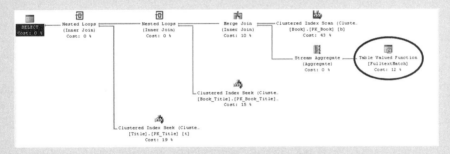

The new full-text search integration provides significant performance and scalability benefits over previous releases.

Measuring Quality

The quality of search results can be measured using two primary metrics: *precision* and *recall*. Precision is the number of hits returned that are relevant versus the number of hits that are irrelevant. If you're having trouble with your car, for instance, and you do a search on *Cressida* on Google, you'll get many hits for the Shakespearian play *Troilus and Cressida* and one of the moons of Uranus, with later results further down the page referring to the Toyota product. Precision in this case is poor. Searching for *Toyota Cressida* gives you only hits related to the Toyota car, with very good or high precision. Precision can be defined mathematically using the formula shown in Figure 1-4, where *p* represents the precision, *n* is the number of relevant retrieved documents, and *d* is the total number of retrieved documents.

$$p = \frac{n}{d}$$

Figure 1-4. *Formula for calculating precision*

Recall is the number of hits that are returned that are relevant versus the number of relevant documents that aren't returned. That is, it's a measure of how much relevant information your searches are missing. Consider a search for the misspelled word *mortage* (a spelling mistake for *mortgage*). You'll get hits for several web sites for mortgage companies. Most web sites don't automatically do spell checking and return hits on corrected spelling mistakes or at least suggest spelling corrections. When you make spelling mistakes, you're missing a lot of relevant hits, or in the language of search, you're getting poor recall. Figure 1-5 is the mathematical definition of recall, where *r* represents recall, *n* is the number of relevant retrieved documents, and *v* is the total number of relevant documents.

$$r = \frac{n}{v}$$

Figure 1-5. *Formula for calculating recall*

Figure 1-6 is a visual demonstration of precision and recall as they apply to search. The large outer box in the figure represents the search space, or database, containing all of the searchable content. The black dots within the box represent individual searchable documents. The shaded area on the left side of the figure represents all of the documents relevant to the current search, while the nonshaded area to the right represents nonrelevant documents.

The complete results of the current search are represented by the documents contained in the dashed oval inside the box. The precision of this search, represented by the shaded area of the oval divided by the entire area of the oval, is low in this query. That is, out of all the documents retrieved, only about half are relevant to the user's needs.

The recall of this search is represented by the shaded area of the oval divided by the entire shaded area of the box. For this particular query, recall was low as well, since a very large number of relevant documents weren't returned to the user.

Precision and recall are normally used in tandem to measure search quality. They work well together and are often defined as having an inverse relationship—barring a complete overhaul of the search algorithm, you can generally raise one of these measures at the expense of lowering the other.

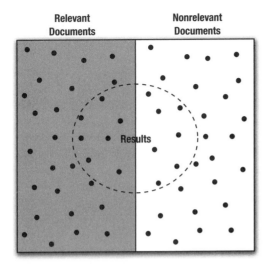

Figure 1-6. *Visual representation of precision and recall in search*

There are other calculations based on precision and recall that can be used to measure the quality of searches. The *weighted harmonic mean*, or *F-measure*, combines precision and recall into a single formula. Figure 1-7 shows the *F1* measure formula, in which precision and recall are evenly weighted. In this formula, *p* represents precision and *r* is the recall value.

$$F = \frac{2 \cdot (p \cdot r)}{p + r}$$

Figure 1-7. *Evenly weighted harmonic mean formula*

The formula can be weighted differently to favor recall or precision by using the weighted F-measure formula shown in Figure 1-8. In this formula, β represents the nonnegative weight that should be applied. A value of β greater than 1.0 favors precision, while a value of β less than 1.0 favors recall.

$$F_\beta = \frac{(1 + \beta^2) \cdot (p \cdot r)}{\beta^2 \cdot p + r}$$

Figure 1-8. *Weighted harmonic mean formula*

Synonymy and Polysemy

Precision and recall are complicated by a number of factors. Two of the most significant factors affecting them are *synonymy* and *polysemy*.

Synonymy: different words that describe the same object or phenomenon. To borrow an example from Michel W. Berry and Murray Browne's book, *Understanding Search Engines*, a *heart attack* is normally referred to in the medical community as *myocardial infarction*. It is said that Inuit Alaskan natives have no words for war, but 10,000 words for snow (I suspect most of these words for snow are obscenities).

Polysemy: words and phrases that are spelled the same but have different meanings. *SOAP*, for instance, has a very different meaning to programmers than to the general populace at large. *Tiny Tim* has one meaning to the Woodstock generation and a completely different meaning to members of younger generations who've read or seen Dickens's *A Christmas Carol.* Another example: one of the authors met his wife while searching for his favorite rock band, Rush, on a web site. Her name came up in the search results and her bio mentioned that she loved Rush. Three years into the marriage, the author discovered that his wife's affection was not for the rock group Rush, but for a radio broadcaster of certain notoriety.

▪**Note** For a more complete discussion of the concepts of synonymy and polysemy, please refer to *Understanding Search Engines-Mathematical Modeling and Text Retrieval* by Michael W. Berry and Murray Browne, (SIAM, ISBN 0-89871-437-0).

There are several strategies to deal with polysemy and synonymy. Among these are two brute force methods, namely:

- Employ people to manually categorize content. The Yahoo! search engine is an example. Yahoo! pays people to surf the Web all day and categorize what they find. Each person has a specialty and is responsible for categorizing content in that category.

- Tag content with keywords that will be searched on. For instance, in support.microsoft.com, you can restrict your search to a subset of the knowledge base documents. A search limited to the SQL Server Knowledge Base will be performed against content pertaining only to SQL Server Knowledge Base articles. These articles have been tagged as knowledge base articles to assist you in narrowing your search.

Currently, research is underway to incorporate automated categorization to deal with polysemy and synonymy in indexing and search algorithms, with particularly interesting work being done by Susan Dumais of Microsoft Research, Michael W. Berry, and others. Microsoft SharePoint, for example, ships with a component to categorize the documents it indexes.

Summary

In this chapter, we introduced full-text search. We considered the advantages of using SQL Server full-text search to search your unstructured content, such as word processing documents, spreadsheets, and other documents.

We gave an overview of the goals and mechanics of full-text search in general, and discussed the SQL Server iFTS implementation architecture, including the indexing and querying processes. As you can see, there are a lot of components involved in the SQL Server iFTS implementation. What we explored in this chapter is a simplified and broad overview of iFTS architecture, which we'll explore further in subsequent chapters.

Finally, we considered search quality concepts and measurements. In this chapter, we introduced the terms and functions that define quality in terms of results.

In subsequent chapters, we'll explore all these concepts in greater detail as we describe the functional characteristics of the SQL Server iFTS implementation.

CHAPTER 2

■■■

Administration

Always have a backup plan.

—Mila Kunis (actress, *That '70s Show*)

SQL Server provides two ways to administer iFTS. You can use the SQL Server Management Studio (SSMS) GUI wizards to create full-text catalogs and full-text indexes, or you can use T-SQL DDL statements to manage iFTS. In this chapter, we'll discuss both methods as well as some advanced configuration features.

Initial Setup and Configuration

It's relatively easy to set up and configure iFTS in SQL Server 2008. The first step is to ensure that iFTS is installed with your SQL Server instance. In the SQL Server installation wizard, you'll see a screen with the iFTS option—make sure this option is checked at install time, as shown in Figure 2-1.

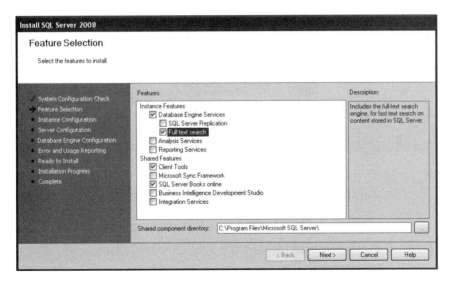

Figure 2-1. *Choosing the Full text search option during installation*

■Tip Though not required by iFTS, we strongly recommend also installing, at a minimum, the SQL Client Tools and SQL Server Books Online (BOL). The code samples shown in this book run in SSMS, which is installed as part of the client tools. BOL is the official Microsoft documentation for SQL Server functionality, including iFTS.

If you're performing an upgrade of a SQL Server 2005 instance with full-text catalogs defined on it, the installer migrates your full-text catalogs to the newly installed SQL Server 2008 instance. In prior versions of SQL Server, full-text search functionality was provided by the full-text engine service, which was external to the SQL Server query engine. In SQL Server 2008, all full-text search functionality is integrated into the query engine. The following items still operate outside of the query engine, however:

- The full-text filter daemon host (fdhost.exe), which manages word breakers, stemmers, and filters is run as a separate process. SQL Server uses the SQL Full-text Filter Daemon Launcher service (fdlauncher.exe) to launch the filter daemon host. Both the filter daemon host process and the launcher service are shown in Figure 2-2.

- The iFTS word breakers, stemmers, and filters are external to the query engine. Prior to SQL Server 2005, full-text search relied on the operating system for these components. In SQL Server 2008, each instance relies on its own set of word breakers, stemmers, and filters.

- The iFTS language-specific thesaurus files are stored in the file system separately. These XML files are loaded when the server is started, or on request via the sys.sp_fulltext_ load_thesaurus_file system stored procedure. We'll discuss thesaurus files in greater detail in Chapter 8.

Figure 2-2. *Full-text daemon host process*

In SQL Server 2005, full-text catalogs contained full-text indexes and weren't created in the database, but rather in a user-specified file path on the local hard drive. Beginning with SQL Server 2008, full-text catalogs are logical constructs that are created in the database to act as containers for full-text indexes, which are also created in the database. Because of this change, the upgrade process will create a new filegroup on the local hard drive and migrate the full-text catalog and its indexes to the SQL Server 2008 instance.

Enabling Database Full-Text Support

In previous versions of SQL Server, it was necessary to explicitly enable and disable full-text search in the database with the sp_fulltext_database system stored procedure. While this stored procedure is still available in SQL Server 2008, it's use is no longer required; in fact, the procedure is deprecated. In SQL Server 2008, all user databases are full-text enabled by default, and full-text support can't be disabled on a per-database basis.

Another backward-compatibility feature is the IsFulltextEnabled database property, exposed through the DATABASEPROPERTYEX function. This database property returns 1 if the database is full-text enabled and 0 if not. This feature is also deprecated, since all user databases on SQL Server 2008 are always full-text enabled. Because of this, you can't rely on the return value of the IsFulltextEnabled database property.

■**Caution** Avoid using deprecated features such as sp_fulltext_database and DATABASEPROPERTYEX ('your_database', 'IsFulltextEnabled') in your development work, since these and other deprecated features will be removed in a future version of SQL Server.

Creating Full-Text Catalogs

Full-text catalogs have changed in SQL Server 2008. While previous versions of SQL Server stored full-text catalogs in the file system, SQL Server 2008 virtualizes the concept of the full-text catalog. A full-text catalog is now simply a logical container for full-text indexes, to make administration and management of groups of full-text indexes easier. You create new full-text catalogs in two ways. The first option is to create a full-text catalog through the SSMS GUI.

■**Note** You can't create full-text catalogs in the tempdb, model, and master system databases.

The New Full-Text Catalog Wizard

The following three steps are required to create a full-text catalog in SSMS:

1. Expand the Storage folder under the target database in the Object Explorer window.

2. Once the Storage folder is expanded, right click on its Full Text Catalogs folder and select New Full-Text Catalog... from the context menu, as shown in Figure 2-3.

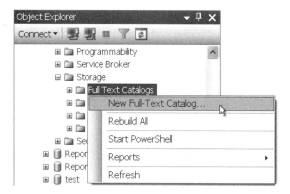

Figure 2-3. *Selecting the New Full-Text Catalog... menu option in SSMS*

3. After you select New Full-Text Catalog... from the context menu, SSMS presents you with the New Full-Text Catalog window, as shown in Figure 2-4.

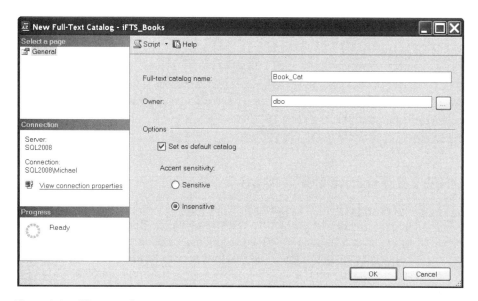

Figure 2-4. *Filling out the New Full-Text Catalog window*

As shown in Figure 2-4, we've specified the following options:

- The Full-text catalog name has been set to Book_Cat. This name must be a valid SQL identifier.

- The Owner has been set to dbo, the user specified in the db_owner role for this database. This owner must be a valid database user or role.

- The Set as default catalog option has been checked in the example. When checked, this option indicates that anytime a full-text index is created in the database without a target full-text catalog explicitly specified in the CREATE FULLTEXT INDEX statement, the full-text index will be created in this catalog.

- The Accent sensitivity setting has been set to Insensitive, indicating that full-text indexing should be insensitive to accents. This means that words such as *resumé* and *resume*, which differ only in their accent marks, will be treated as equivalent by full-text search. Turning off search accent sensitivity returns accent-insensitive matches. Basically any diacritic marks in the search term and indexed word are stripped out, so accent-insensitivity doesn't necessarily return expected results for languages that are heavy on diacritic marks.

The CREATE FULLTEXT CATALOG Statement

The second way to create a full-text catalog is through the T-SQL CREATE FULLTEXT CATALOG statement. Listing 2-1 shows the T-SQL statement that creates a full-text catalog using all the same options as in the previous SSMS GUI example.

Listing 2-1. *Creating a Full-Text Index with T-SQL*

```
CREATE FULLTEXT CATALOG Book_Cat
WITH ACCENT_SENSITIVITY = OFF
AS DEFAULT
AUTHORIZATION dbo;
```

In addition to the options shown, you can also specify a filegroup on which to create the full-text catalog with the ON FILEGROUP clause. You might want to create a separate filegroup on a separate hard drive for improved performance.

■**Tip** While you can still specify the IN PATH clause of the CREATE FULLTEXT CATALOG statement for backward compatibility, SQL Server 2008 ignores this clause.

SQL Server provides the ALTER FULLTEXT CATALOG statement. This allows you to mark an existing full-text catalog as the default with the AS DEFAULT option, rebuild an entire full-text catalog with the REBUILD clause (optionally changing the accent-sensitivity settings), or initiate a master merge and optimization of indexes in the full-text catalog with the REORGANIZE clause. A *master merge* is the process by which SQL Server merges smaller index fragments into a single large index. A rebuild or master merge of a full-text catalog may take a considerable amount of time depending on the amount of indexed data. Listing 2-2 initiates a rebuild of the full-text catalog created in Listing 2-1.

Listing 2-2. *Rebuilding a Full-Text Catalog*

```
ALTER FULLTEXT CATALOG Book_Cat
REBUILD WITH ACCENT_SENSITIVITY = OFF;
```

The `DROP FULLTEXT CATALOG` statement deletes an existing full-text catalog. You can't drop a full-text catalog that contains any full-text indexes.

Upgrading Full-Text Catalogs

Since full-text catalogs in prior versions of SQL Server were stored in the file system, not in the database itself, upgrading an existing full-text catalog involves essentially moving the full-text catalog data from the file system into the database. An full-text catalog upgrade is required if you do any of the following:

- Perform an upgrade of a SQL Server instance

- Back up a SQL Server 2000 or 2005 database and restore it to a SQL Server 2008 instance

- Detach an existing database and attach it to a SQL Server 2008 instance

- Copy a database with the SQL Server Copy Database wizard

All of these SQL Server upgrade methods are detailed in BOL.

The iFTS team has given us a number of options for upgrading SQL Server 2000 and 2005 full-text catalogs, including the following:

- *Import full-text indexed data*: This option directly imports the data from your existing full-text catalog into your SQL Server 2008 full-text indexes. This is the default option and will normally be the fastest upgrade path. However, there have been improvements to several of the SQL Server 2008 word breakers and stemmers, and they may generate different output than their SQL Server 2005 counterparts. Table 2-1 lists the languages that use the same word breakers as SQL Server 2005. If your existing full-text catalogs use only the languages listed in Table 2-1, you can safely import your full-text indexed data.

Table 2-1. *Languages with Identical Word Breakers in SQL Server 2005 and 2008*

Language	LCID
Chinese (Hong Kong)	3076
Chinese (Macau)	5124
Chinese (Singapore)	4100
Danish	1030
English	1033
Korean	1042
Polish	1045
Simplified Chinese	2052
Thai	1054
Traditional Chinese	1028
Turkish	1055
UK (International) English	2057

- *Reset your full-text catalogs*: This option deletes the existing full-text catalogs for the database you're upgrading. This method turns off change tracking and automatic population for your full-text catalog. Use this when you want to schedule a full population of an upgraded full-text catalog for off-peak hours.

- *Perform full population*: This option rebuilds your full-text catalog, kicking off a full population of the full-text catalog after the upgrade. Although this method guarantees that all your full-text data will be indexed using the most current SQL Server 2008 word breakers you have installed, full population can be resource-intensive for large full-text catalogs.

Creating Full-Text Indexes

The full-text index is the basis of iFTS. When you perform a SQL Server iFTS query, the query engine uses the full-text index to quickly locate relevant rows. SQL Server uses a word-level, inverted index data structure that stores information about the indexed word, the location of the word within the indexed data, and the primary key referencing the proper row in the source table. As with full-text catalogs, SQL Server 2008 provides two options for creating full-text indexes: an SSMS GUI wizard and T-SQL statements. Words are stored in the index in Unicode format, in lowercase. The decision to store them in lowercase is for display reasons, because lowercase words are easier to read than all-uppercase words.

The Full-Text Indexing Wizard

To use the SSMS GUI to create a full-text index, expand the Tables folder under your database in the Object Explorer and right-click on the target table. To access the Full-Text Indexing Wizard, choose the Full-Text index ➤ Define Full-Text Index... option from the pop-up context menu, as shown in Figure 2-5.

Figure 2-5. *Accessing the Create Full-Text Index Wizard in SSMS*

A splash screen appears, welcoming you to the Full-Text Indexing Wizard, as shown in Figure 2-6. You can disable the splash screen for future invocations of the wizard by checking the appropriate box.

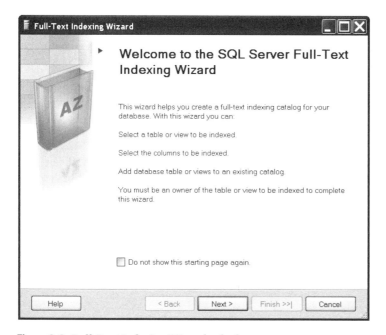

Figure 2-6. *Full-Text Indexing Wizard splash screen*

Click Next to move past the splash screen, and follow the wizard's instructions:

1. Select a single-column unique index defined on the table. The unique index is used by the full-text index to relate index entries back to the source table. It's best to select an int primary key or unique index to fulfill this function, as we've done in Figure 2-7.

2. Next, select the columns from the table that you want to add to the full-text index, as shown in Figure 2-8. All eligible columns are listed, including character, Unicode, binary, and large object (LOB) data type columns.

3. In Figure 2-8, we've chosen to add the Book_Content and Book_Name columns to the full-text index. The Book_Content column is defined as a varbinary(max) column. When you use a varbinary column to hold your indexed content, you must also define a *type column* that declares the type of content held in the varbinary column. In this example, we've chosen the Book_File_Ext column as the type column. This column contains the file extensions associated with the documents in the full-text indexed varbinary column (in this case, Book_Content). The Book_File_Ext column contains entries such as .doc for Microsoft Word documents, .txt for plain text documents, and .xml for XML documents, among others.

4. On this screen, we've also chosen the English language word breaker. All the columns you add to the full-text index must use the same language word breaker or your full-text queries will return errors.

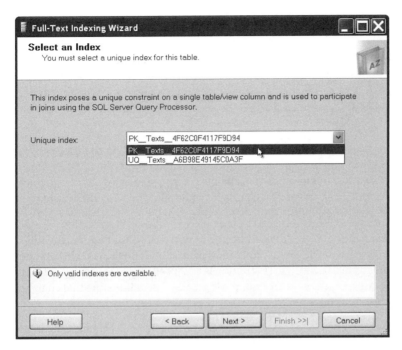

Figure 2-7. *Selecting a unique index in the Full-Text Indexing Wizard*

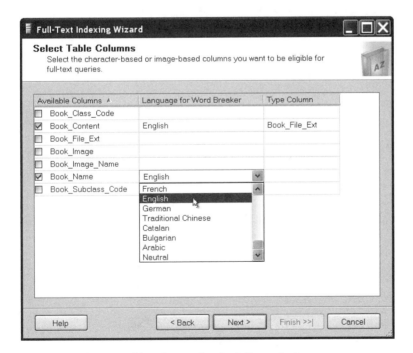

Figure 2-8. *Selecting table columns for the full-text index*

5. Figure 2-9 shows the next step in the wizard—selecting a change tracking option. The choices include the following:

- *Automatically*: Changes are tracked automatically and the full-text index is updated automatically. The automatic updating of the full-text index isn't necessarily immediate, and there may be a delay between when a change is made and when the full-text index is updated. This option is useful for situations in which you don't expect a large volume of changes.

- *Manually*: Changes are tracked automatically by SQL Server, but no changes are applied to the full-text index until you start index population with the appropriate ALTER FULLTEXT INDEX statement. Manual change tracking allows SQL Server to track changes, even during peak server usage periods, while allowing you to schedule regular updates for off-peak hours.

- *Do not track changes*: SQL Server doesn't track changes and doesn't update the full-text index. You must manually start a population with the ALTER FULLTEXT INDEX statement to update your full-text index. This option is best used when the majority of your data changes at discrete intervals, for example if you have an online store that changes its product descriptions once a month.

6. For this example, we've chosen to let SQL Server automatically track changes and apply updates to the full-text index.

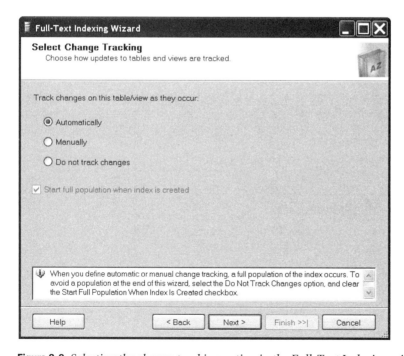

Figure 2-9. *Selecting the change tracking option in the Full-Text Indexing wizard*

7. The wizard asks you to select a full-text catalog in which to create the index, a filegroup, and a stoplist (see Figure 2-10). If you don't have an existing full-text catalog, the wizard allows you to create one in this step. Unless you choose another filegroup to contain your full-text index, the wizard uses the default filegroup.

8. The wizard also defaults to the system stoplist, which is a list of words ignored by word breakers. The system stoplist contains many simple words that are normally considered unhelpful to full-text search, such as *a, the*, and *and*.

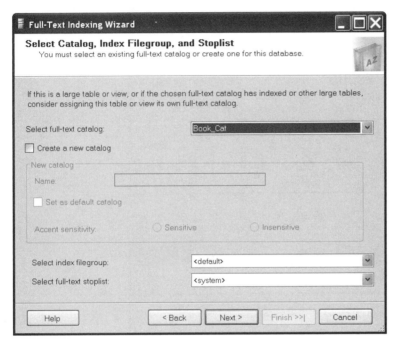

Figure 2-10. *Choosing a catalog, filegroup, and stoplist in the wizard*

9. The next screen of the wizard, shown in Figure 2-11, allows you to define a population schedule for your full-text catalog or index. This step is only necessary if you aren't using change tracking (the Do not track changes option). We'll describe this feature in greater detail in the "Scheduling Population" section later in this chapter.

10. The wizard gives you a summary screen that allows you to view all the options you've selected. This gives you a chance to hit the Back button to change your full-text indexing wizard options, or confirm your index creation options and build the full-text index by pressing the Next button. The summary screen is shown in Figure 2-12.

11. The final screen of the wizard shows the progress of the full-text index creation, including a final success or failure notice at the end of the creation attempt. Figure 2-13 shows the final Full-Text Indexing Wizard progress and status screen.

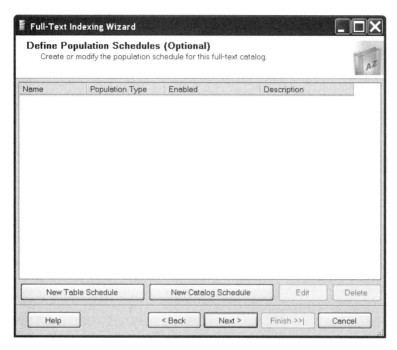

Figure 2-11. *Defining population schedules in the wizard*

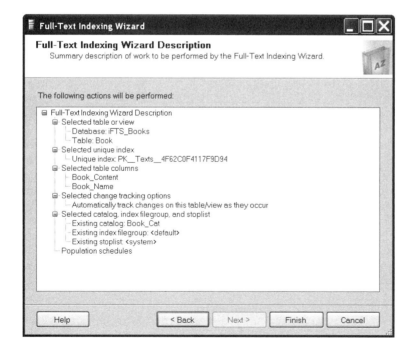

Figure 2-12. *Full-Text Indexing wizard summary screen*

Figure 2-13. *Final wizard progress and status screen*

When the wizard progress screen indicates success with a green checkmark icon, your full-text index has been successfully created. You can verify this by expanding the Storage ➤ Full-Text Catalogs folder under the target database and right-clicking on the chosen full-text catalog. When the pop-up context menu appears, choose Properties and look at the Tables/Views page in the Full-Text Catalog Properties window. This window shows all full-text indexes that are in the full-text catalog, with additional details about the full-text indexes. Figure 2-14 shows the Book_Cat full-text catalog properties, featuring details about the full-text index just created on the Book table.

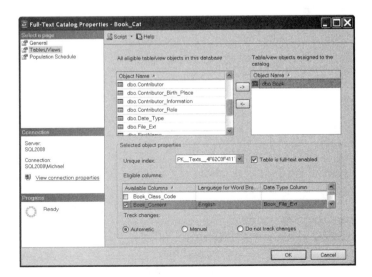

Figure 2-14. *Full-Text Catalog Properties for Book_Cat catalog*

The DROP FULLTEXT INDEX statement drops a specified full-text index from the database.

FULL-TEXT METADATA

SQL Server creates and stores a lot of metadata around your full-text indexes in several internal tables. You can't directly query these internal tables, as they're exclusively for SQL Server's use. There are two main internal tables that are specific to iFTS metadata:

- The sys.fulltext_index_map internal table stores the mappings between full-text key columns and internal document IDs that uniquely identify documents.

- The sys.fulltext_catalog_freelist internal table stores unused document IDs.

In addition, SQL Server creates several more internal data structures to support individual full-text indexes. You can view the metadata for these internal data structures in tabular format with a query like the following that uses the sys.internal_tables catalog view:

```
SELECT
  SCHEMA_NAME(t.schema_id) AS user_table_schema,
  OBJECT_NAME(fti.object_id) AS user_table,
  fti.object_id AS user_table_name,
  it.name AS internal_table_name,
  it.object_id AS internal_table_id,
  it.internal_type_desc
FROM sys.internal_tables AS it
INNER JOIN sys.fulltext_indexes AS fti
  ON it.parent_id = fti.object_id
INNER JOIN sys.tables t
  ON t.object_id = fti.object_id
WHERE it.internal_type_desc LIKE 'FULLTEXT%'
ORDER BY user_table;
```

The results might resemble the following figure:

	user_tab...	user_table	user_table_...	internal_table_name	internal_tabl...	internal_type_desc
1	dbo	Book	2105058535	fulltext_index_docidstatus_2105058535	1013578649	FULLTEXT_DOCID_STATUS
2	dbo	Book	2105058535	fulltext_docidfilter_2105058535	1029578706	FULLTEXT_DOCID_FILTER
3	dbo	Book	2105058535	fulltext_indexeddocid_2105058535	1045578763	FULLTEXT_INDEXED_DOCID
4	dbo	Book	2105058535	fulltext_avdl_2105058535	1061578820	FULLTEXT_AVDL
5	dbo	Book	2105058535	ifts_comp_fragment_2105058535_18	226099846	FULLTEXT_COMP_FRAGMENT
6	dbo	Book	2105058535	ifts_comp_fragment_2105058535_20	964198485	FULLTEXT_COMP_FRAGMENT
7	dbo	Commentary	101575400	fulltext_index_docidstatus_101575400	1077578877	FULLTEXT_DOCID_STATUS
8	dbo	Commentary	101575400	fulltext_docidfilter_101575400	1093578934	FULLTEXT_DOCID_FILTER
9	dbo	Commentary	101575400	fulltext_indexeddocid_101575400	1109578991	FULLTEXT_INDEXED_DOCID
10	dbo	Commentary	101575400	fulltext_avdl_101575400	1125579048	FULLTEXT_AVDL
11	dbo	Commentary	101575400	ifts_comp_fragment_101575400_3	2099048	FULLTEXT_COMP_FRAGMENT
12	dbo	Contributor_Bi...	165575628	fulltext_index_docidstatus_165575628	1141579105	FULLTEXT_DOCID_STATUS
13	dbo	Contributor_Bi...	165575628	fulltext_docidfilter_165575628	1157579162	FULLTEXT_DOCID_FILTER
14	dbo	Contributor_Bi...	165575628	fulltext_indexeddocid_165575628	1173579219	FULLTEXT_INDEXED_DOCID
15	dbo	Contributor_Bi...	165575628	fulltext_avdl_165575628	1189579276	FULLTEXT_AVDL
16	dbo	Contributor_Bi...	165575628	ifts_comp_fragment_165575628_3	2069582411	FULLTEXT_COMP_FRAGMENT
17	dbo	Contributor_In...	229575856	fulltext_index_docidstatus_229575856	1205579333	FULLTEXT_DOCID_STATUS
18	dbo	Contributor_In...	229575856	fulltext_docidfilter_229575856	1221579390	FULLTEXT_DOCID_FILTER
19	dbo	Contributor_In...	229575856	fulltext_indexeddocid_229575856	1237579447	FULLTEXT_INDEXED_DOCID

As you can see, SQL Server creates several types of iFTS-specific internal tables. The name of each internal table has the object_id of the user table it's associated with appended to it. We'll discuss DMVs, DMFs, catalog views, and other methods of accessing iFTS-specific metadata in greater detail in Chapter 9.

The DocId Map

You can use most any indexable data type as the unique index on your full-text indexed table. You can use a `uniqueidentifier` or `varchar` column, for instance. However, when you define the unique index using a non-`int` data type, SQL Server has to create a document ID (`DocId`) map that maps your unique index values to internally managed `int` values. This translates into an additional step that the query engine must perform in your full-text search queries, making them less efficient than they could be. If you define the unique index on an `int` column, SQL Server can use the column value as the `DocId` directly without an intermediate mapping step. This can result in a significant increase in efficiency, particularly when you're indexing a table with a large number of rows. We strongly recommend using an `int` column as your unique index for purposes of full-text indexing.

The CREATE FULLTEXT INDEX Statement

You can also create full-text indexes on tables or indexed views via T-SQL with the `CREATE FULLTEXT INDEX` statement. Scripting allows you to automate full-text index creation and gives you the ability to apply the same full-text index across multiple databases and environments. For instance, it's not uncommon to create a full-text index in a development environment, test it, and then re-create the same full-text index in a user acceptance testing (UAT) environment. Once the full-text index has been tested in UAT, it can be recreated in a production environment. Listing 2-3 shows a T-SQL script that creates and enables the same full-text index on the Book table that we previously demonstrated with the Full-Text Indexing Wizard.

Listing 2-3. *Scripting Full-Text Index Creation*

```
CREATE FULLTEXT INDEX ON dbo.Book
(
  Book_Content TYPE COLUMN Book_File_Ext LANGUAGE English,
  Book_Name LANGUAGE English
)
KEY INDEX PK_Book
ON
(
  Book_Cat
)
WITH
(
  CHANGE_TRACKING = AUTO,
  STOPLIST = SYSTEM
);
GO

ALTER FULLTEXT INDEX
ON dbo.Book ENABLE;
GO
```

The CREATE FULLTEXT INDEX statement shown in Listing 2-3 begins by indicating the table you wish to create the index on, followed by the columns to index in parentheses.

```
CREATE FULLTEXT INDEX ON dbo.Book
(
  Book_Content TYPE COLUMN Book_File_Ext LANGUAGE English,
  Book_Name LANGUAGE English
)
```

Note You can use language keywords (such as English) or LCIDs in some situations, for example in the CREATE FULLTEXT INDEX statement LANGUAGE clauses. The LCID equivalent for English is 1033.

The Book_Content column definition in the example uses the TYPE COLUMN clause to define the type of data stored in each corresponding row of the Book table. The Book_File_Ext column contains a filename extension to indicate the type of content in the Book_Content column. The value of the Book_File_Ext column determines which filter iFTS applies to the content. A value of .doc in the Book_File_Ext column, for instance, means that the Book_Content column contains a Microsoft Word document, while a value of .xml indicates an XML document.

Tip You can retrieve the entire list of document types supported by an instance of SQL Server 2008 by querying the sys.fulltext_document_types catalog view.

The LANGUAGE clause of the column definitions specifies English, or Language Code Identifier (LCID) 1033, as the language to be used. You can retrieve the entire listing of supported full-text languages and LCID codes by querying the sys.fulltext_languages catalog view.

The KEY INDEX clause specifies which unique index on the Book table iFTS will use to relate full-text index entries back to the source table. In this instance, we've chosen to use the int primary key. The ON clause that follows specifies which full-text catalog this full-text index will be created on—in this example the Book_Cat catalog:

```
KEY INDEX PK_Book
ON
(
  Book_Cat
)
```

The WITH clause in the example sets the change-tracking mode for the full-text index. In this case, we've set it to AUTO. The STOPLIST option has also been set to SYSTEM in the example:

```
WITH
(
  CHANGE_TRACKING = AUTO,
  STOPLIST = SYSTEM
);
```

The available options for CHANGE_TRACKING are AUTO, MANUAL, and OFF, each corresponding to the similarly named options in the Full-Text Indexing Wizard. The OFF mode has an optional NO POPULATION clause, which indicates that the full-text index shouldn't be populated after creation. While your index will be queryable, no results will be returned in your queries, as nothing has been indexed yet. If you set change tracking to OFF with the NO POPULATION clause, you must manually start population of your full-text index with the ALTER FULLTEXT INDEX statement.

The STOPLIST option can be set to one of SYSTEM, OFF, or the name of a user-created stoplist, indicating the system stoplist, no stoplist, or a user-defined stoplist, respectively.

The final ALTER FULLTEXT INDEX statement includes the ENABLE clause to enable the full-text index after it's created:

```
ALTER FULLTEXT INDEX
ON dbo.Book ENABLE;
```

Full-Text Index Population

Once full-text indexes are created, there's the small matter of populating them. When full-text indexes are created, they're automatically populated unless you create them with the CHANGE_ TRACKING = OFF, NO POPULATION option. Even after a full-text index is created and initially populated, however, it still needs to be updated from time to time. We'll discuss full-text index population in this section.

If you create a full-text index with change tracking set to AUTO, as we did in our example, SQL Server handles the details of tracking changes to the base table and updating the full-text index on an as-needed basis. You may determine that the overhead associated with automatic change tracking is too costly for your system. You can reach this decision for a variety of reasons— if you expect full-text index change tracking to consume too many server resources during peak periods of server activity, for instance. In that case, you can set the CHANGE_TRACKING option to OFF or MANUAL and begin full-text index populations with the ALTER FULLTEXT INDEX statement.

SQL Server provides three types of full-text index populations through the ALTER FULLTEXT INDEX statement: full population, incremental population, and update population.

■**Tip** If a full-text index population is in progress when you try to start a new population, SQL Server returns a warning message and doesn't start the new population. The population that is currently in process continues unaffected though.

Full Population

The START FULL POPULATION clause of the ALTER FULLTEXT INDEX statement starts a full population of your index. When you start a full population on a full-text index, SQL Server retrieves every row of the source table or indexed view and adds all entries to the index. A full population can cause excessive locking during the index process, which might conflict with user queries and DML statements, since the full-text engine must access every row of the source table to populate the index. Normally, a full population is run immediately after full-text index creation and might be scheduled at regular intervals (normally off-peak hours) if you've chosen to set change tracking to MANUAL or OFF. A full population on a table that already has a populated full-text index won't break the existing full-text index—it will still be queryable while the new full population is in process. Listing 2-4 demonstrates how to start a full population on a full-text index.

Listing 2-4. *Starting Full Population of a Full-Text Index*

```
ALTER FULLTEXT INDEX ON dbo.Book
START FULL POPULATION;
```

Incremental Population

When you start an incremental population with the START INCREMENTAL POPULATION clause of the ALTER FULLTEXT INDEX statement, the population process retrieves only the rows modified since the last full-text index population completed. It then has to enumerate all rows in the table to determine which rows have been deleted and remove references to these rows from the full-text index. If a large percentage of your data has changed, incremental populations are generally faster than full populations, as they only make one pass of the base table. If you encounter excessive server resource usage or user query and DML statement locking, you might decide to schedule full populations or update populations for off-peak hours instead of using incremental populations with AUTO change tracking.

To use the incremental population option, the source table must have a rowversion data type column. If the table doesn't have a rowversion column and you specify incremental population, SQL Server will start a full population. Note that when you initially start change tracking, a full population will be done. If you subsequently kick off change tracking on a table, an incremental population may be done instead of a full-population if the table has a rowversion column and a prior full population has completed.

■**Tip**   The rowversion data type is a synonym for the timestamp data type. The name timestamp for this data type is deprecated. You should use the name rowversion in future development.

When you start an incremental population, SQL Server uses the rowversion column of the base table or indexed view to determine which rows have changed since the last population. In the incremental population strategy, SQL Server only considers rows that have changed since the last population when updating the full-text index. Listing 2-5 shows how to start an incremental population.

Listing 2-5. *Starting Incremental Population of a Full-Text Index*

```
ALTER FULLTEXT INDEX ON dbo.Book
START INCREMENTAL POPULATION;
```

Update Population

You can start an update population with the START UPDATE POPULATION clause of the ALTER FULLTEXT INDEX statement. An update population (formerly called a *change-tracking population* in prior releases of SQL Server) relies on a record of the updates, inserts, and deletes to the base table or indexed view, which is maintained by SQL Server between populations. These changes are maintained by SQL Server in a change-tracking index. When you start an update population, SQL Server applies all the changes in the change-tracking index to the full-text index. In order to use update populations, your full-text index needs to be set to MANUAL change tracking. Update populations don't require a rowversion column like incremental populations do. Again, if you're using an update population and are encountering excessive locking or resource problems, you may decide to schedule your populations for off-peak hours. Listing 2-6 demonstrates how to start an update population.

Listing 2-6. *Starting Update Population of a Full-Text Index*

```
ALTER FULLTEXT INDEX ON dbo.Book
START UPDATE POPULATION;
```

Additional Index Population Options

You can also stop, pause, or resume a population with the STOP POPULATION, PAUSE POPULATION, and RESUME POPULATION clauses of the ALTER FULLTEXT INDEX statement. The STOP POPULATION clause stops any population in progress, but allows auto change tracking to continue. (To stop change tracking, you must use the SET CHANGE_TRACKING OFF option.) PAUSE POPULATION pauses a full population, and RESUME POPULATION resumes a previously paused full population. The index will remain queryable while the full-text population has been stored or paused. These two options are only applicable to a full population.

The ALTER FULLTEXT INDEX statement also allows you to alter the change-tracking mode for your full-text index with the SET CHANGE_TRACKING clause. If your full-text index has change tracking turned off, for instance, you can change it to AUTO or MANUAL with this clause.

ALTER FULLTEXT INDEX also provides the ENABLE and DISABLE clauses to enable or disable a full-text index, respectively. You can change the full-text stoplist via the SET STOPLIST clause, and can add columns to an index via the ADD clause or drop columns with the DROP clause.

Catalog Rebuild and Reorganization

In addition to managing full-text index populations on an individual basis with the ALTER FULLTEXT INDEX statement, you can use ALTER FULLTEXT CATALOG to rebuild or reorganize an entire full-text catalog. Rebuilding a full-text catalog repopulates every full-text index that the catalog contains. Listing 2-7 shows how to rebuild a full-text catalog.

Listing 2-7. *Rebuilding a Full-Text Catalog*

```
ALTER FULLTEXT CATALOG Book_Cat
REBUILD WITH ACCENT_SENSITIVITY = OFF;
```

In this example, the optional WITH ACCENT_SENSITIVITY clause of the REBUILD clause sets the accent sensitivity for the catalog to OFF. You can use this option to change the accent sensitivity of your full-text catalog.

During the process of populating a full-text index, SQL Server can generate multiple small indexes, which it subsequently combines into one large index—a process known as a *master merge*, or index reorganization. You can tell SQL Server to perform a master merge to optimize internal full-text index and catalog structures. Periodic reorganization can improve full-text index performance, particularly if your catalog changes frequently. Listing 2-8 demonstrates reorganization of a full-text catalog.

Listing 2-8. *Reorganizing a Full-Text Catalog*

```
ALTER FULLTEXT CATALOG Book_Cat
REORGANIZE;
```

Scheduling Populations

You can schedule full-text index populations using the Full-Text Indexing Wizard, as we previously mentioned in this chapter. When you use the Full-Text Indexing Wizard to create a schedule, it creates a SQL Server Agent job to perform full-text index population according to the schedule you define. Figure 2-15 shows the wizard schedule window, in which we've defined a recurring population task that will kick off every day at 1 a.m.

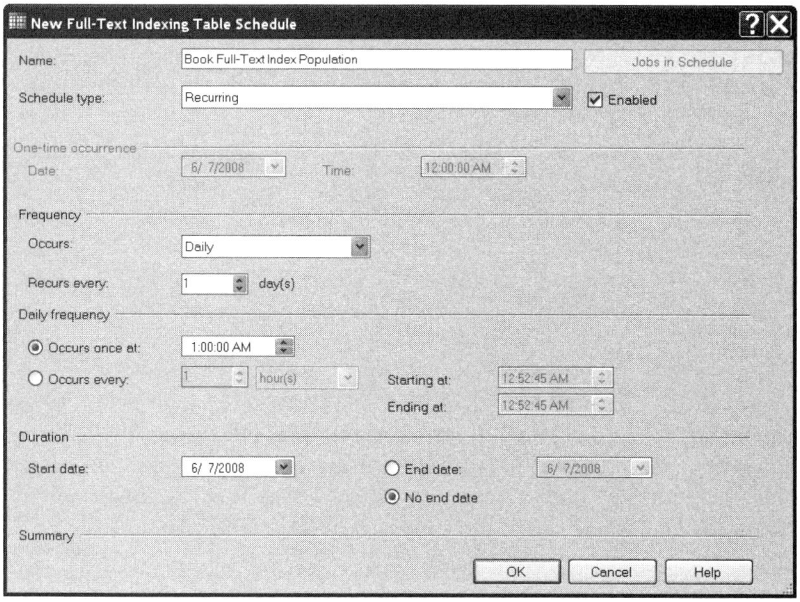

Figure 2-15. *Full-Text Indexing Wizard schedule wizard*

■**Note** Since the Full-Text Indexing Wizard schedules jobs via SQL Server Agent, you need to ensure that the SQL Server Agent service is turned on. You can verify this with the SQL Server Configuration Manager utility or in the Control Panel under Services.

If you've already created your full-text indexes, you can schedule your own SQL Server Agent jobs to execute ALTER FULLTEXT INDEX statements to populate them without going through the Full-Text Indexing wizard GUI.

Management

SQL Server 2008 provides several tools to help you manage your full-text indexes and catalogs. In this section, we'll look at backing up SQL Server full-text catalogs and indexes, as well as SQL Server Profiler events that are useful for iFTS management, performance tuning, and troubleshooting.

Backups

Prior to SQL Server 2008, full-text catalogs and indexes were stored in the file system, separate from their associated databases. In SQL Server 2000, you needed a separate strategy to back up your full-text indexes separately from your databases. SQL Server 2005 also stored full-text catalogs in the file system, but improved backups by allowing you to back up your catalogs with the database.

SQL Server 2008 ups the ante by creating your full-text indexes and catalogs in the database. This simplifies backing them up, since they're automatically backed up during normal database backups. Listing 2-9 shows a simple BACKUP DATABASE statement that performs a full database backup, including full-text catalogs.

Listing 2-9. *Full Database Backup*

```
BACKUP DATABASE iFTS_Books
TO DISK = N'C:\iFTS_Books\iFTS_Books.bak'
  WITH DESCRIPTION = N'iFTS_Books backup example including full-text catalogs',
    NOFORMAT,
    INIT,
    NAME = N'iFTS_Books-Full Database Backup',
    SKIP,
    NOREWIND,
    NOUNLOAD,
    STATS = 10;
```

You can restore your database, including full-text catalogs and indexes, with the RESTORE DATABASE statement, as shown in Listing 2-10.

Listing 2-10. *Full Database Restore*

```
RESTORE DATABASE iFTS_Books
  FROM DISK = N'C:\iFTS_Books\iFTS_Books.bak'
    WITH FILE = 1,
    NOUNLOAD,
    REPLACE,
    STATS = 10;
```

If you created your full-text indexes on a different filegroup, or if you have multiple full-text indexes on separate filegroups, you can identify the filegroups that contain your full-text indexes to perform filegroup backups and restores.

■**Tip** Your first backup for a filegroup has to be a full file backup; subsequent backups of the filegroup can be differential file backups.

Logs

The iFTS crawler keeps crawl logs in the MSSQL\Log directory for each SQL Server instance. These are text log files with names that begin with sqlft* and end with the extension .log. The crawl logs contain entries that give you information about full-text population start events, stop events, and errors. The following are some sample crawl log entries:

```
2008-06-02 23:29:48.94 spid26s    Informational: Full-text Full population
 initialized for table or indexed view '[iFTS_Books].[dbo].[Book]'
 (table or indexed view ID '706101556', database ID '11'). Population
 sub-tasks: 1.

2008-06-02 23:30:17.97 spid26s    Warning: No appropriate filter was found
 during full-text index population for table or indexed view
 '[iFTS_Books].[dbo].[Book]' (table or indexed view ID '706101556',
 database ID '11'), full-text key value 0x34. Some columns of the row were not
 indexed.

2008-06-02 23:30:18.01 spid32s    Informational: Full-text Full population
 completed for table or indexed view '[iFTS_Books].[dbo].[Book]' (table
 or indexed view ID '706101556', database ID '11'). Number of documents
 processed: 25. Number of documents failed: 0. Number of documents that were
 retried: 0.
```

This sample shows the initialization and completion of a full-text population. In between is a warning that no appropriate filter was found for a specific entry (in this case an Adobe Acrobat PDF file), so the indexer skipped it. The crawl logs are a useful tool for locating information about specific iFTS population and indexing problems.

SQL Profiler Events

SQL Profiler contains three full-text search events that you can view in the Trace Properties, as shown in Figure 2-16.

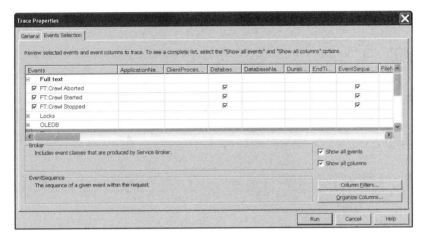

Figure 2-16. *Full-text events in SQL Profiler*

The events you can trace in SQL Profiler are related to full-text index population, namely the process known as the full-text index *crawl*. The crawl process performs the following iFTS tasks:

1. The crawl first retrieves rows from the base table or indexed view.

2. Once rows are retrieved, a binary stream is sent to the IFilters, which extract text and properties.

3. The IFilters send data to the word breakers, which tokenize the words in the columns covered by the index.

4. Finally, the full-text index is populated with the tokenized words.

SQL Profiler can capture the following events that are useful for troubleshooting full-text population issues:

- The *FT:Crawl Started* event is fired whenever a full-text population begins.

- The *FT:Crawl Stopped* event is fired whenever a full-text population stops because of a successful completion or a fatal error.

- The *FT:Crawl Aborted* event is fired when there's an error (usually a fatal error) during a full-text population.

You can access these same events in Windows System Monitor (perfmon.exe) under the SQLServer:Trace Event Statistics performance object.

> **■Tip** In the event of a full-text population error, the SQL Server log, the crawl log, and the Windows Event Log will contain additional information about the cause of the error.

System Procedures

SQL Server 2008 deprecates many of the FTS-specific system stored procedures that were used in previous versions. Most have been replaced by catalog views and dynamic management views and functions. In fact, there are only a handful of system stored procedures specific to iFTS that aren't deprecated in SQL Server 2008. The sp_fulltext_service procedure changes server properties related to full-text search on SQL Server. There are several properties that can be changed or retrieved with the sp_fulltext_service procedure, as shown in Table 2-2.

Table 2-2. *The sp_fulltext_service Properties*

Property	Description
load_os_resources	Determines whether SQL Server uses instance-specific or operating systemwide word breakers, stemmers, and filters. This property can be set to one of the following values:
	0 = SQL Server uses only word breakers, stemmers, and filters specific to the server instance. This is the default setting.
	1 = SQL Server uses operating system word breakers, stemmers, and filters. This allows the use of Microsoft Indexing Service resources and language types that don't have instance-specific resources.
pause_indexing	Allows you to pause or resume full-text indexing operations on a SQL Server instance. This property can be set to one of the following values:
	0 = Resume full-text indexing operations for the instance.
	1 = Pause full-text indexing operations for the instance.
update_languages	Updates the list of languages registered with iFTS.
upgrade_option	Controls how full-text indexes are migrated during an upgrade from SQL Server 2000 or SQL Server 2005. This property can be set to one of the following values:
	0 = Causes full-text catalogs to be rebuilt using SQL Server 2008 word breakers.
	1 = Resets full-text catalogs, causing the catalog contents to be emptied and the full-text indexes to be disabled.
	2 = Imports full-text catalogs without rebuilding them using SQL Server 2008 word breakers.
verify_signature	Enables or disables whether unsigned binaries (such as word breakers) can be loaded by the full-text search engine. This property can be set to one of the following values:
	0 = Do not verify whether binaries are signed.
	1 = Load only signed, trusted binaries. This is the default.

The `clean_up`, `connect_timeout`, `data_timeout`, and `resource_usage` properties of the `sp_fulltext_service` procedure are all provided for backward compatibility, but they don't perform any function in SQL Server 2008. The values for these properties are always 0 in SQL Server 2008. Avoid using these properties in SQL Server 2008. In addition, SQL Server provides the system stored procedures listed in Table 2-3.

Table 2-3. *Full-Text Search System Stored Procedures*

Procedure	Description
`sp_fulltext_key_mappings`	Returns the internal mappings between document identifiers (DocIds) and full-text key values.
`sp_help_fulltext_system_components`	Returns information about registered word breakers, filters, and protocol handlers.
`sp_fulltext_load_thesaurus_file`	Loads language-specific iFTS thesaurus file.
`sp_fulltext_pending_changes`	Returns unprocessed changes for a table that's full-text indexed using change tracking.
`sp_fulltext_service`	Sets full-text service properties for the SQL Server instance.

The remaining full-text search system stored procedures are deprecated. You should avoid using them in future development work and instead use the catalog views and data management views provided by SQL Server 2008.

■**Note** We'll discuss full-text search-specific catalog views and dynamic management views in detail in Chapter 9.

Summary

In this chapter, we covered several topics specific to the creation and management of full-text catalogs and indexes. We talked about selecting full-text search in the SQL Server installation wizard and some of the tasks the installation wizard takes during an upgrade from SQL Server 2000 or 2005. We then talked about how to create full-text catalogs and full-text indexes using the SSMS wizards and scripted T-SQL statements.

Then we discussed full-text index population methods, including full population, update population, and incremental population. We also presented catalog rebuild and reorganization options and discussed scheduling population jobs with SQL Server Agent.

We rounded out this chapter with a discussion of some of the administration tools available for full-text search management. We discussed database backups, crawl logs, SQL Profiler events, and system stored procedures. Many of the iFTS-specific system stored procedures have been deprecated in SQL Server 2008 in favor of catalog views and dynamic management views, which we'll detail in Chapter 9. In the next chapter, we'll discuss basic and advanced full-text queries on SQL Server 2008.

■■■

Basic and Advanced Queries

I did not look for any specific thing. I only hoped to find, and find I have, all that there was, only some letters and a few memoranda . . .

—Bram Stoker's *Dracula*

Once you've built and populated full-text indexes in your database, you can begin querying them to retrieve relevant data. This chapter is designed to provide an introduction to the features available through full-text search predicates and functions, and as a guide to the powerful search query grammar of SQL Server iFTS. SQL Server provides powerful full-text search querying capabilities, from the most basic phrase search to extremely complex searches involving Boolean operators, proximity searches, and weighted search terms. We begin our discussion of SQL Server iFTS with an introduction to the two available SQL Server search predicates, CONTAINS and FREETEXT.

iFTS Predicates and Functions

SQL Server iFTS provides two search predicates, both based on *SearchSQL*, which is an extension to the SQL language promoted by the ISO and ANSI committees. These predicates are the following:

- The CONTAINS predicate provides access to phrase search, proximity search, strict search, and advanced query capability.

- The FREETEXT predicate provides fuzzy search and basic query capabilities.

■**Tip** These two search predicates are supported by all Microsoft Search products, including Microsoft Index Server as well as most other search engines.

What is a *predicate*? Simply put, a predicate is a comparison operator in the WHERE clause of a SQL statement. In SQL Server iFTS, predicates take a format similar to the SQL EXISTS predicate, with no explicit comparison operators required, as shown in Listing 3-1.

Listing 3-1. *Simple iFTS Queries*

```
USE iFTS_Books;
GO

SELECT b.Book_ID
FROM dbo.Book b
WHERE CONTAINS
(
  *,
  N'fish and chips'
);

SELECT b.Book_ID
FROM dbo.Book b
WHERE FREETEXT
(
  *,
  N'love''s or money'
);
```

■**Tip** The queries in Listing 3-1 work in the sample iFTS_Books database available from the downloads section of the Apress web site (www.apress.com).

As with other SQL statements, single quotation marks in search phrase strings must be doubled up. Single quotes don't need to be doubled if they're coming from client applications that pass search phrase strings as parameters to stored procedures and parameterized queries. Take care when writing query phrases containing single quotation marks, as they'll cause your query to bomb with an error message similar to the following:

```
Msg 102, Level 15, State 1, Line 1
Incorrect syntax near 'm'.
Msg 105, Level 15, State 1, Line 1
Unclosed quotation mark after the character string ')
'.
```

UNICODE SEARCH PHRASES

Your search phrases should always be declared as Unicode (nvarchar, nchar). When you don't declare them as Unicode, SQL Server implicitly converts them to Unicode, so it's a good idea to explicitly declare them as Unicode from a performance perspective. Declaring them as Unicode also helps prevent parameter sniffing. Furthermore, with the trend toward globalization, restricting your full-text-indexed columns to specific non-Unicode collations can prove short-sighted and result in the need for a drastic and expensive system overhaul down the line. We've used Unicode throughout the iFTS_Books sample database to support the international character sets used to store the documents and book metadata.

The functionality of the FREETEXT and CONTAINS predicates are also exposed by the rowset functions, FREETEXTTABLE and CONTAINSTABLE. These are complementary functions that accept parameters including a search phrase. Unlike their predicate counterparts, however, these functions return rowsets consisting of two columns—a key column appropriately named KEY and a rank column named RANK. The rowsets returned by these functions can be returned to the client application or used server-side to join against the source table (or another related table). You can sort the results in descending order to push the most relevant results to the top of the result set. We'll explore the details of how these predicates work and the algorithms they use in this chapter. We'll cover the FREETEXT predicate and FREETEXTTABLE function first, as they're the simplest. We'll then tackle the more advanced options available via the CONTAINS predicate and CONTAINSTABLE function.

FREETEXT and FREETEXTTABLE

One of the most common problems DBAs have when deploying search applications is low recall (the searches miss relevant results). The most common causes for this are that either the content hasn't been indexed correctly or the search phrase hasn't been constructed appropriately.

The most common reason a searcher can't find what she's looking for is because the search is being too strict—for example, the user's searching for documents containing the word *book* and frustrated when documents containing the word *books* aren't returned, or when searching for *jog* and the results don't return documents containing the word *jogging*.

The FREETEXT predicate and FREETEXTTABLE function searches automatically expand your search terms to include all noun conjugations (including plurals, gender, and case) and declensions (verb forms) of the root of the original search term. So a search for the word *jog* is expanded to a search for the following:

- *jog*

- *jogging*

- *jogged*

A search for the word *book* is expanded to include the following:

- *books*

- *booked*

- *booking*

- *book*

In the case of the word *book*, both verb and noun forms are included. FREETEXT queries also automatically apply all thesaurus expansions and replacements for the language being used in the query, as well as the global thesaurus entries for all languages. As an example, you might include thesaurus entries to expand the word *jog* to include the words *run* and *sprint* as well. We'll discuss thesaurus expansions and replacements in detail in Chapter 8.

Another feature of a FREETEXT query is that *nearness*, or separation distance, is factored into rank. Nearness is a measure of how close individual search tokens are to one another in the matching content. By default, a multitoken search using the CONTAINS predicate will only return rows where the tokens or words are adjacent to one another—that is, there are no words in between tokens. You can override this behavior with the NEAR operator or by including a Boolean operator (AND, OR, or AND NOT) between search tokens. As an example, a default CONTAINS search for *University of California* won't match with *University California*, but in a FREETEXT search it will match.

NEARNESS AND RANK

With regard to nearness and rank, the behavior of SQL Server 2008 iFTS has changed somewhat from SQL Server 2005 FTS. In SQL Server 2008, the closer any two search terms are to one another, the higher the ranking. As an example, the phrase *dollar is not a sign* has a three-word separation distance between the terms *dollar* and *sign*. In SQL Server 2005, if the search token separation distance was greater than 3,978 words, the rows weren't returned in search results. In SQL Server 2008, as long as all search tokens are in the content, they will be returned in searches and nearness is factored into rank. We tested separation distances up to one million words and confirmed this to be true.

FREETEXT is sometimes referred to as the "natural way to search"; however, many users complain about FREETEXT, as it often returns far too many irrelevant results, and result retrieval can be relatively slow. In actuality, FREETEXT is only marginally slower than CONTAINS searches, and the perceived slowness of FREETEXT tends to be a result of the large number of documents returned by a FREETEXT search.

■**Note** Microsoft switched the default search type in its Indexing Service product from CONTAINS to FREETEXT in version 2.0. That switch reportedly raised an inordinate number of support incidents reported to PSS (Product Support Services, now called Customer Support Services) in which users complained about irrelevant results. Before you implement a search solution using FREETEXT, ensure that it will be appropriate for your users.

In general, we don't recommend using FREETEXT in search applications that serve up technical documentation or knowledge base articles where the keywords are generally technical terms or nouns that don't have verb forms. In other words, avoid using FREETEXT for keyword-based searches. For catalogs or news service applications, FREETEXT is the recommended method, as the searches tend to be phrase-based as opposed to keyword-based. As an example, Google uses a FREETEXT-type algorithm for default searches. (Note that Google doesn't use SQL iFTS to power its searches, but rather a proprietary search engine.)

A FREETEXT search accepts up to three arguments. They are, in order:

- The first argument is a column list.

  - You can qualify columns using two-part names.

  - You can use the wildcard * character to indicate that all full-text-indexed columns should be included in the search.

  - You can use parentheses to enclose a comma-separated list containing multiple column names.

- The second argument is the search phrase, which should be a Unicode string using the appropriate iFTS FREETEXT or CONTAINS search predicate syntax.

- The third argument is an optional language setting specifier preceded by the LANGUAGE keyword.

Listing 3-2 demonstrates a simple FREETEXT search on a single column of the dbo.Book table, with results shown in Figure 3-1.

Listing 3-2. *FREETEXT Search on a Single Column*

```
SELECT b.Book_ID
FROM dbo.Book b
WHERE FREETEXT
(
  *,
  N'mutton'
);
```

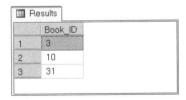

Figure 3-1. *Results of FREETEXT single-column search*

Alternatively, you can search on multiple specific columns as shown in Listing 3-3, with results shown in Figure 3-2.

Listing 3-3. *FREETEXT Search on Multiple Columns*

```
SELECT *
FROM dbo.Commentary c
WHERE FREETEXT
(
  (c.Commentary, c.Article_Content),
  N'Aristotle'
);
```

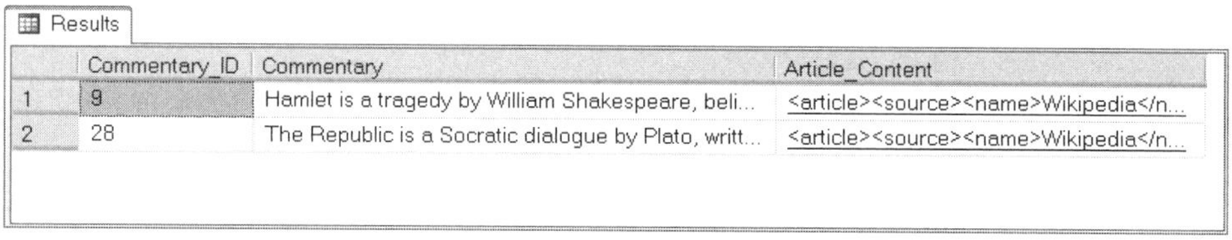

	Commentary_ID	Commentary	Article_Content
1	9	Hamlet is a tragedy by William Shakespeare, beli...	\<article\>\<source\>\<name\>Wikipedia\</n...
2	28	The Republic is a Socratic dialogue by Plato, writt...	\<article\>\<source\>\<name\>Wikipedia\</n...

Figure 3-2. *Result of multiple column FREETEXT search*

In Listing 3-3, we specified the exact columns that we wanted to search. Note that we also qualified columns using their two-part names: c.Commentary and c.Article_Content. Though this isn't strictly necessary in our example, it's useful to eliminate ambiguity when your queries are joining multiple tables.

When you full-text index a table, as described in Chapter 2, only the columns that you specify are actually included in the index. If you specify a column that isn't part of the full-text index in your search predicate, SQL Server will raise an error similar to the following:

```
Msg 7601, Level 16, State 3, Line 1
Cannot use a CONTAINS or FREETEXT predicate on column 'NonIndexedColumn' because
it is not full-text indexed.
```

Another option is to use the wildcard * symbol to search all full-text-indexed columns on a table, as shown in Listing 3-4. Results are shown in Figure 3-3.

Listing 3-4. *FREETEXT Query on All Indexed Columns*

```
SELECT b.Book_ID
FROM dbo.Book b
WHERE FREETEXT
(
  *,
  N'geometry'
);
```

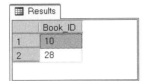

Figure 3-3. *Result of FREETEXT query on all indexed columns*

MULTIPLE LANGUAGE CODE ERRORS

Take care with language specifications when indexing your content. Normally, you'll want to index all of the columns in a table using a single language identifier or LCID. If you specify multiple LCIDs across different columns of a single table, you can't search them all in a single full-text search predicate. If your search query and target table meet all of the following conditions, your query will fail:

- There are multiple full-text indexed columns in a query.

- The full-text indexed columns are defined to be indexed by different language word breakers.

- A language is not specified in your query.

A query that fails for these reasons will generate an error message like the following:

```
Msg 7525, Level 16, State 1, Line 1
Full-text table or indexed view has more than one LCID among its
full-text indexed columns.
```

Chapter 5 delves into the concept of multilingual searches and explains how to circumvent this problem and search in multiple languages.

Adding a Language Specification

The optional *language* argument consists of the LANGUAGE keyword followed by an LCID or language name in single quotes. The *language* argument proves to be a common conceptual stumbling block. This argument is intended to be used when you're storing multilingual content in your full-text index columns and want to search the columns using a specific language. The common assumption is that if you search in English (LCID 1033), only documents written in English will be returned. The expectation among search users (and many developers) is that SQL Server iFTS is clever enough to figure out the language of your query and only return documents written in the language you specify. This is not the case.

The results returned are actually documents that contain any of the stemmed versions of your search phrase. A search on multilingual content will return all rows containing the search phrase (and any thesaurus expansions or substitutions as well as any conjugations and declensions of the search phrase).

As an example, if you search for *gift*, you'll get rows that contain the words *gifted, gift, gifts,* and *gifting. Gift* in German, however, means *poison.* This means you'll get rows with English content containing the word *gift,* but also rows in German that refer to the German word for poison. Listing 3-5 demonstrates a FREETEXT search for books containing the word *gift,* specifying English (LCID 1033) as the query language. Figure 3-4 shows that the results include German (LCID 1031) content containing the word *gift* as well.

Listing 3-5. *FREETEXT Search for "Gift", with English Language Specified*

```
SELECT b.Book_ID,
  b.Book_LCID
FROM dbo.Book b
WHERE FREETEXT
(
  b.Book_Content,
  N'gift',
  LANGUAGE 1033
);
```

	Book_ID	Book_LCID
1	3	1033
2	5	1033
3	6	1033
4	8	1033
5	9	1033
6	10	1033
7	11	1033
8	13	1033
9	15	1033
10	19	1031
11	23	1031
12	26	1033
13	27	1033
14	28	1033
15	31	1033
16	32	1033
17	39	1033

Figure 3-4. *English and German content returned by a FREETEXT query with English language specified*

In the example, you'll get some results that are exact word matches, but are completely irrelevant and probably not in a language the searcher understands. The name for these classes of words are *false friends* or *false conjugates*, not to be confused with *wanderworts*, which are words that are spelled the same (or pronounced the same) in different languages and have the same meaning (for example *wine*). We'll discuss false friends and wanderworts in greater detail in Chapter 5.

Using the language parameter is the best option when you're forced to store multilingual content in the same column, even though rows will be returned in a different language than what the user is searching in. Note that you can add an LCID column to specify the language of each row's content, as we've done in the dbo.Book table. To return only German content, you can add a Book_LCID = 1031 predicate to your WHERE clause in addition to specifying the language argument.

The key to understanding the language argument is the fact that language rules are applied during index time as well as at query time. These language rules are applied by the word breakers that tokenize content. When you specify the language you want your content indexed by, the appropriate language-specific word breaker is invoked at index time. You can specify this in the wizard or by using the LANGUAGE clause of the CREATE FULLTEXT INDEX statement. If you don't use the LANGUAGE clause, the default full-text language setting for your server is used. You can retrieve this setting via the sp_configure system stored procedure, as shown in Listing 3-6.

Listing 3-6. *Retrieving the Server Default Full-Text Language*

```
EXECUTE sp_configure 'default full-text language';
```

Keep in mind that certain filters override these settings if your content is stored in varbinary(max) or xml columns. The word breakers for Microsoft Office documents, XML documents, and HTML documents will override the default server settings and query-specific options, and will instead defer to language-specific settings stored within these documents. The word breakers for these types of documents apply language rules while extracting the content, also performing some expansion of words. The simple expansion that's performed at index time is not as comprehensive as the word stemming that's performed at query time. As an example, the types of index expansions that are performed on English content can be grouped into four categories, as follows:

1. *Hyphenation*: Words with hyphens are indexed as the base words, and then the base words are concatenated. For example, the word *data-base* will be indexed as *data, base*, and *database*. (This hyphenated spelling of the word *database* was prevalent in academic papers of the mid-to-late 20th century.)

2. *Acronyms*: Capitalized acronyms are indexed as the individual letters and as a unit. For example, the acronym *F.B.I.* is indexed as *fbi*, and *f.b.i.* On the other hand, *fbi* is indexed only as *fbi*. The lowercase acronym *f.b.i.* is only indexed as the individual letters *f, b*, and *i*. A search for the uppercase acronym *F.B.I.* finds documents containing *F.B.I., f.b.i., fbi*, and *FBI*. A search for *f.b.i.* will locate only documents containing *f.b.i.* and *F.B.I.*

3. *Currency and numbers*: Currencies are stored as the currency value and also using a special *nnCurrency* format. The value *$1.00* is indexed as *$1.00* and also as *nn1$*; *$1,23.45* is indexed as *$1,234.56* and *nn1,234dd56*. Non-currency numbers are indexed as the number and also using a format known as *nnNumber*. The number *3.14159* is indexed as both *3.14158* and *nn3dd14159*. This indexing scheme helps maintain consistency with other Microsoft search products that index numbers, to allow you to perform value-based searches on them. In other Microsoft search products, you could search for Word documents with a page count property greater than 100 pages. In SQL Server, all indexed properties are treated as strings in your searches.

4. *Date*: If a date to be indexed follows the format *MM/DD/YYYY* or any variant of that format (with the exception of dates with month names spelled out such as *January 31, 2008*), the date will be indexed in both a string format and a special *ddDate* format. The date *01/31/2008*, for example, is indexed as both *01/31/2008* and *dd20080131*.

Not all languages follow the same rules for hyphenation and acronyms, however. For some languages, compound words are indexed alongside alternate word forms. Indexing the German word *Haftzugsfestigkeitsprüfungsprotokoll* causes no less than six alternate word forms to be indexed. The query in Listing 3-7 uses the sys.dm_fts_parser DMF to display the alternate words for *Haftzugsfestigkeitsprüfungsprotokoll*. Results are shown in Figure 3-5. We'll explore the sys.dm_fts_parser DMF, and other useful views and functions, in Chapter 9.

Listing 3-7. *Parsing a German Search Term with a German Word Breaker*

```
SELECT *
FROM sys.dm_fts_parser
(
  N'Haftzugsfestigkeitsprüfungsprotokoll',
  1031,
  0,
  0
);
```

	special_term	display_term	source_term	occurrence
1	Exact Match	haftzugsfestigkeitsprufungsprotokoll	Haftzugsfestigkeitsprüfungsprotokoll	1
2	Exact Match	haft	Haftzugsfestigkeitsprüfungsprotokoll	1
3	Exact Match	zugs	Haftzugsfestigkeitsprüfungsprotokoll	2
4	Exact Match	festigkeit	Haftzugsfestigkeitsprüfungsprotokoll	3
5	Exact Match	prufung	Haftzugsfestigkeitsprüfungsprotokoll	4
6	Exact Match	protokoll	Haftzugsfestigkeitsprüfungsprotokoll	5

Figure 3-5. *Alternate word forms of a single German word*

When you search for one of the alternate word forms shown in Figure 3-5, the source term will be matched as well. Compound words aren't exclusive to German; they also exist in Finnish, Swedish, and other languages. Each language may have different rules concerning hyphenation and other specific word-breaking details.

The Dutch language, for instance, treats hyphenation differently than most other languages. In most languages, a hyphen implies that a word should be treated as a single unit, and the unit will sometimes appear unhyphenated. As we described previously, the English word *data-base* is indexed as *data*, *base*, and *database*. In Dutch, hyphenation is for the most part preserved, so that *kop-van-jut* is indexed as three separate words: *kop*, *van*, and *jut*. There are some exceptions, though, such as the word *kop-hals-rompboerderij*, which is indexed as *kop-hals-rompboerderij*, *kop-hals-romp*, *boerderij*, *kop-hals-rompboerderij*, and *kophalsrompboerderij*. Listing 3-8 contains a few sample queries to illustrate Dutch hyphenation, with results shown in Figure 3-6.

Listing 3-8. *Dutch Word Breaker Hyphenation in Action*

```
SELECT
  special_term,
  display_term,
  source_term,
  occurrence
FROM sys.dm_fts_parser
(
  N'kop-van-jut',
  1043,
  0,
  0
);
GO

SELECT
  special_term,
  display_term,
  source_term,
  occurrence
FROM sys.dm_fts_parser
(
  N'pianiste-componiste',
  1043,
  0,
  0
);
GO

-- The above are indexed as separate words. The following demonstrates how
-- the entire token is indexed as a unit, both with and without hyphens in place
```

```
SELECT
  special_term,
  display_term,
  source_term,
  occurrence
FROM sys.dm_fts_parser
(
  N'kop-hals-rompboerderij',
  1043,
  0,
  0
);
GO
```

Figure 3-6. *Results of Dutch word-breaker hyphenation*

Because of differences in how various word breakers handle hyphenation and index hyphenated words, we advise against stripping hyphens out of your search queries.

Keep in mind that when querying, you should specify the same language settings you used to create the index. If you indexed your content in Dutch and you search for the word *data-base* using the English language word breaker, the search will attempt to locate the words *data* and *base*; you won't find content containing the word *database*. If your content was indexed using the US English word breaker, however, you would find content containing the word *database*.

Returning the Top N by RANK

In many search applications, only a small percentage of search results are returned. This is done mainly for performance reasons, and it works well because users tend to find what they're looking for in the first page of results. If the first page of results doesn't contain the required results, users will generally refine their search and try again. Although most users don't check secondary pages of search results, there are some search applications where users have a greater probability of reading beyond the first page. For example, in most job search applications, users can be counted on to view several pages.

When large numbers of search results are returned, it may not be practical to transfer the entire result set to the client for client-side paging. You can use the *top_n_by_rank* argument to limit results in such cases. The *top_n_by_rank* argument is a fourth optional argument available only with the FREETEXTTABLE and CONTAINSTABLE functions. Listing 3-9 illustrates how this works, with the results shown in Figure 3-7.

Listing 3-9. *Retrieving the Top Five Search Results by Rank*

```
SELECT
  t.*,
  k.[RANK]
FROM dbo.Book b
INNER JOIN dbo.Book_Title bt
  ON b.Book_ID = bt.Book_ID
INNER JOIN dbo.Title t
  ON bt.Title_ID = t.Title_ID
INNER JOIN FREETEXTTABLE
(
  dbo.Book,
  *,
  N'fish',
  5
) AS k
  ON k.[KEY] = b.Book_ID
WHERE t.Is_Primary_Title = 1
ORDER BY k.[RANK] DESC;
```

	Title_ID	Title_LCID	Is_Primary_Ti...	Title	RANK
1	42	1033	1	Legends of the Gods, The Egyptian Texts, Edited With Translation	977
2	63	1033	1	The American Standard Version of the Holy Bible	973
3	21	1033	1	The "Aldine" Edition of the Arabian Nights Entertainments	961
4	10	1033	1	Bulfinch's Mythology: The Age of Fable	945
5	40	1033	1	Alice's Adventures In Wonderland	944

Figure 3-7. *Top N by Rank FREETEXT query results*

In this example, the *top_n_by_rank* argument is set to 5, ensuring that only the first five results in descending order of RANK are returned.

■**Note** In SQL Server 2005, there was an additional setting for "precompute rank" that gave a performance boost for FREETEXTTABLE queries in which the *top_n_by_rank* argument was used. This setting is deprecated in SQL 2008 and is not operational—it doesn't do anything. This feature is no longer required, as the iFTS query engine is now fully integrated with SQL Server.

CONTAINS

CONTAINS returns exact or literal matches for a search phrase. Queries for the word *run*, for instance, will only match content containing the exact word *run* and not *runs* or *runt*. Only content containing character-for-character matches is returned. However, you can select the degree of imprecision, closeness, or fuzziness in your search using additional query string options. Taken to its extreme, you can make CONTAINS functionally equivalent to FREETEXT. Listing 3-10 demonstrates a simple CONTAINS query, with the result shown in Figure 3-8.

Listing 3-10. *Simple CONTAINS Query*

```
SELECT b.Book_ID
FROM dbo.Book b
WHERE CONTAINS
(
  *,
  N'leaf'
);
```

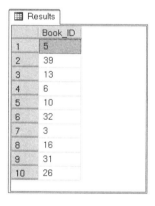

Figure 3-8. *Result of simple CONTAINS query*

As with the FREETEXT search, the CONTAINS predicate supports the ability to specify whether to search a single column, multiple columns, or all columns. The CONTAINS predicate supports several types of modifiers, including the following:

- Phrase

- Boolean

- Prefix

- Generational

- Proximity

- Weighted

We'll describe each of these search modifiers in turn in the following sections.

Phrase Searches

You can search for phrases as opposed to a single word. To specify a phrase in a CONTAINS search, you have to wrap the entire phrase in double quotes. Listing 3-11 is a simple CONTAINS search for the phrase "*cats and dogs*". The result is shown in Figure 3-9.

Listing 3-11. *Simple CONTAINS Phrase Search*

```
SELECT b.Book_ID
FROM dbo.Book b
WHERE CONTAINS
(
  *,
  N'"cats and dogs"'
);
```

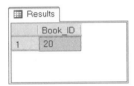

Figure 3-9. *Result of simple CONTAINS phrase search*

If you look at the Messages tab in SSMS after running this query, you'll notice that SQL Server returned an informational warning message because the search phrase in Listing 3-11 contains the noise word *and*. The warning message looks like the following:

```
Informational: The full-text search condition contained noise word(s).
```

The issue of full-text search conditions that contain noise words can be problematic when one token in a Boolean search is a stopword, as shown in Listing 3-12, which is a slightly modified version of the query in Listing 3-11.

Listing 3-12. *Boolean Search with a Stopword*

```
SELECT b.Book_ID
FROM dbo.Book b
WHERE CONTAINS
(
  *,
  N'"cats" and "and"'
);
```

By default this query returns no results, even though there are documents that contain the word *cats*. This is because the word *and* is on the English stoplist, so no documents will ever match the Boolean condition `"cats" and "and"`. You have three possible options to get around this behavior, as listed following:

1. Strip stopwords out of search conditions before submitting them to the server. This could be done in a client application prior to performing the SQL iFTS query.

2. Remove stopwords you want to include in searches from the stopword list. In SQL Server 2008, you could create a custom stoplist (possibly based on an existing system stoplist), remove the stopwords you want to include in queries, and assign the newly created stoplist to a full-text index. We discuss stoplists in depth in Chapter 7.

3. Enable stopword transformations via server settings. Note that SQL Server 2008 still refers to this as "noise word" transformations. You can change this setting via `sp_configure`:

```
EXECUTE sp_configure 'show advanced options', 1;
RECONFIGURE WITH OVERRIDE;
GO

EXECUTE sp_configure 'transform noise words', 1;
RECONFIGURE WITH OVERRIDE;
GO
```

After you change the `transform noise words` server option, SQL Server replaces stopwords with a wildcard asterisk (*) in search conditions. This means the search condition shown in Listing 3-11 is transformed to `'"cats" and "*"'`, and will return results.

Boolean Searches

As we discussed briefly in the previous section, you can use Boolean operators in your search condition (such as AND, AND NOT, and OR for each term of your search condition). In this book we'll capitalize Boolean operators; however, they're treated as case-insensitive. Boolean operators allow you to search for combinations of multiple search tokens and phrases that might not be contiguous (right next to each other), as Listing 3-13 demonstrates. The results include documents that contain both the words *sword* and *shield*, regardless of where they occur in the document content, as shown in Figure 3-10.

Listing 3-13. *Searching for Phrases with the AND Boolean Operator*

```
SELECT b.Book_ID
FROM dbo.Book b
WHERE CONTAINS
(
  *,
  N'"sword" and "shield"'
);
```

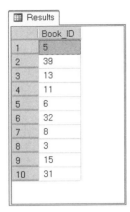

Figure 3-10. *Results of Boolean AND search*

■Tip You can also use symbolic abbreviated forms of the Boolean operators: & for AND, | for OR, and &! for AND NOT. The Boolean operator combination OR NOT has no significance in iFTS and is not supported.

In some cases, you may wish to search for multiple variants of a single word; for example, *center* is sometimes spelled *centre*, so a search for *center* won't return content that uses the alternate spelling *centre*. Listing 3-14 shows how you can use a Boolean OR operator to search for documents containing either spelling. Results are shown in Figure 3-11.

Listing 3-14. *Using OR to Search for Phrases with Different Spellings*

```
SELECT Book_ID
FROM dbo.Book
WHERE CONTAINS
(
  *,
  N'"center" OR "centre"'
);
```

You can also combine search terms using multiple Boolean expressions and group them with parentheses. Listing 3-15 combines the phrases *performing, center,* and *centre* using the Boolean AND and OR operators, with results shown in Figure 3-12.

Results

	Book_ID
1	5
2	9
3	6
4	10
5	32
6	8
7	14
8	27
9	3
10	22
11	15
12	16
13	31
14	26
15	7
16	20
17	24
18	28

Figure 3-11. *Results of Boolean OR search*

Listing 3-15. *Searching with Multiple Boolean Expressions*

```
SELECT Book_ID
FROM dbo.Book
WHERE CONTAINS
(
  *,
  N'"performing" AND ("center" OR "centre")'
);
```

Results

	Book_ID
1	5
2	10
3	32
4	16
5	26
6	28

Figure 3-12. *Results of search with multiple Boolean expressions*

In some cases, you may need to filter your search to exclude a given term. For example, in a search for *fish*, you might not want to see any references to *hook*. In this case, you can use the Boolean AND NOT operator to filter out any results containing the term *hook*. This particular search would look like Listing 3-16. Although the sample database contains 16 books with the word *fish* in them, only four of those don't contain the word *hook*, as shown in Figure 3-13.

Listing 3-16. *Using AND NOT to Exclude Search Terms*

```
SELECT Book_ID
FROM dbo.Book
WHERE CONTAINS
(
  *,
  N'"fish" AND NOT "hook"'
);
```

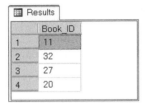

Figure 3-13. *Results of Boolean AND NOT search*

Prefix Searches

The CONTAINS predicate also allows you to do basic wildcard prefix searches. This is indicated by the wildcard asterisk (*) operator. A wildcard prefix search for the term *run** returns documents containing the words *run, runs, runt, running, runner*—in short, anything that matches the first part of the search argument up to the *. No stemming is done in a prefix search, so that a search on *mice** doesn't return content containing the word *mouse*, for instance. The query shown in Listing 3-17 returns matches for all words that begin with the prefix *chl**, such as *chlorophyll, chlorine*, and *chloride*. Results are shown in Figure 3-14.

Listing 3-17. *Prefix Search Example*

```
SELECT Book_ID
FROM dbo.Book
WHERE CONTAINS
(
  *,
  N'"chl*"'
);
```

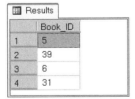

Figure 3-14. *Results of prefix search*

■**Note** For wildcard searches to work, you must wrap the terms in double quotes. If you don't include the search term in double quotes, SQL Server treats the trailing asterisk as part of the search term and attempts to match the search term exactly, trailing asterisk included. Also note that if your search phrase includes multiple words, all of the words in the phrase are treated as wildcard prefixes. That is, a search for *"al* anon"* performs a prefix search for words that begin with *al** followed immediately by words that begin with *anon**, including *Al Anon, alcoholics anonymous, Allan Anonymous*, and many others.

One commonly requested wildcard feature is suffix searches—using the wildcard character at the start of a search term like **ing* to match all words ending in the suffix *ing*. SQL iFTS doesn't allow this type of search. If you absolutely need this type of search functionality, one approach is to store all of your content in reverse, so "*The rain in Spain stays mainly in the plain*" could be stored as "*nialp eht ni ylniam syats niapS ni niar ehT*". Then if you wanted to search for words ending in *ain*, you could simply reverse the search suffix and append the wildcard character to the end like this: *nia**. It's not clear why the FTS engine doesn't support suffix-based wildcard searching, as some other RDBMS search components do (including both DB2 and Oracle).

Generational Searches

Generational searches are searches in which either, or all, of the following occur:

- Words are stemmed, which simply means that additional forms of the words are generated and matched, including plural nouns and verb forms. This is known as *inflectional term generation*.

- Search terms are replaced via language-specific thesaurus replacement sets. This is included in *thesaurus term generation*.

- Search terms are expanded via language-specific thesaurus expansion sets. This is also part of thesaurus term generation.

Though the FREETEXT predicate that we discussed previously will automatically perform word stemming and thesaurus expansions and replacements, the CONTAINS predicate does not. In order to perform generational searches with CONTAINS, you have to use the FORMSOF operator and indicate whether you want to use INFLECTIONAL or THESAURUS forms. Listing 3-18 uses the CONTAINS inflectional term generation to match inflectional forms of the word *punch*, including *punch, punches, punched*, and *punching*. Results are shown in Figure 3-15.

Listing 3-18. *Inflectional Term Generation with CONTAINS*

```
SELECT Book_ID
FROM dbo.Book
WHERE CONTAINS
(
  *,
  N'FORMSOF(INFLECTIONAL, punch)'
);
```

Figure 3-15. *CONTAINS inflectional term generation search*

Proximity Searches

SQL Server iFTS also allows you to perform searches that require search terms to be in close proximity to one another. Suppose you want to locate books about the presidential role of commander-in-chief of the armed forces. You might choose to search for the words *president* and *army*, as shown in Listing 3-19. As you can see in Figure 3-16, the results include several books that probably have little or nothing to do with your topic of choice. Instead, most of the books probably refer to your keywords in passing at some point in their text.

Listing 3-19. *Searching for the Phrases "president" and "army"*

```
SELECT
  ct.[KEY],
  ct.[RANK],
  t.Title
FROM CONTAINSTABLE
(
  dbo.Book,
  *,
  N'"president" AND "army"'
) ct
INNER JOIN dbo.Book_Title bt
  ON ct.[KEY] = bt.Book_ID
INNER JOIN dbo.Title t
  ON bt.Title_ID = t.Title_ID
WHERE t.Is_Primary_Title = 1;
```

	KEY	RANK	Title
1	3	2	A Connecticut Yankee in King Arthur's Court
2	5	1	Bulfinch's Mythology: The Age of Fable
3	10	1	The "Aldine" Edition of the Arabian Nights Entertainments
4	13	1	Antony and Cleopatra
5	14	1	Big Dummy's Guide to the Internet, v. 2.2
6	16	8	The Campaigns of the British Army at Washington and New Orleans 1814-1815
7	26	2	Legends of the Gods, The Egyptian Texts, Edited With Translation
8	31	1	Mothers' Remedies
9	32	4	Life and Public Services of John Quincy Adams

Figure 3-16. *Results of search for "president" and "army"*

As you can imagine, *Mothers' Remedies* (a book about home health) is not exactly the type of book that addresses the chief executive's role in relation to the armed forces. You can use proximity searches, via the NEAR operator, to return more relevant results. The theory behind proximity search is that documents with search terms that are close to one another (like *president* and *army* used in the example) are probably more relevant to the search topic. The NEAR operator returns a higher RANK for matching documents when the search terms are in close proximity to one another, and a lower RANK when the search terms are far apart. When the search terms are separated by more than 50 words, the RANK drops to 0. Listing 3-20 performs a proximity search and restricts the results to those with a RANK greater than 0. The results, in Figure 3-17, show the more relevant documents found.

Listing 3-20. *NEAR Proximity Search for "president" and "army"*

```
SELECT
  ct.[KEY],
  ct.[RANK],
  t.Title
FROM CONTAINSTABLE
(
  dbo.Book,
  *,
  N'"president" NEAR "army"'
) ct
INNER JOIN dbo.Book_Title bt
  ON ct.[KEY] = bt.Book_ID
INNER JOIN dbo.Title t
  ON bt.Title_ID = t.Title_ID
WHERE t.Is_Primary_Title = 1
  AND ct.[RANK] > 0;
```

	KEY	RANK	Title
1	16	1	The Campaigns of the British Army at Washington and New Orleans 1814-1815
2	32	1	Life and Public Services of John Quincy Adams

Figure 3-17. *Books about the president and the army*

The two titles returned by the query in Listing 3-20 are more likely to be relevant to the role of president as civilian leader of the military than most of the other previous results.

■**Tip** As an alternative, you can use the ~ operator instead of the NEAR keyword to perform a proximity search.

Proximity search in iFTS has some limitations, including the following:

- The `NEAR` operator is internally mapped to the `AND` operator. The further apart your search terms are from one another, the lower the ranking of matches returned by your proximity search. This has a big implication for your proximity searches: the `NEAR` operator is basically useless with the iFTS `CONTAINS` and `FREETEXT` predicates (it's no different from using the `AND` operator). To get a true proximity search, you need to use `CONTAINSTABLE` or `FREETEXTTABLE` and restrict the results with a `WHERE` clause. Your `WHERE` clause predicate should specify that the `RANK` column returned by the iFTS function needs to be greater than 0 (for any proximity search match), or greater than some other value for a higher quality match.

- The `CONTAINS` and `FREETEXT` predicate proximity operators operate differently from the `CONTAINSTABLE` and the `FREETEXTTABLE` proximity operators. In the iFTS functions, proximity is calculated into the rank. In other words, with `CONTAINSTABLE` and `FREETEXTTABLE`, the closer your search terms are to one another, the higher the rank (all other things being equal). By contrast, the order in which `CONTAINS` and `FREETEXT` results are returned does not in any way reflect the separation distance of the search terms. You may find the first row of results returned by the iFTS predicates has the search terms farthest apart, and the next row has the search terms closest together.

- There's no way to change the definition of "closeness" that proximity search uses. The iFTS team worked hard to include a method to define distance separation by word, sentence, paragraph, and so on. This functionality would've let you search documents for the search phrase *Dick Cheney* within five words of *Halliburton*, for instance. Unfortunately, due to time constraints, this feature was cut late in the SQL Server 2008 development cycle. The authors are hopeful that this much-needed feature will ship in a service pack, or in the next version of SQL Server.

Additionally, if you use the same search term twice in a proximity search, as in `"africa"` `NEAR` `"africa"`, iFTS looks for two distinct instances of the search term (in this case `"africa"`) in close proximity to one another in the searched content. Documents containing only one instance of the search term are not returned by the proximity search.

Weighted Searches

Sometimes you need to do a search in which two topics are hopelessly intertwined, and yet you want to search for one topic alone. Using a Boolean `AND NOT` operator isn't an option, because it will filter out some relevant hits. What you need is a way to maximize the impact of the term you want to include while minimizing the contribution of the term you want to exclude. In iFTS terms, what you want is a weighted search. In this type of search, you apply weights to your tokens to make some tokens more relevant than others.

Let's consider a search for *Ike Turner* (Tina's ex-husband). Ike was a prominent musician and producer in his own right, but Internet searches on him return results that are mostly about his more famous ex-wife *Tina Turner* (a Google search, for example, returns about 1.3 million hits). Excluding *Tina* returns almost 1/2 million hits. However, these results are primarily about Ike's life after Tina, leaving out a lot of relevant information. In other words, you don't want to exclude *Tina Turner* from the search completely.

For our purposes, we'll locate books about *Caesar*, the Roman emperor. There are several books that mention Caesar in passing (Caesar not being the topic of the book). For instance, Shakespeare's *Hamlet* mentions Caesar: *"Imperious Caesar, dead and turn'd to clay."* You can add additional search terms such as *Rome* to the search and apply a weight to each term to increase the relevance of the results. Listing 3-21 demonstrates. The results are shown in Figure 3-18.

Listing 3-21. *Weighted ISABOUT Search for Caesar and Rome*

```
SELECT
  ct.[KEY],
  ct.[RANK],
  t.Title
FROM CONTAINSTABLE
(
  dbo.Book,
  *,
  N'ISABOUT("Caesar" WEIGHT(1), "Rome" WEIGHT(.1))'
) ct
INNER JOIN dbo.Book_Title bt
  ON ct.[KEY] = bt.Book_ID
INNER JOIN dbo.Title t
  ON bt.Title_ID = t.Title_ID
WHERE t.Is_Primary_Title = 1
  ORDER BY ct.[RANK] DESC;
```

	KEY	RANK	Title
1	13	552	Antony and Cleopatra
2	25	417	Julius Caesar
3	12	376	Antony and Cleopatra
4	39	34	The American Standard Version of the Holy Bible
5	24	10	Julius Caesar
6	5	5	Bulfinch's Mythology: The Age of Fable
7	9	3	Hamlet
8	32	3	Life and Public Services of John Quincy Adams
9	27	2	孫子兵法
10	31	0	Mothers' Remedies
11	11	0	All's Well That Ends Well
12	3	0	A Connecticut Yankee in King Arthur's Court
13	16	0	The Campaigns of the British Army at Washingt...
14	20	0	Alice's Adventures In Wonderland
15	21	0	Hamlet
16	22	0	Hamlet

Figure 3-18. *Results of search for books about Caesar of Rome*

As you can see, the weighted values ensure that the documents returned contain the keywords with weights applied to them. The weighted terms are factored into the final RANK, with the higher RANK values representing better quality matches. Shakespeare's *Antony and Cleopatra*, for instance, is a much better match than *Alice's Adventures in Wonderland*, even though both documents mention *Caesar* or *Rome*.

The WEIGHT value ranges from 0 to 1, with 1 being the highest. The weights you assign to your search terms also affect the result rankings generated by the CONTAINSTABLE function. Weighted terms are also valuable when you're doing a taxonomy-based search. SQL Server iFTS doesn't natively support such advanced taxonomy searches, but they can be implemented via third-party software in data mining and client search applications.

CONTAINSTABLE Searches

The CONTAINS and FREETEXT predicates don't give you any method of limiting the number of rows returned in your result sets. This has two implications: First, you may get more results than you need, which will degrade performance on your system, and second, the results aren't returned in any particular order. CONTAINSTABLE and FREETEXTTABLE help alleviate this problem by assigning a rank to each result and giving you the ability to use the *top_n_by_rank* argument to only return the top *n* results. Listing 3-22 shows a typical usage of the CONTAINSTABLE function. Note that the results are joined back to relevant tables using the KEY column of the result set, and the results are ordered in descending order by the RANK column. Results are shown in Figure 3-19.

Listing 3-22. *Simple CONTAINSTABLE Function Usage*

```
SELECT
  c.[KEY],
  c.[RANK],
  t.Title
FROM dbo.Book_Title bt
INNER JOIN dbo.Title t
  ON bt.Title_ID = t.Title_ID
INNER JOIN CONTAINSTABLE
(
  dbo.Book,
  Book_Content,
  N'monster'
) c
  ON bt.Book_ID = c.[KEY]
WHERE t.Is_Primary_Title = 1
ORDER BY c.[RANK] DESC;
```

	KEY	RANK	Title
1	8	74	The Golden Fleece and the Heroes Who Lived Before Achilles
2	5	44	Bulfinch's Mythology: The Age of Fable
3	10	28	The "Aldine" Edition of the Arabian Nights Entertainments
4	28	7	Πολιτεία
5	26	6	Legends of the Gods, The Egyptian Texts, Edited With Translation
6	6	4	The Odyssey of Homer Done Into English Prose
7	39	4	The American Standard Version of the Holy Bible
8	31	1	Mothers' Remedies
9	32	1	Life and Public Services of John Quincy Adams
10	3	1	A Connecticut Yankee in King Arthur's Court
11	13	1	Antony and Cleopatra
12	14	1	Big Dummy's Guide to the Internet, v. 2.2
13	16	1	The Campaigns of the British Army at Washington and New Orleans 1814-1815

Figure 3-19. *Results of CONTAINSTABLE search*

You can also add the optional *top_n_by_rank* argument, as shown in Listing 3-23. In this example, only the top five rows from the results in Figure 3-19 are returned. The results are also sorted in descending order by rank.

Listing 3-23. *CONTAINSTABLE with the top n by rank Argument*

```
SELECT
  c.[KEY],
  c.[RANK],
  t.Title
FROM dbo.Book_Title bt
INNER JOIN dbo.Title t
  ON bt.Title_ID = t.Title_ID
INNER JOIN CONTAINSTABLE
(
  dbo.Book,
  Book_Content,
  N'monster',
  5
) c
  ON bt.Book_ID = c.[KEY]
WHERE t.Is_Primary_Title = 1;
```

If you return the rank, you'll see that it's a value between 0 and 1000. The rank value is derived from a statistical method that attempts to assign a value to the relevance of each result. The higher the rank, the more relevant your result; 1000 indicates a perfect match. SQL Server iFTS uses a formula known as the Jaccard coefficient in the rank calculation.

Advanced Search Topics

In this section, we'll discuss advanced search topics, including how to use the XQuery `contains()` function in conjunction with iFTS and weighted column searches. In addition, we'll introduce taxonomy-based search and text mining concepts.

Using XQuery contains() Function

You can use the iFTS `CONTAINS` and `FREETEXT` predicates in conjunction with the XQuery `contains()` function when searching XML data. One important fact to remember is that, while iFTS is case insensitive, the XQuery `contains()` function is case sensitive. Ideally, you'd use `contains()` to determine precisely which node of your XML document holds the matching text. Consider the query in Listing 3-24.

Listing 3-24. *Using the XQuery contains() Function*

```
SELECT Article_Content
FROM dbo.Commentary
WHERE CONTAINS
(
  Article_Content,
  N'Bible'
)
AND Article_Content.exist(N'/article/title[contains(., "Bible")]') = 1;
```

The `dbo.Commentary` table has three XML articles in the `Article_Content` column that contain the word *Bible*. In this example, we use the iFTS `CONTAINS` predicate to retrieve the initial result set of all XML commentary entries that contain the word *Bible*. We then use the `xml` data type `exist()` method in conjunction with the XQuery `contains()` function to further narrow down the results to only those that have the word *Bible* in their `title` element.

Column Rank-Multiplier Searches

A frequent request on the newsgroups is the ability to search a table and return documents with different columns weighted differently. For example, one of the authors was approached by a web site designed to allow users to search publications by location.

The requirement the web site was struggling with was that a search for *England* (for example) should return rows ranked high where the hit occurred in the `City` column, slightly less in the `Publication_Name` column, and finally the `Description` column should be ranked low. The particular formula they came up with was that a hit coming from the `City` should have a rank multiplier of 5, a `Publication_Name` hit would be assigned a rank multiplier of 2, and a multiplier of 1 would be applied to hits coming from the `Description` column.

Listing 3-25 is a simple example of how to conduct such a search against the content in the `iFTS_Books` database. For this example, we're using a hit multiplier of 10 for hits anywhere in the `dbo.Contributor_Birth_Place` table, a multiplier of 5 for hits in the `Commentary` column of the `dbo.Commentary` table, and a multiplier of 1 for hits in the `Article_Content` column of the same table. Results are shown in Figure 3-20.

Listing 3-25. *Sample Column Rank-Multiplier Search*

```
SELECT *
FROM
(
  SELECT
    Commentary_ID,
    SUM([Rank]) AS Rank
  FROM
  (
    SELECT
      bc.Commentary_ID,
      c.[RANK] * 10 AS [Rank]
    FROM FREETEXTTABLE
    (
      dbo.Contributor_Birth_Place,
      *,
      N'England'
    ) c
    INNER JOIN dbo.Contributor_Book cb
      ON c.[KEY] = cb.Contributor_ID
    INNER JOIN dbo.Book_Commentary bc
      ON cb.Book_ID = bc.Book_ID
    UNION ALL
    SELECT
      c.[KEY],
      c.[RANK] * 5
    FROM FREETEXTTABLE
     (
      dbo.Commentary,
      Commentary,
      N'England'
    ) c
    UNION ALL
    SELECT
      ac.[KEY],
      ac.[RANK]
    FROM FREETEXTTABLE
     (
      dbo.Commentary,
      Article_Content,
      N'England'
    ) ac
  ) s
  GROUP BY Commentary_ID
) s1
INNER JOIN dbo.Commentary c1
  ON c1.Commentary_ID = s1.Commentary_ID
ORDER BY [Rank] DESC;
```

	Commentary_ID	Rank	Commentary_ID	Commentary	Article_Content
1	4	4714	4	The Authorized King James Version is an English ...	`<article><source><name>Wikipedia</name><url>htt...`
2	9	2520	9	Hamlet is a tragedy by William Shakespeare, belie...	`<article><source><name>Wikipedia</name><url>htt...`
3	19	2284	19	Julius Caesar is a tragedy by William Shakespear...	`<article><source><name>Wikipedia</name><url>htt...`
4	15	2100	15	The Hound of the Baskervilles is a crime novel by ...	`<article><source><name>Wikipedia</name><url>htt...`
5	20	1100	20	Alice's Adventures in Wonderland (1865) is a wor...	`<article><source><name>Wikipedia</name><url>htt...`
6	12	1100	12	Antony and Cleopatra is a play by William Shakes...	`<article><source><name>Wikipedia</name><url>htt...`
7	27	1086	27	The Art of War is a Chinese military treatise that w...	`<article><source><name>Wikipedia</name><url>htt...`
8	16	743	16	The history of the British Army spans over three a...	`<article><source><name>Wikipedia</name><url>htt...`
9	3	694	3	A Connecticut Yankee in King Arthur's Court is an ...	`<article><source><name>Wikipedia</name><url>htt...`
10	11	550	11	All's Well That Ends Well is a play by William Shak...	`<article><source><name>Wikipedia</name><url>htt...`
11	26	550	26	Ancient Egyptian religion encompasses the religio...	`<article><source><name>Wikipedia</name><url>htt...`

Figure 3-20. *Results of column rank-multiplier search*

Taxonomy Search and Text Mining

Third-party providers sell taxonomies and thesauruses that define vectors for search terms. A vector for the search term *cholesterol* might look like the following.

```
{
  (Cholesterol,10),
  (milligrams, 3),
  (reducing, 2),
  (lipoprotein, 3),
  (prevents,2),
  (cholesterol levels, 3),
  (narrowing, 2),
  (fats, 3),
  (hdl cholesterol, 3),
  (factors, 4),
  (ldl receptors, 3),
  (fatty,3),
  (ldl cholesterol, 6),
  (deciliter, 3),
  (heart disease, 7),
  (risk of heart attack, 3),
  (risk, 8),
  (saturated 3),
  (lipid, 3)
}
```

The numbers in this sample vector are called *signatures*. If the relative frequencies of occurrence of these terms in a given body of text are close to the relative weights in this vector, the body of text (or a portion of it) is about *cholesterol*. This sample vector comes from Intellisophic (`intellisophic.com`), a vendor of taxonomies. Given a body of text, a user can do a weighted search using this vector (normalized for a max weight of 1) and the results would likely be about *cholesterol*.

Another company, Triplehop (`triplehop.com`, now part of Oracle), offers technology to generate vectors that can help achieve higher relevance in search results. As an example, if someone searches for the word *bank*, are they actually searching for a *financial institution*, a *river bank*, a *blood bank*, an *aircraft maneuver*, or an *expression of trust*? Triplehop can run search results through their vectors to understand the context of the search term in the search results and subsequently categorize the search results.

Taxonomies and vectors such as these are used in text-mining operations. Text mining operates on the principal that a topic can be reduced to a set of features, and then this set of features can be compared to documents to see which documents meet these features. The probability is higher that documents that closely match the features are about the given topic.

In text mining, we collect vectors or features of a topic (for example, *women*). These features are derived from a known training set (for example, a body of documents written by or about women). Once we've derived a training set, we run the training set against a document collection and score it for accuracy. If we get a high degree of accuracy (over 90% for example), we believe our vector is good and can use this vector in searches to find documents about the topic.

Using vector-based searches to determine context or features is sometimes referred to as a *bag of words* approach. Demographics can be inferred by searching for terms that are exclusive to females (for example, *my husband*, *my breasts*, and so on), and then determining other features that are exclusive to women from a document collection. After this, vectors can be created to do weighted searches to determine gender. To continue our example, research has been done that indicates women use more adverbs and adjectives in their writing than men. This information can be used to create additional training sets to generate vectors.

Summary

In this chapter, we looked at using the CONTAINS and FREETEXT predicates, and the CONTAINSTABLE and FREETEXTTABLE rowset functions. For keyword-type searches, use CONTAINS and CONSTAINSTABLE. For other types of searches, use FREETEXT and FREETEXTTABLE. If you want ranked results, you have to use the CONTAINSTABLE and FREETEXTTABLE rowset functions. CONTAINS and CONTAINSTABLE have many parameters that allow you to control how strict or fuzzy you want your searches to be. In general, CONTAINS and CONTAINSTABLE are faster than FREETEXT and FREETEXTTABLE, as the algorithm is marginally faster and CONTAINS searches generally return fewer rows.

CHAPTER 4

■■■

Client Applications

Everything should be made as simple as possible, but not simpler.

——Albert Einstein (attributed)

One of the challenges you'll face when designing iFTS-enabled applications is making them as simple as possible for your end users to access the full power of full-text search. While it's a relatively simple matter to perform a basic FREETEXT or CONTAINS query for user-supplied search terms or phrases, Web-based search engines have had a huge impact on the level of user sophistication. Users of search applications now demand features above and beyond basic term or phrase searches, including hit highlighting and access to advanced options through a simple interface. In this chapter, we'll discuss some methods to make your IFTS-enabled client applications simple yet powerful.

Hit Highlighting

Hit highlighting is standard fare for search applications. Simply put, hit highlighting is the process of highlighting key words or phrases in search results to make it apparent to your users that there was in fact a good match, along with an indication where one or more matches occurred in the results. With the new sys.dm_fts_parser dynamic management function (DMF), you can add simple SQL Server-based hit highlighting functionality to your applications, to provide additional context to your iFTS results.

The Procedure

Hit highlighting can be performed through stored procedures, client-side SQL code, or client-side or middle-tier client code (using .NET for example). Listing 4-1 is a simple stored procedure that performs hit highlighting using T-SQL on the server. The advantage to this method is that the hit highlighting logic, which must access the raw document data, is physically located close to the data. This eliminates the overhead associated with transferring large documents between the server and middle-tier or client-side applications.

Listing 4-1. *Simple Hit Highlighting Procedure*

```
CREATE PROCEDURE SimpleCommentaryHighlight
  @SearchTerm nvarchar(100),
  @Style nvarchar(200)
AS
BEGIN
  CREATE TABLE #match_docs
  (
    doc_id bigint NOT NULL PRIMARY KEY
  );

  INSERT INTO #match_docs
  (
    doc_id
  )
  SELECT DISTINCT
    Commentary_ID
  FROM Commentary
  WHERE FREETEXT
  (
    Commentary,
    @SearchTerm,
    LANGUAGE N'English'
  );

  DECLARE @db_id int = DB_ID(),
    @table_id int = OBJECT_ID(N'Commentary'),
    @column_id int =
    (
      SELECT
        column_id
      FROM sys.columns
      WHERE object_id = OBJECT_ID(N'Commentary')
        AND name = N'Commentary'
    );

  SELECT
    s.Commentary_ID,
    t.Title,
    MIN
    (
      N'...' + SUBSTRING
      (
        REPLACE
          (
            c.Commentary,
            s.Display_Term,
```

```
              N'<span style="' + @Style + '">' + s.Display_Term + '</span>'
          ),
        s.Pos - 512,
        s.Length + 1024
      ) + N'...'
  ) AS Snippet
FROM
  (
    SELECT DISTINCT
      c.Commentary_ID,
      w.Display_Term,
      PATINDEX
        (
          N'%[^a-z]' + w.Display_Term + N'[^a-z]%',
          c.Commentary
        ) AS Pos,
      LEN(w.Display_Term) AS Length
    FROM sys.dm_fts_index_keywords_by_document
      (
        @db_id,
        @table_id
      ) w
    INNER JOIN dbo.Commentary c
      ON w.document_id = c.Commentary_ID
    WHERE w.column_id = @column_id
      AND EXISTS
        (
          SELECT 1
          FROM #match_docs m
          WHERE m.doc_id = w.document_id
        )
      AND EXISTS
        (
          SELECT 1
          FROM sys.dm_fts_parser
            (
              N'FORMSOF(FREETEXT, "' + @SearchTerm + N'")',
              1033,
              0,
              1
            ) p
          WHERE p.Display_Term = w.Display_Term
        )
  ) s
INNER JOIN dbo.Commentary c
  ON s.Commentary_ID = c.Commentary_ID
```

```
INNER JOIN dbo.Book_Commentary bc
  ON c.Commentary_ID = bc.Commentary_ID
INNER JOIN dbo.Book_Title bt
  ON bc.Book_ID = bt.Book_ID
INNER JOIN dbo.Title t
  ON bt.Title_ID = t.Title_ID
WHERE t.Is_Primary_Title = 1
GROUP BY
  s.Commentary_ID,
  t.Title;

DROP TABLE #match_docs;

END;
```

■**Note** Although this procedure focuses on searching the `dbo.Commentary` table, it can be modified to search other tables as well. This procedure exists in the `iFTS_Books` sample database.

The `SimpleCommentaryHighlight` procedure accepts two parameters: a search term and an HTML style to use in highlighting matches. Listing 4-2 shows a simple example of how to call the stored procedure from Listing 4-1 to search for the term *write*. The results are shown in Figure 4-1.

Listing 4-2. *Calling the Hit Highlighting Stored Procedure*

```
EXECUTE SimpleCommentaryHighlight N'write',
  N'background-color:yellow; font-weight:bold';
```

	Commentary_ID	Title	Snippet
1	20	Alice's Adventures In Wonderland	...Alice's Adventures in Wonderland (1865) is a work of literary nonsense <span styl...
2	11	All's Well That Ends Well	...All's Well That Ends Well is a play by William Shakespeare, originally classified as ...
3	14	Big Dummy's Guide to the Internet...	...oject in September of 1991. The idea was to write a guide to the Internet for folks...
4	33	Elementare Arithmetik und Algebra	...Algebra is a branch of mathematics concerning the study of structure, relation and...
5	36	Grimm's Fairy Tales	...In 1803, the Grimms met the Romantics Clemens Brentano and Ludwig Achim von ...
6	9	Hamlet	...Hamlet is a tragedy by William Shakespeare, believed to have been <span style="...
7	19	Julius Caesar	...Julius Caesar is a tragedy by William Shakespeare, believed to have been <span ...
8	6	The Odyssey of Homer Done Into ...	...The Odyssey is one of two major ancient Greek epic poems attributed to Homer. ...
9	1	The Small Catechism of Martin Lut...	...Luther's Small Catechism was <span style="background-color:yellow; font-weight:b...
10	28	Πολιτεία	...The Republic is a Socratic dialogue by Plato, <span style="background-color:yello...
11	38	Στοιχεῖα	...Euclid's Elements is a mathematical and geometric treatise consisting of 13 books ...
12	27	孫子兵法	...The Art of War is a Chinese military treatise that was <span style="background-col...

Figure 4-1. *Results of hit highlighting procedure*

The procedure in Listing 4-1 performs a full-text search against the Commentary column of the dbo.Commentary table for the search terms you supply, storing the IDs of the matching documents in a temporary table:

```
CREATE TABLE #match_docs
(
  doc_id bigint NOT NULL PRIMARY KEY
);

INSERT INTO #match_docs
(
  doc_id
)
SELECT DISTINCT
  Commentary_ID
FROM Commentary
WHERE FREETEXT
(
  Commentary,
  @SearchTerm,
  LANGUAGE N'English'
);
```

The procedure then retrieves the current database ID, the object ID for the dbo.Commentary table, and the column ID of the Commentary column. All of this information will be used later in the procedure by the DMFs:

```
DECLARE @db_id int = DB_ID(),
  @table_id int = OBJECT_ID(N'Commentary'),
  @column_id int =
  (
    SELECT
      column_id
    FROM sys.columns
    WHERE object_id = OBJECT_ID(N'Commentary')
      AND name = N'Commentary'
  );
```

The final query—shown next—retrieves information about the match and a 1KB snippet of the text that contains matching terms. The SELECT clause of the query returns information about the match, including the ID of the commentary entry, the title of the book that the commentary item relates to, and a snippet of text from the matching commentary. The <span style="..."> HTML tag with the specified style is added to the matching terms:

```
SELECT
  s.Commentary_ID,
  t.Title,
  MIN
```

```
(
  N'...' + SUBSTRING
  (
    REPLACE
      (
        c.Commentary,
        s.Display_Term,
        N'<span style="' + @Style + '">' + s.Display_Term + '</span>'
      ),
      s.Pos - 512,
      s.Length + 1024
    ) + N'...'
) AS Snippet
```

The FROM clause uses the sys.dm_fts_index_keywords_by_document DMF to retrieve matching terms directly from the full-text index. The query uses sys.dm_fts_parser to grab all the inflectional and thesaurus forms of the search term to ensure that inflectional forms are matched. The PATINDEX function is used to locate matches for the inflectional forms within the text of the Commentary column. Finally, the query joins to other tables as necessary to retrieve book title information. The following is the FROM clause showing the logic just described, as well as the joins:

```
FROM
  (
    SELECT DISTINCT
      c.Commentary_ID,
      w.Display_Term,
      PATINDEX
        (
          N'%[^a-z]' + w.Display_Term + N'[^a-z]%',
          c.Commentary
        ) AS Pos,
      LEN(w.Display_Term) AS Length
    FROM sys.dm_fts_index_keywords_by_document
      (
        @db_id,
        @table_id
      ) w
    INNER JOIN dbo.Commentary c
      ON w.document_id = c.Commentary_ID
    WHERE w.column_id = @column_id
      AND EXISTS
        (
          SELECT 1
          FROM #match_docs m
          WHERE m.doc_id = w.document_id
        )
      AND EXISTS
```

```
        (
          SELECT 1
          FROM sys.dm_fts_parser
            (
              N'FORMSOF(FREETEXT, "' + @SearchTerm + N'")',
              1033,
              0,
              1
            ) p
          WHERE p.Display_Term = w.Display_Term
        )
    ) s
INNER JOIN dbo.Commentary c
  ON s.Commentary_ID = c.Commentary_ID
INNER JOIN dbo.Book_Commentary bc
  ON c.Commentary_ID = bc.Commentary_ID
INNER JOIN dbo.Book_Title bt
  ON bc.Book_ID = bt.Book_ID
INNER JOIN dbo.Title t
  ON bt.Title_ID = t.Title_ID
WHERE t.Is_Primary_Title = 1
GROUP BY
  s.Commentary_ID,
  t.Title;
```

HIT HIGHLIGHTING EFFICIENCY

Microsoft Index Server, through which SQL Server iFTS's lineage can be traced, provides built-in hit highlighting functionality that can be accessed through Internet Information Server (IIS) extensions. Surprisingly enough, this hit highlighting functionality is very similar to the methods presented here. Essentially, Index Server reparses matching documents using the relevant word breakers and stemmers to find hits. It then adds HTML tags to matching terms and returns the result. As you can imagine, this isn't the most efficient solution, particularly for large documents. A much more efficient solution for hit highlighting would be to store the exact character position of the matching term in the full-text index and expose it to your developers. This would eliminate the need to reprocess complete documents just to find hit locations. The tradeoff, of course, is the additional storage space required to save this additional information. You could, however, create your own inverted index on top of SQL Server 2008's to store the character positions of matching terms. But this would result in the storage of a not insignificant amount of duplicate information, as well as duplicated effort. The authors hold out the hope that the iFTS team will see the wisdom of exposing the start character position of matching terms in documents to make hit highlighting faster, more efficient, and more precise. We hope that this functionality, or similar functionality, will be added to a future version of SQL Server.

Calling the Procedure

On the client side, you can use the .NET SqlClient, SqlCommand, and SqlDataReader to perform hit highlighting queries and display results. The simple Windows Forms hit highlighting application we included in the sample downloads uses the stored procedure in Listing 4-1 to return hit highlighted results. Listing 4-3 is the heart of the procedure—it calls the hit highlighting procedure and displays the results. After a client query, the results are formatted in HTML and displayed in a Windows Forms WebBrowser control. Figure 4-2 shows the hit-highlighted results of a search for the term *write*.

Listing 4-3. *Client Call to Hit Highlighting Procedure*

```
string sqlConString = "SERVER=SQL2008;" +
  "INITIAL CATALOG=iFTS_Books;" +
  "INTEGRATED SECURITY=SSPI;";

private void SearchButton_Click(object sender, EventArgs e)
{
  SqlConnection sqlCon = null;
  SqlCommand sqlCmd = null;
  SqlDataReader sqlDr = null;

  try
  {
    sqlCon = new SqlConnection(sqlConString);
    sqlCon.Open();
    sqlCmd = new SqlCommand
    (
      "dbo.SimpleCommentaryHighlight",
      sqlCon
    );

    sqlCmd.CommandType = CommandType.StoredProcedure;

    sqlCmd.Parameters.Add
    (
      "@SearchTerm",
      SqlDbType.NVarChar,
      100
    ).Value = SearchText.Text;

    sqlCmd.Parameters.Add
    (
      "@Style",
      SqlDbType.NVarChar,
      200
    ).Value = "background-color:yellow; font-weight:bold;";
```

```
      sqlDr = sqlCmd.ExecuteReader();
      string Results = "";
      int RowCount = 0;

      while (sqlDr.Read())
      {
        RowCount++;
        if (RowCount % 2 == 1)
          Results += "<p style='background-color:#ffffff'>";
        else
          Results += "<p style='background-color:#C0C0C0'>";
        Results += "<b>" + sqlDr["Title"].ToString() + "</b><br>";
        Results += sqlDr["Snippet"].ToString() + "</p>";
      }

      Results = "<html><body>" +
        String.Format
        (
          "<p style='background-color:#FBB917'>" +
          "<b>Total Results Found: {0}</b></p>",
          RowCount
        ) +
        Results +
        "</body></html>";

      ResultWebBrowser.DocumentText = Results;
    }
    catch (Exception ex)
    {
      Console.WriteLine(ex.Message);
    }
    finally
    {
      if (sqlDr != null)
        sqlDr.Dispose();
      if (sqlCmd != null)
        sqlCmd.Dispose();
      if (sqlCon != null)
        sqlCon.Dispose();
    }
}
```

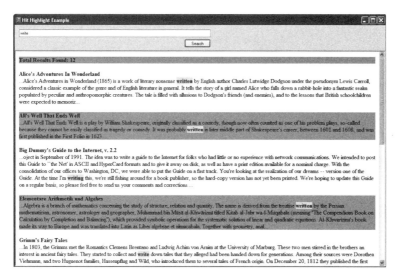

Figure 4-2. *Sample query with hit-highlighted results*

The concept of hit highlighting is simplified in this example, and you'll undoubtedly find situations in which the highlighted text returned is not the actual text that matched the search term (though it will be similar). An example is the search term *men*, which highlights *Clemens* in the commentary for the book *Grimm's Fairy Tales*. An actual match for the term *men* also exists in this particular commentary, and it is this match that's returned by iFTS queries. The hit highlighting procedure, however, uses a simple method of locating matches that can result in some nonmatching terms being partially highlighted.

Search Engine–Style Search

You have three main options when designing a front-end interface for your iFTS-based search applications:

1. You can ignore SQL Server's advanced iFTS search features and instead allow only simple FREETEXT or basic CONTAINS searches of lists of keywords entered by your users. This option doesn't allow users to perform searches that exclude words or phrases, return proximity-based matches, or use other advanced iFTS search features. Many front-end search applications for SQL Server full-text search implement this type of simplistic search functionality because it's quick and easy to implement, with little support required.

2. You can force users to learn advanced iFTS search clause features. This option allows users to perform more advanced searches, but also introduces a greater possibility for errors and higher support costs. The problem is that users have to learn a new search syntax, loaded down with additional keywords and a somewhat strict grammar. Consider the following simple query, which searches for inflectional forms of the words *fish* and *hook*:

```
CONTAINS(*, ' FORMSOF(INFLECTIONAL, fish) & FORMSOF(INFLECTIONAL, hook) '
```

In addition to getting the somewhat complex syntax exactly right, your users have to learn all the new keywords and a whole new method of searching for content with this option.

3. You can build on the knowledge that your users already have. In other words, allow your users to enter search queries in the syntax of their favorite search engine and programmatically convert it to the more complex iFTS CONTAINS syntax required by SQL Server behind the scenes. This option makes for an intuitive and simple user interface, making a more pleasurable overall user experience. You also gain greater control over user input, while allowing users to take advantage of whatever advanced functionality you deem necessary. The downside to this is that you have to do some development work, although the development work can be greatly simplified with the proper tools.

Thanks to Internet search engines such as Yahoo! and Google, search application users are more sophisticated and demanding than ever. Modern users have a wealth of search knowledge, and they know how search should work. By implementing option 3 from the prior list, you can put that knowledge of search to use within your organization. You'll save on training and support costs and create easy-to-use search applications your users will be able to sit down and use right out of the box. In this section, we'll discuss how to create your own search engine style interface.

The key to a successful search engine–style interface is to make the syntax simple but full-featured. Consider the Google search box for a moment. This search box is the essence of simplicity, using very few operators. Google's operators are intuitive. The preceding – unary operator, for instance, excludes a term from the search, while the OR keyword allows you to find pages containing either of the search terms on both sides of the operator. Our goal in designing a search engine style interface for iFTS will be to implement the same type of intuitive search syntax and operators.

We'll actually be creating a small toy language for defining Google-style queries. There are two important aspects to language: *syntax*, or the rules of language construction, and *semantics*, or what the components of the language actually do. We'll describe the language, including both syntax and semantics, in the following sections.

Defining a Grammar

A *grammar* is simply a set of rules that define the syntax of a language, whether it's a computer language or natural (human) language. The syntax doesn't have any inherent implied meaning or perform any actions by itself; that's the domain of semantics, which we'll cover later in this chapter. Fortunately for us, computer language grammars tend to be more rigid in their rules and construction than human language. You can actually define an explicit syntax for even the most complex Google-style queries, quite simply, using standard notations. We'll build that grammar here and use it as the building block for our Google-style query engine.

The first step in defining our grammar is to decide the operators and constructs we'll allow. To keep in line with our goal of making the interface simple to use, we'll use the popular Google search engine query syntax as the basis for our query engine. We'll support all of the operators in Table 4-1.

Table 4-1. *Custom Search Engine Operators*

Operator	Description
term	A search term is a single word. Search terms will be searched for using the iFTS inflectional search option.
term*	The trailing asterisk wildcard character on a term will perform a prefix search.
"*phrase*"	A phrase is one or more words enclosed in quotes. A phrase will be searched for using an iFTS phrase search.
+	A term or phrase prefixed with the plus operator performs an exact search; no inflectional or thesaurus forms will be found.
-	A term or phrase prefixed with the minus operator excludes the term or phrase from the search. This is equivalent to the iFTS AND NOT operator.
~	A term prefixed with the tilde operator performs a thesaurus synonym search.
<...>	Multiple terms or phrases can be included in angle brackets. The query engine will generate iFTS proximity searches using the NEAR operator for these terms and phrases.
and	The and keyword, or the symbol &, can be used between terms and phrases to indicate a logical AND operation. If you don't include a logical operator between terms and phrases, and will be the default.
or	The or keyword, or the symbol |, can be used between terms and phrases to indicate a logical OR operation. The logical AND operator takes precedence over logical OR.
(...)	Parentheses can be used to group expressions and to change the order of precedence of operators.

This simple set of operators and constructs includes most of the basic operators available via the Google search engine, with a few slight changes and additions to take advantage of additional iFTS functionality. For example, we've made the following changes to Google's basic syntax:

- The <...> syntax takes advantage of iFTS proximity search functionality.

- The (...) syntax is an intuitive syntax for changing the order of precedence of logical operators.

- The \| and & symbols, in addition to the and and or keywords, give the user additional simple options based on their personal preferences.

- The wildcard * character has a slightly modified behavior compared to the Google wildcard.

▪Tip The *Google Help: Cheat Sheet*, which describes the Google search query syntax that we used as a basis for our grammar, is located at http://www.google.com/help/cheatsheet.html.

Note that in our example we won't override or circumvent normal SQL iFTS behavior in our query engine to make it operate in a more Google-like fashion—all iFTS query rules and behaviors still apply. We will, however, supplement the interface by providing end users with a syntax that is simpler and more intuitive than the standard iFTS syntax.

Extended Backus-Naur Form

After we define our operators, the next step is to explicitly define the syntax of the grammar. The standard method for defining a grammar is *Extended Backus-Naur Form (EBNF)*. In EBNF, named *productions* are shown to the left of a ::= operator, while the components that make up those productions are shown to the right. You can think of the ::= operator in the EBNF form as meaning "is composed of," where the nonterminal symbol on the left side is composed of the symbols on the right side. We'll use a simplified variation of EBNF to express our grammar here:

```
Query ::= OrExpression

OrExpression ::= AndExpression
              | OrExpression ( 'or' | '|' ) AndExpression

AndExpression ::= PrimaryExpression
              | AndExpression { 'and' | '&' } PrimaryExpression

PrimaryExpression ::= Term
                  | '~' Term
                  | Phrase
                  | '(' OrExpression ')'
                  | '<' ( Term | Phrase )+ '>'

ExactExpression ::= '+' Term
                  | '+' Phrase

Term ::= ('A'...'Z'|'0'...'9'|'!'|'@'|'#'|'$'|'%'|'^'|'*'|'_'|'''|'.'|'?')+

Phrase ::= '"' (string characters)+ '"'
```

The following details apply to this grammar representation:

- The pipe symbol | is used on the right side of the ::= symbol to indicate that the non-terminal on the left side can be any of the items on the right side. This symbol can be read to represent "or."

- Parentheses ( ) are used to group choices on the right side, indicating that one of the items in parentheses should be selected to complete the production.

- Braces { } are used to indicate optional items on the right side.

- Apostrophes ' ' are used to enclose character literals, so that '<' indicates that the literal character < is required to complete the production.

- The plus sign + is used to indicate that one or more of the preceding items is required to complete the production. For example, the production (`Term` | `Phrase`)+ indicates that one or more combinations of `Term` and `Phrase` nonterminals need to be present to complete the production. You can think of the trailing plus sign as having the same meaning as the regular expression + ("one or more") symbol.

- The abbreviation `string characters` is used to indicate that any printable characters are allowed within the production.

As you can see from the EBNF form, the grammar we're trying to produce here is fairly simple in nature, containing only seven logical productions. By contrast, the EBNF grammar specification for the T-SQL language is extremely complex, taking dozens of pages to print out in full.

■**Tip** For reference, you can view the T-SQL language grammar in BOL. It's actually spread out over hundreds of pages, in manageable chunks, in the "Syntax" section at the top of pages in the "Transact-SQL Reference" section.

Implementing the Grammar with Irony

After we've defined our grammar, it's time to get into the implementation details. After researching several alternatives, we decided to use the Irony .NET parser created by .NET guru Roman Ivantsov. We chose Irony because of its simplicity and because it automatically produces an *abstract syntax tree (AST)*, which is an in-memory tree structure we'll need to convert the user's input to something intelligible by SQL Server. We'll talk more about the AST later.

Our first step is to download and compile the Irony .NET library from http://www.codeplex.com/irony. Then we create a new C# project and add a reference to `Irony` as shown in Figure 4-3.

Figure 4-3. *Adding a reference to the Irony library to a C# project*

After adding a reference to the Irony library, we add a reference to the Irony.Compiler namespace in the code and then define the query engine grammar in a class named SearchGrammar, as shown in Listing 4-4. Note that the SearchGrammar class is derived from the Irony Grammar class.

Listing 4-4. *Search Grammar in Irony Form*

```
...
using Irony.Compiler;
...

public class SearchGrammar : Grammar
{
  public SearchGrammar()
  {
    // Terminals
    var Term = new IdentifierTerminal("Term", "!@#$%^*_'.?",
      "!@#$%^*_'.?0123456789");
    var Phrase = new StringLiteral("Phrase");

    // NonTerminals
    var OrExpression = new NonTerminal("OrExpression");
    var OrOperator = new NonTerminal("OrOperator");
    var AndExpression = new NonTerminal("AndExpression");
    var AndOperator = new NonTerminal("AndOperator");
    var ExcludeOperator = new NonTerminal("ExcludeOperator");
    var PrimaryExpression = new NonTerminal("PrimaryExpression");
    var ThesaurusExpression = new NonTerminal("ThesaurusExpression");
    var ThesaurusOperator = new NonTerminal("ThesaurusOperator");
    var ExactOperator = new NonTerminal("ExactOperator");
    var ExactExpression = new NonTerminal("ExactExpression");
    var ParenthesizedExpression = new NonTerminal("ParenthesizedExpression");
    var ProximityExpression = new NonTerminal("ProximityExpression");
    var ProximityList = new NonTerminal("ProximityList");

    this.Root = OrExpression;
    OrExpression.Rule = AndExpression
                      | OrExpression + OrOperator + AndExpression;
    OrOperator.Rule = Symbol("or") | "|";
    AndExpression.Rule = PrimaryExpression
                       | AndExpression + AndOperator + PrimaryExpression;
    AndOperator.Rule = Empty
                     | "and"
                     | "&"
                     | ExcludeOperator;
    ExcludeOperator.Rule = Symbol("-");
```

```
    PrimaryExpression.Rule = Term
                           | ThesaurusExpression
                           | ExactExpression
                           | ParenthesizedExpression
                           | Phrase
                           | ProximityExpression;
    ThesaurusExpression.Rule = ThesaurusOperator + Term;
    ThesaurusOperator.Rule = Symbol("~");
    ExactExpression.Rule = ExactOperator + Term
                         | ExactOperator + Phrase;
    ExactOperator.Rule = Symbol("+");
    ParenthesizedExpression.Rule = "(" + OrExpression + ")";
    ProximityExpression.Rule = "<" + ProximityList + ">";
    MakePlusRule(ProximityList, Term);

    RegisterPunctuation("<", ">", "(", ")");
  }
  ...
}
```

The Irony grammar follows the EBNF grammar fairly closely; however, to implement some of the productions the Irony implementation requires more nonterminals.

With the `SearchGrammar` class in place, Irony can parse our grammar, recognizing and returning nonterminals and tokens with which it will build an AST. The AST is a treelike data structure that Irony builds with the tokens you supply. Consider the sample Google-style query string +fish (sticks or hook) -catfish. The AST produced by this query, after Irony performs lexical analysis on the string, is shown in Figure 4-4.

■**Tip** The AST shown in Figure 4-4 was produced by the Irony Grammar Explorer, which is also available for download from http://www.codeplex.com/irony.

As you can see in the AST, Irony parses the tokens and symbols out of the input string and places them in a proper hierarchical structure. It is through this hierarchical tree structure that we'll generate the final iFTS `CONTAINSTABLE` clause to query the database.

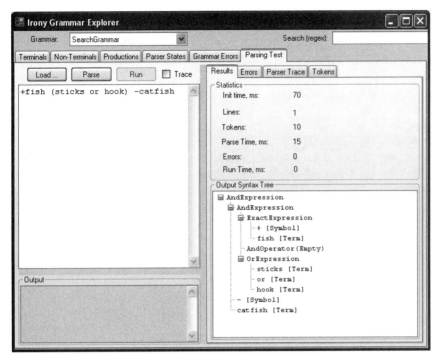

Figure 4-4. *AST produced by a sample query fed into the new search query grammar*

Generating the iFTS Query

The final step in the process is to convert the nodes of the AST into an iFTS CONTAINS clause to query the database. There are several methods of parsing an AST, including advanced techniques such as implementing the visitor pattern with separate classes for every type of node.

Because our grammar is simple, however, we'll go the easy route and implement a simple recursive function that will begin parsing the AST at the root node and will call itself recursively traversing every node of the tree. Listing 4-5 is the ConvertQuery function, which accepts the root node of the AST and returns the constructed CONTAINSTABLE search query string. We'll show how to call this function and utilize the results in the following sections.

Listing 4-5. *Converting a Recursive AST Traversal Function*

```
public static string ConvertQuery(AstNode node, TermType type)
{
  string result = "";
  // Note that some nonterminals don't actually get into the AST tree,
  // because of some of Irony's optimizations - punctuation stripping and
  // node bubbling. For example, in ParenthesizedExpression parentheses
  // symbols get stripped off as punctuation, and the child expression node
  // (parenthesized content) replaces the parent ParExpr node (the
  // child is "bubbled up").
  switch (node.Term.Name)
```

```
{
  case "OrExpression":
    result = "(" + ConvertQuery(node.ChildNodes[0], type) + " OR " +
      ConvertQuery(node.ChildNodes[2], type) + ")";
    break;

  case "AndExpression":
    AstNode tmp2 = node.ChildNodes[1];
    string opName = tmp2.Term.Name;
    string andop = "";

    if (opName == "-")
    {
      andop += " AND NOT ";
    }
    else
    {
      andop = " AND ";
    }
    result = "(" + ConvertQuery(node.ChildNodes[0], type) + andop +
    ConvertQuery(node.ChildNodes[2]) + ")";
    break;

  case "PrimaryExpression":
    result = "(" + ConvertQuery(node.ChildNodes[0], type) + ")";
    break;

  case "ProximityList":
    string[] tmp = new string[node.ChildNodes.Count];
    type = TermType.Exact;
    for (int i = 0; i < node.ChildNodes.Count; i++)
    {
      tmp[i] = ConvertQuery(node.ChildNodes[i], type);
    }
    result = "(" + string.Join(" NEAR ", tmp) + ")";
    type = TermType.Inflectional;
    break;

  case "Phrase":
    result = '"' + ((Token)node).ValueString + '"';
    break;

  case "ThesaurusExpression":
    result = " FORMSOF (THESAURUS, " +
      ((Token)node.ChildNodes[1]).ValueString + ") ";
    break;
```

```
    case "ExactExpression":
      result = " \"" + ((Token)node.ChildNodes[1]).ValueString + "\" ";
      break;

    case "Term":
      switch (type)
      {
        case TermType.Inflectional:
          result = ((Token)node).ValueString;
          if (result.EndsWith("*"))
            result = "\"" + result + "\"";
          else
            result = " FORMSOF (INFLECTIONAL, " +  result + ") ";
          break;

        case TermType.Exact:
          result = ((Token)node).ValueString;
          break;
      }
      break;

    // This should never happen, even if input string is garbage
    default:
      throw new ApplicationException("Converter failed: unexpected term: " +
        node.Term.Name + ". Please investigate.");

  }
  return result;
}
```

SPECIAL HANDLING IN THE AST

One tradeoff that's sometimes made in simple grammar implementations is putting special handling in the AST traversal and parsing routines instead of trying to code everything directly in the grammar itself. As an example, to keep our grammar implementation simple, we've left some rules out of the grammar and instead handled them in the AST traversal/iFTS query creation function.

In one instance, we decided that special handling for the trailing wildcard * character in search terms should be handled during AST traversal instead of directly in the grammar definition itself. Differentiating between the unary - operator and the logical AND operators is also performed in the AST traversal function, since the unary - operator maps directly to the iFTS AND NOT operator.

Converting a Google-Style Query

Using the Irony grammar we've created is relatively simple. You basically need to create a couple of object instances and call a few methods of those instances. A simple call to the ConvertQuery function consists of first creating a SearchGrammar and a LanguageCompiler object:

```
SearchGrammar _grammar;
LanguageCompiler _compiler;
```

You then pass the source query to the LanguageCompiler object, which returns a fully formed AST. Then, assuming no errors occurred, you call the ConvertQuery method of the SearchGrammar object to convert the AST to a proper iFTS query:

```
AstNode root = _compiler.Parse(SourceQueryText.Text.ToLower());
if (!CheckParseErrors()) return;
FtsQueryTextBox.Text = SearchGrammar.ConvertQuery
(
  root,
  SearchGrammar.TermType.Inflectional
);
```

Finally, you call the static ExecuteQuery method of the SearchGrammar class to actually execute the iFTS query against the target database. In the following sample code, we use the ExecuteQuery method to populate a DataTable, which we then display in a DataGridView control:

```
DataTable dt = SearchGrammar.ExecuteQuery(FtsQueryTextBox.Text);
ResultsDataGridView.DataSource = dt;
```

Querying with the New Grammar

In the sample download files, we've included a sample Windows Forms application that puts the sample grammar we've built in this section to use. The application accepts a search engine–style query, converts it to an iFTS CONTAINSTABLE query, displays the iFTS version of the query, and executes the query against dbo.Book table of the iFTS_Books database. Results are returned in a DataGridView control, as shown in Figure 4-5.

■**Tip** We chose to implement a simple Windows application in this example to avoid the set up and configuration associated with web applications, but there's no reason similar .NET code can't be created using ASP.NET to provide similar web- or intranet-based search functionality against SQL Server.

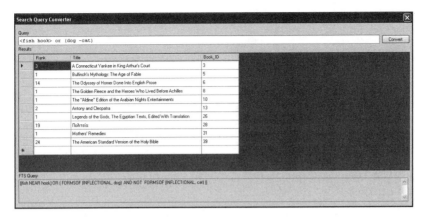

Figure 4-5. *Sample search engine–style query converted to iFTS query*

The static `ExecuteQuery` method of the `SearchGrammar` class is responsible for opening a database connection, executing the iFTS query against the database, and returning the results as a `DataTable`. The `CONTAINSTABLE` SQL query generated and executed by the `ExecuteQuery` method looks like the following:

```
SELECT ct.[RANK] AS Rank,
    t.Title,
    b.Book_ID
FROM CONTAINSTABLE
(
    dbo.Book,
    *,
    @ftsQuery
) AS ct
INNER JOIN dbo.Book b
    ON ct.[KEY] = b.[Book_ID]
INNER JOIN dbo.Book_Title bt
    ON b.Book_ID = bt.Book_ID
INNER JOIN dbo.Title t
    ON bt.Title_ID = t.Title_ID
WHERE t.Is_Primary_Title = 1
    AND ct.[RANK] > 0;
```

Note that we generate a `CONTAINSTABLE` query and check for `RANK` > 0. This is important for the use of the iFTS `NEAR` operator, since it's essentially useless with the normal `CONTAINS` operator. Also note that the results of the `CONTAINSTABLE` function are joined back to the `dbo.Book` table and other supporting tables to retrieve related information about the results.

The example in Figure 4-5 demonstrates the following simple search engine–style query:

```
<fish hook> or (dog -cat)
```

This query indicates the user wants to locate all documents in which either of the following conditions are true:

- The words *fish* and *hook* appear in close proximity to one another.

- The word *dog* appears but the word *cat* does not appear.

The resulting iFTS CONTAINS query looks like the following:

```
((fish NEAR hook) OR ( FORMSOF (INFLECTIONAL, dog)
  AND NOT FORMSOF (INFLECTIONAL, cat) ))
```

The following are some additional queries that demonstrate the conversion capabilities of the query conversion engine.

- *Trying to find*: the exact word *love*, inflectional forms of the word *money*, and excluding the word *diamond*.

    Search query: +love money -diamond

    iFTS query: (("love" AND FORMSOF (INFLECTIONAL, money)) AND NOT FORMSOF (INFLECTIONAL, diamond))

- *Trying to find*: the exact phrase *dogs and cats*, or the exact phrase *cats and dogs*.

    Search query: "cats and dogs" or "dogs and cats"

    iFTS query: ("cats and dogs" OR "dogs and cats")

- *Trying to find*: all words that begin with *fish*, excluding the exact word *fishing*.

    Search query: fish* -"fishing"

    iFTS Query: ("fish*" AND NOT "fishing")

- *Trying to find*: all documents with any inflectional form of the word *president*, and either of the following: thesaurus forms of the word *run* or the words *election* and *primary* in close proximity to one another.

    Search query: president (~run or <election primary>)

    iFTS Query: (FORMSOF (INFLECTIONAL, president) AND (FORMSOF (THESAURUS, run) OR (election NEAR primary)))

By using Irony and a well-constructed grammar, you can allow your users to generate complex and intricate queries using a relatively simple syntax that they're already familiar with.

Summary

In this chapter, we looked at some of the nifty client-side features that you can add to iFTS to make database searches easier and more intuitive for your end users. This will give you several benefits. You can minimize end user training, ramp-up time, and ongoing support; and you can also improve overall productivity by providing your end users with a more intuitive and easier to use interface.

First we looked at simple hit highlighting of iFTS results. For data from which the plain text is accessible, you can easily add this common feature that search users expect. While we demonstrated this functionality using simple T-SQL statements and functions, more advanced functionality can be achieved through use of SQL CLR functions. Additionally, other methods can be employed to optimize hit highlighting functionality for speed (with a tradeoff of more storage, however).

To round out the chapter, we looked at another bit of commonly requested functionality: Google-style search queries. For our example, we created a simple Google-based search query grammar that we implemented in C# with the Irony parser. Adding this type of functionality adds a whole new level of functionality for your end users, providing them with the right mix of power and simplicity that they've come to expect.

The authors would like to thank Roman Ivantsov, creator of Irony and C# programmer extraordinaire, for reviewing and advising on our initial Irony grammar and the initial draft of the AST traversal function.

CHAPTER 5

■ ■ ■

Multilingual Searching

Drawing on my fine command of the English language, I said nothing.

—Robert Benchley

We've focused largely on English as spoken in the United States throughout this book, owing largely to the fact that it's the authors' native tongue. We've given some brief examples of queries in other languages. SQL Server 2008 iFTS natively supports 48 languages (three additional languages are supported but disabled by default), and can support even more languages through the use of third-party filters and word breakers.

While it can't hurt to be a polyglot (someone who speaks many languages), it's unlikely that the members of your DBA and development teams are fluent in the 48 languages that shipped with SQL Server 2008 iFTS. Fortunately for us, knowledge of several different languages is not essential to developing a multilingual full-text search solution. Instead, having team members who have an understanding of language fundamentals is probably one of the most useful tools for taking advantage of SQL Server iFTS multilingual options.

This is not to belittle the advantages of having staff members who are fluent in the languages your SQL FTS search solution supports. For example, if a Chinese user searches for Chinese content on your web site and doesn't find what she's looking for, she'll go to a web site that does. If she's a customer and doesn't find the product she's looking for on your web site, but finds it somewhere else, the odds are good she won't return to your site again.

CHINESE LANGUAGE BUG FIXES

In our example at the beginning of this section, we specifically chose to cite the Chinese language not only because of the large potential customer base, but because there were some bugs in the Chinese word breaker that shipped with SQL Server 2005. These bugs have been fixed in SQL Server 2008 iFTS. The fact that there were bugs in the SQL Server 2005 Chinese language word breaker was brought to our attention by a developer who is a fluent speaker of Chinese. This developer couldn't retrieve specific content indexed in Chinese on SQL Server 2005, but with his help we were able to use the new dynamic management functions (DMFs) in SQL Server 2008 to validate that the situation has been corrected.

In this chapter, we'll dig deeper into the concept of multilingual full-text searching in SQL Server 2008. After reading this chapter, you'll have a good understanding of how iFTS multilingual features work and some information you can use to implement your own iFTS-enabled multilingual search solutions. But we begin with a short history of written language to provide background on some of the issues that iFTS faces when indexing and searching multilingual content.

A Brief History of Written Language

Wikipedia defines written language as "the representation of a language (symbols of communication and the elements used to manipulate them) by means of a writing system." Evolutionary linguists speculate that the earliest forms of communication consisted of prehistoric pictorial representations of objects—picture drawings known as *pictograms*. Cave drawings dating back to more than 32,000 years ago provide some of the earliest known pictograms. Figure 5-1 is a prehistoric cave drawing of a horse from the Lascaux cave complex in France. The drawing is estimated to be more than 16,000 years old.

Figure 5-1. *Prehistoric cave painting from Lascaux, France*

As man advanced in sophistication, pictogram systems increased in complexity to the point that they became unwieldy. Pictograms were subsequently replaced with Neolithic proto-writing systems of the 7th millennium B.C.E. These proto-writing systems replaced complex pictographic writing systems with simpler *logographic* systems that utilized ideographic and mnemonic symbols. The Vinča signs of southeastern Europe are one of the most famous examples of a Neolithic proto-writing system. Figure 5-2 is a depiction of a clay vessel with Vinča asigns on it.

Figure 5-2. *Depiction of an unearthed clay vessel with Vinča signs drawn on it*

Over time, even these advancements in written communication proved inadequate. While ideographic symbols may be adequate to represent physical objects, they aren't up to the task of describing abstract concepts such as justice and beauty. Most writing systems, over time, evolved into using alphabetic characters that were used to represent phonetic sounds, syllables, or ideas; or in some cases, all three. Egyptian hieroglyphs, for instance, used a phonetic-based alphabet in which symbols represented sounds. Figure 5-3 shows the name *Cleopatra* written in Egyptian hieroglyphs.

Figure 5-3. *"Cleopatra" written in Egyptian hieroglyphs*

The formal Egyptian hieroglyph alphabet was unwieldy; so much so that the Egyptian scribes used a simpler *demotic* alphabet for informal correspondence. Modern languages incorporate a wide range of ideas from ancient languages. Western written languages tend to consist of alphabets that roughly represent *phonemes*, the smallest structural units of a language that have meaning. Eastern languages, such as Traditional Chinese, are logographic in nature; individual characters represent entire words or ideas. Figure 5-4 shows the Traditional Chinese symbol for *Tree* and the English word representing the same.

Figure 5-4. *Traditional Chinese and English words for "Tree"*

iFTS and Language Complexity

In addition to different alphabets and writing systems, iFTS must deal with myriad issues that increase the complexity of indexing and querying textual content. Every language has rules of syntax to define the structural relationships between symbols. SQL Server iFTS must first deal with these syntactical constructs at the symbol level via language-specific word breakers. Word breakers encapsulate a wide array of complex language-specific rules that are applied to break textual data into words and tokens. We'll discuss the rules that affect word breaking, tokenization, and querying in the sections that follow.

Writing Symbols and Alphabets

Because of the diversity of languages, the SQL Server iFTS indexer must be able to handle many different alphabets and writing systems to allow users to find what they're looking for. For most writing systems, this means using whitespace and punctuation to break the text stream into tokens. In Chinese, and some other Far Eastern alphabets, a single character may express a complete idea that requires multiple alphabetic characters in a Western language. With Chinese, the indexer must do more work to extract searchable tokens from character strings. Consider the following Chinese character string:

这篇 11 页的文章讨论 *Microsoft SQL Server 2008 如何为存储非结构化数据提供灵活的解决方案，并将其与关系型数据组合来构建包含组织所有数据的全面解决方案*

In English, this translates to the following:

This 11-page paper discusses how Microsoft SQL Server 2008 provides a flexible solution for storing unstructured data and combining it with relational data to build comprehensive solutions that encompass the full range of data across an organization.

The whitespace in the Chinese version is sparse and doesn't map well to indexing the dozens of words and ideas in the translated English version. In addition, the Chinese word breaker has to deal with both single-character and multicharacter tokens. The Traditional Chinese (LCID 1028) word breaker derives 42 tokens from the Chinese text, as shown:

11, 2008, microsoft, server, sql, 与 , 为 , 储 , 全面 , 关 , 其 , 决 , 包含 , 化 , 合 , 型 , 如何 , 存 , 将 , 并 , 建 , 所有 , 据 , 提供 , 数 , 文章 , 方案 , 来 , 构 , 活 , 灵 , 的 , 篇 , 系 , 组 , 织 , 结 , 解 , 讨 , 论 , 这 , 非 , and 页

As you can see, the Chinese word breaker handles the concept of word boundaries much differently than the English word breaker. While the English word breaker can rely heavily on punctuation and whitespace to define word boundaries, the Chinese language offers no such luxury.

Languages such as Arabic are at the other extreme. In Arabic, whitespace generally delimits words, but some letters such as the Arabic *A* (*alif*) are nearly always followed by whitespace—even in the middle of word. The Arabic phrase *Allahu akbar* (*God is greatest*) demonstrates the use of whitespace after the letter alif (‏ا‏).

الله اكبر

In some cases, a word is used to indicate a sentence end in Arabic. For example, the following two Arabic tokens represent the exact same word, both meaning *house* in English:

بيت

بــيــت

The difference between these Arabic words is that the second form is used exclusively at the end of sentences. Language-specific word breakers must take these word breaking rules into consideration at both index and query time.

Bidirectional Writing and Capitalization

While many languages such as Spanish and English are written from left to right, other languages such as Arabic and Hebrew are written from right to left. Language-specific rules in the word breaker must deal with these differences in writing direction to ensure that words are read and tokenized in the same direction that they were written.

Also, for many languages, capitalization doesn't inherently affect word-breaking activity. In the English language, the token *Marie-Claire* generates exactly four inflectional form tokens: *marie, claire, marieclaires,* and *marieclaire.* Likewise, the lowercase form, *marie-claire,* generates the same four tokens. To the English word breaker, capitalization is unimportant to the word-breaking process.

▧**Note** Although capitalization is inherently unimportant for word breaking in most languages, we'll discuss some instances in which iFTS imposes its own rules on handling capitalization later in this section.

There are exceptions to every rule, however; and in this case the exception is French. The French word breaker generates six inflectional forms of the token *Marie-Claire* when the phrase is capitalized. When the token is not capitalized, as in *marie-claire,* the French word breaker generates no less than 49 inflectional forms. Listing 5-1 invokes the French word breaker to break both the capitalized and noncapitalized forms of the token *Marie-Claire,* proving once and for all that the French take their capitals very seriously. Partial results are shown in Figure 5-5.

Listing 5-1. *Breaking Marie-Claire in French*

```
SELECT *
FROM sys.dm_fts_parser
(
  N'FORMSOF(FREETEXT, marie-claire)',
  1036,
  NULL,
  0
);

SELECT *
FROM sys.dm_fts_parser
(
  N'FORMSOF(FREETEXT, Marie-Claire)',
  1036,
  NULL,
  0
);
```

Figure 5-5. *Partial results of breaking the token "Marie-Claire" in French*

Although capitalization is unimportant for word-breaking purposes in most languages, SQL Server iFTS imposes its own rules on capitalization of acronyms. The English word breaker will tokenize the capitalized acronym *F.B.I.* as both *FBI* and *F.B.I.* This is done to maximize recall, since users might search for either token when looking for documents related to the Federal Bureau of Investigation. By contrast, the lowercase version of the acronym, *f.b.i.*, indexes only the individual characters *f*, *b*, and *i*. Similarly, the lowercase token *fbi* will only be indexed as *fbi*.

■**Tip** These capitalization rules are different for different languages. While the English word breaker returns *f*, *b*, and *i* when breaking *f.b.i.*, the French word breaker returns both *f.b.i.* and *fbi*.

The reasoning behind these somewhat exotic capitalization rules is based in large part on popular style guide recommendations. The idea is that when a user types in an all-uppercase acronym, she's really searching for an acronym; when searching for all-lowercase characters, the assumption is that she's searching for a something other than an acronym—a "real word." These somewhat complicated rules are designed to help minimize the number of false positives returned by iFTS. As we pointed out in the preceding tip, these particular rules do vary widely from one language to another.

Hyphenation and Compound Words

Each word breaker handles hyphenation issues based on the rules of the target language. Some languages such as Dutch simply break a hyphenated word into its constituent components and proceed to index the constituent words. The Dutch word breaker will break the token *merry-go-round* into three separate words: *merry*, *go*, and *round*. The English word breaker, on the other hand, generates four tokens: *merry*, *go*, *round*, and *merrygoround*.

Some languages have intricate rules built in to handle compound and composite word indexing. Consider the German word *Herzkreislaufwiederbelebung* (literally "heart cycle revival," also known as CPR to the English-speaking world). The German word breaker breaks this word into four constituent German words: *herzkreislaufwiederbelebung, herz, kreislauf,* and *wieder-belebung.* The idea is that a search for any of these constituent words should return documents containing the composite word as well, increasing recall. The English word breaker, on the other hand, refuses to acknowledge the German rules, and returns only a single token of the full word for indexing.

Nonalphanumeric Characters and Accent Marks

Language-specific word breakers also defer to the base language in dealing with whitespace and nonalphabetic characters. In English, the period character is used as a decimal point in numeric values; however, in some European countries the comma character is used for the same purpose. As an example, the German word breaker turns the token *3,14* into *3,14* and *nn3d14.* The English word breaker, on the other hand, treats the comma as a token separator and generates four tokens from *3,14*; namely *3, nn3, 14,* and *nn14.* We previously discussed numeric token indexing in Chapter 3.

The word breakers for most languages break words at whitespace and punctuation. The English word breaker will break the phrase *four score and ten* at whitespace and return the tokens *four, score, and,* and *ten.* A token like *http://www.microsoft.com* is indexed as *http, www, microsoft,* and *com* by the English word breaker. A search for *Microsoft* will return content containing the URL `http://www.microsoft.com`, which is a desirable behavior. The English word breaker divides *sergey@google.com* into three tokens: *sergey, google,* and *com.*

The rules for characters followed by nonalphanumeric characters are somewhat convoluted (at least in English). The English word breaker accepts the token *C#* and returns *C#.* The lowercase token *c#,* however, is indexed as *c* with the *#* character stripped off. The uppercase token *C++* and lowercase token *c++,* on the other hand, are both indexed as *c++.*

Accent and diacritic marks carry varying degrees of significance for different languages. At one extreme is the English language, in which accents and diacritics are by and large unimportant and unnecessary. Except for a few imported words used in the occasional Madison Avenue advertising campaign or as the name for a trendy restaurant, accent marks have fallen out of favor in the English language. At the other end of the scale is the French language, in which an accent mark can mean the difference between eating *salty* peanuts (*arachides salés*) and eating *dirty* peanuts (*arachides sales*). We highly recommend sticking to the salty peanuts.

Token Position Context

Different languages may apply context to token position in the source text. Consider the Chinese phrase 繁體中文版 (*Traditional Chinese Version* in English). This phrase is broken up by the Chinese word breaker into three separate symbols: 繁體 , 中文 , and 版 . By rearranging the characters in the phrase to read 文繁體版中 (a somewhat nonsensical translation of *In article traditional form version*), the Chinese word breaker generates four separate symbols: 文 , 繁體 , 版 , and 中 . By contrast, in English the phrase *Traditional Chinese Version* is broken up into the words *Traditional, Chinese,* and *Version.* Changing the order of tokens in the English phrase (*Chinese Version Traditional,* for example) doesn't change the tokens that are output by the English word breaker.

INDEXING METHODOLOGIES

In passing, we should note that some search engines use various methods to locate and index the stems of the words it retrieves from the source text. The iFTS team has chosen not to use this method to index words, as it tends to lower precision. Indexing stems of words, such as the stem *interest* for the word *interesting*, also introduces additional complexities during the lexical analysis phase of indexing. Other search utilities, such as Lucene, do provide this type of functionality via add-ons. But even on Lucene and other search engines, this isn't the preferred indexing methodology.

Generational Forms

Generational forms encompass both inflectional forms (for example, verb conjugations and plural nouns) and thesaurus replacements and expansions. Inflectional forms are language-specific, consisting of potentially thousands of rules for stemming words.

Consider the Arabic language, which has some complex semantics associated with it. Statistical studies have shown that on average, there are four different concepts expressed in the derivatives of a single Arabic root. In some cases, Arabic roots such as لبق have as many as a dozen or more derivatives (in English: *accept, okay, subscribe, kiss*, and so on). Because Arabic is a highly derivational and inflectional language, the Arabic word breaker includes additional logic to group word derivatives and then to limit results returned to only those derivatives that fall into the same group as the search term itself.

Other languages, such as English, greatly simplify plural noun generation and verb conjugation through the use of affix (suffix) rules. All languages in general—and English in particular—are full of exceptions. Consider the infinitive *go*, one of two suppletive English verbs (the other is *be*). While many simple past tense verbs can be created by adding the affix *-ed* to the infinitive (for example, *fished, cooked, watched*), the past simple tense of *go* is *went*, a word with no apparent relationship to the infinitive form. The English word breaker and stemmer must maintain lists of these types of exceptions and the logic to properly apply them in order to be effective.

Thesaurus replacements and expansions are another story. These types of generational forms are essentially user-defined, and are useful for implementing custom search functionality. For instance, if your users tend to search for domain-specific specialized words (such as legal and medical terms), you can map them to their more mundane equivalents using thesauruses. Likewise, if you need to add functionality to search for words that aren't covered by the word breaker and stemmer for your language (such as slang terms), the thesaurus can help you fulfill this need. We discuss thesaurus expansion and replacement in Chapter 8.

Gender

Though English largely ignores gender-specificity in words, with the exception of nouns and pronouns specifically defined to evoke gender-specific ideals, gender plays an important role in other languages. In English, we see throwbacks to gender-specific idioms, such as the words *fisherman* and *mailman*, and an implicit association of certain ideals with gender (such as referring to *sailing ships* with feminine pronouns). In the worst case, these gender-specific words can be overcome through the use of thesauruses. For instance, you could include an expansion rule in your thesaurus to automatically expand your search for the word *fisherman* to include the word *fisherwoman*.

SQL Server iFTS automatically includes stemming logic that accommodates gender rules for other languages where gender plays a more important role. Consider the word *flaco* (*skinny*, masculine). When the Spanish stemmer sees this word, it generates inflectional forms that include both the masculine gendered versions of the word (*flaco*, *flacos*) and the feminine gendered versions (*flaca*, *flacas*). If you referred to a man with the word *flaca*, odds are good that he would take offense at being called a *skinny girl*.

Gender plays a role in nouns as well. Consider the Spanish words *barco* and *barca*, which both mean *ship*. If you asked for a *barco*, you'd get a big ship, whereas a *barca* would be much smaller. Though not as important for English (where a *ship* is a *ship*), gender plays an important role when querying multilingual content in many languages.

Storing Multilingual Data

Now that we have an understanding of the issues and complexities involved in searching multilingual text, it's time to dive into the details of storage and search. There are several methods you can use to prepare your database to store multilingual data; in this section, we'll introduce the methods and tools at your disposal. SQL Server iFTS supports 48 languages by default (and three additional languages not installed by default) as listed in Table 5-1.

Table 5-1. *SQL Server 2008 iFTS-Supported Languages*

Language Name		
Arabic	Bengali (India)	Brazilian
British English[1]	Bulgarian	Catalan
Chinese (Hong Kong SAR, PRC)[1]	Chinese (Macau SAR)[1]	Chinese (Singapore)[1]
Croatian	Danish[2]	Dutch
English[1]	French	German
Gujarati	Hebrew	Hindi
Icelandic	Indonesian	Italian
Japanese	Kannada	Korean[1]
Latvian	Lithuanian	Malay - Malaysia
Malayalam	Marathi	Neutral
Norwegian (Bokmål)	Polish[2]	Portuguese
Punjabi	Romanian	Russian
Serbian (Cyrillic)	Serbian (Latin)	Simplified Chinese[1]
Slovak	Slovenian	Spanish
Swedish	Tamil	Telugu
Thai[1]	Traditional Chinese[1]	Turkish[2]
Ukrainian	Urdu	Vietnamese

[1] *Word breaker is unchanged from the SQL Server 2005 version.*
[2] *Language is supported in SQL Server 2008, but not installed by default.*

Storing Plain Text

One of the first tasks you'll need to consider when storing multilingual data is your choice of character sets. When storing purely textual data, you must choose the correct code page. Code pages are used to map a specific set of characters to numeric code-point values. Most code pages support only small 7- or 8-bit code points, allowing you to represent only 128 or 256 characters. By contrast, the Chinese language Kagnxi dictionary contains more than 49,000 characters (although it's estimated that full Chinese language literacy requires a working knowledge of only three to four thousand characters). When designing multilingual database applications that store textual data, it's advantageous to store text as Unicode. Unicode can map more than 1 million characters to its code points, enough to represent every written language known to man with plenty of room to spare.

SQL provides two data types designed to store Unicode: nchar and nvarchar. These data types require double the storage space of their non-Unicode counterparts, char and varchar, but can represent all your multilingual and internationalized text. We've demonstrated the use of nvarchar and nchar in several tables in the iFTS_Books sample database. For instance, the Commentary column of the dbo.Commentary table is defined as nvarchar, so that multilingual text can be adequately represented. Listing 5-2 shows the CREATE TABLE statement that builds the dbo.Commentary table.

Listing 5-2. *Create dbo.Commentary Table*

```
CREATE TABLE [dbo].[Commentary]
(
  Commentary_ID int NOT NULL CONSTRAINT PK_Commentary PRIMARY KEY CLUSTERED,
  Commentary nvarchar(max) NOT NULL,
  Article_Content xml NULL
);
GO
```

Storing XML

XML data can be stored in an xml data type column or a varbinary column. We'll cover the details of storing XML data in Chapter 6. The XML word breaker goes above and beyond the plain-text word breakers, in that it allows you to store data from multiple languages in the same XML document. The XML filter actually respects the xml:lang attribute, which allows you to specify the language of the content of your XML element. When the XML filter encounters an xml:lang attribute, it launches the appropriate word breaker for the language indicated. Consider the XML document in Listing 5-3, which uses the xml:lang attribute to specify that the XML content is Japanese.

Listing 5-3. *Sample Japanese XML Content*

```
<article xml:lang = "ja">
  <date>2008-06-15</date>
  <title> ユークリッド原論 </title>
```

```
<section id = "Lead">
  <para>
    『原論』( げんろん、ΣΤΟΙΧεία, 英 :Elements ) は、紀元前 3 世紀ごろにエジプ
    トのアレクサンドリアで活躍した数学者エウクレイデス  （英語式には Euclid
    （ユークリッド ）） によって編纂された数学書である。
    論証的学問としての数学の地位を確立したギリシア数学を代表する名著。
  </para>
  <para>
    その内容は現在もユークリッド幾何学として広く知られるものを含んでいるが、
    原論そのものは幾何学のみを扱うものではない。全 13 巻、内容は以下の通り。
  </para>
  <para>
    <list>
      1. 巻： 平面図形の性質
      2. 巻： 面積の変形 （幾何的代数 ）
      3. 巻： 円の性質
      4. 巻： 円に内接・外接する多角形
      5. 巻： 比例論
      6. 巻： 比例論の図形への応用
      7. 巻： 数論
      8. 巻： 数論
      9. 巻： 数論
      10. 巻： 無理量論
      11. 巻： 立体図形
      12. 巻： 面積・体積
      13. 巻： 正多面体
    </list>
  </para>
</section>
</article>
```

The XML filter will recognize the `xml:lang = "ja"` attribute in the article tag, and it will subsequently launch the Japanese language word breaker. There's currently no comprehensive list of `xml:lang` tags that map to LCIDs available, so we decided to compile one based on currently available information. Table 5-2 lists the iFTS supported languages and their equivalent `xml:lang` attribute values. We also created a table in the iFTS_Books database, called `dbo.Xml_Lang_Code`, which includes the `xml:lang` to LCID mappings as well.

■**Tip** Most of the codes appended to the end of the `xml:lang` language codes are two-character country codes taken from the ISO 3166 standard. There are some exceptions, however. The `zh-Hans` and `zh-Hant` codes, which represent Simplified Chinese and Traditional Chinese alphabets, respectively, are two examples. In the past, `zh-CN` was used to indicate Simplified Chinese and `zh-TW` was used to indicate Traditional Chinese. These uses have been deprecated in favor of the new tags.

Table 5-2. *Commonly Used xml:lang Attribute Values and Corresponding LCIDs*

xml:lang Value	LCID	Description	xml:lang Value	LCID	Description
ar	1025	Arabic	bg	1026	Bulgarian
bn	1093	Bengali (India)	ca	1027	Catalan
de	1031	German	en-GB	2057	UK (International) English
en-US	1033	US English	es	3082	Spanish
fr	1036	French	gu	1095	Gujarati
he	1037	Hebrew	hi	1081	Hindi
hr	1050	Croatian	id	1057	Indonesian
is	1039	Icelandic	it	1040	Italian
ja	1041	Japanese	kn	1099	Kannada
ko	1042	Korean	lt	1063	Lithuanian
lv	1062	Latvian	ml	1100	Malayalam
mr	1102	Marathi	ms	1086	Malay (Malaysia)
nl	1043	Dutch	no	1044	Norwegian
pa	1094	Punjabi	pt	2070	Portugese
pt-BR	1046	Brazilian	ro	1048	Romanian
ru	1049	Russian	sk	1051	Slovak
sl	1060	Slovenian	sr-Cyrl	3098	Serbian (Cyrillic)
sr-Latn	2074	Serbian (Latin)	sv	1053	Swedish
ta	1097	Tamil	te	1098	Telugu
th	1054	Thai	vi	1066	Vietnamese
uk	1058	Ukranian	ur	1056	Urdu
zh-Hans	2052	Simplified Chinese	zh-Hant	1028	Traditional Chinese
zh-HK	3076	Chinese (Hong Kong, People's Republic of China)	zh-MO	5124	Chinese (Macau, Special Administrative Region)
zh-SG	4100	Chinese (Singapore)			

The XML filter can launch the appropriate language-specific word breaker at indexing time, but it has no effect on breaking and stemming at query time. In other words, if you index the Japanese language XML in Listing 5-3, the content will be properly indexed according to the Japanese language word breaking and indexing rules. However, if you attempt to perform a search and specify English as the search language, the English language word breaking and stemming rules will be applied to your query string. This mismatch between indexing language and query language can result in poor recall of your multilingual documents.

Storing HTML Documents

HTML documents can be stored as varbinary documents with an .html document type identifier. You can use the MS.LOCALE meta tag to define the language of the entire HTML document. The downside is that for HTML documents written in multiple languages, the language specifies that the document is written in only one language. Like the XML filter, the HTML filter launches the appropriate language-specific word breaker to tokenize your HTML content. Listing 5-4 shows a simple German language HTML document with the MS.LOCALE meta tag.

Listing 5-4. *German-Language HTML Document with MS.LOCALE Meta Tag*

```
<html>
  <head>
    <title>Deutsches Wörterbuch</title>
    <meta name = "MS.LOCALE" content = "DE"/>
  </head>
  <body>
    <h1>Deutsches Wörterbuch</h1>
    <p>
      Das <b>Deutsche Wörterbuch</b> (DWB) oder auch <b>Der Grimm</b>
      ist das größte deutsche Wörterbuch, mit insgesamt 33 Bänden. Es
      wurde von den Brüdern Grimm begonnen und erst 1960, nach über 120
      Jahren, vollendet.
    </p>
    <h2>Aufgabe und Entstehungsgeschichte</h2>
    <p>
      Die Herausgabe des Deutschen Wörterbuchs war das ehrgeizigste
      sprachwissenschaftliche Arbeitsvorhaben, dem sich die Brüder Grimm,
      die deutschen Philologen Jacob und Wilhelm Grimm, stellten.
    </p>
    <p>
      Es handelt sich um ein klassisches Belegwörterbuch, das in aller
      Gründlichkeit die Herkunft jedes deutschen Wortes und seinen Gebrauch
      erläutern will. Das Ziel des DWB, so stellten es sich die Brüder vor,
      sollte es sein, dass sich der einfache Bürger der nationalen
      Gemeinsamkeit in der deutschen Sprache vergewissern konnte, da es zu
      Beginn der Arbeit am DWB noch kein politisch vereinigtes Deutschland,
      sondern nur viele Kleinstaaten gab.
    </p>
  </body>
</html>
```

The `<meta name = "MS.LOCALE" content = "DE"/>` tag specifies that the content of the HTML document is written in German. This meta tag causes the HTML filter to launch the German language word breaker to index this content.

Storing Microsoft Office Documents

Several Microsoft Office documents, most notably MS Word documents, allow you to mark text or documents as language-specific. Microsoft Office documents are stored in `varbinary` columns with a type indicator column that specifies that type of document stored in the content column. We introduced this in Chapter 3, and we'll discuss the details of storing binary document data in Chapter 6. The Microsoft Office document filter respects the language settings you indicate within your document, and it will launch the appropriate filters during the indexing process.

Storing Other Document Types

Other document types, specifically those that are indexed with third-party filters, have varying levels of support for indexing multilingual content. The Adobe PDF filter, for instance, is known to have limited support for indexing multilingual documents. All of these document types are essentially stored as varbinary content with a type indicator column. If you want to determine whether third-party filters for specific document types support multilanguage indexing, you'll have to check the documentation provided by the manufacturer.

Detecting Content Language

You may not always have the luxury of knowing in advance what language your content is written in. There are some sophisticated language detection algorithms available for automating the process of determining the language of your content. Most of these methods involve looking at the content and detecting words and character fragments that are specific to different languages, then tagging the content as such. Dale Gerdemann of the University of Tübingen evaluated language identification methods in a lecture, available at `http://www.sfs.uni-tuebingen.de/iscl/Theses/kranig.pdf`.

A quick and dirty approach that works well for the "big six" western languages (English, French, German, Italian, Spanish, and Dutch) is to count letter sequences, accents, and noise word occurrences in the content (or a small portion of it, such as the first 500 or 1,000 characters). You can analyze text for specific documents, but keep in mind that frequently Web-based content will contain a large amount of English content, even when the author's primary language is not English. For instance, many Taiwanese bloggers post in combinations of both English and Traditional Chinese. This makes automated language identification more difficult.

Designing Tables to Store Multilingual Content

When iFTS indexes content, it doesn't store any language-specific metadata with the tokens it adds to the full-text index. This means that there's no mechanism for applying language-specific rules to indexed content after it's already been indexed. In fact, language-specific rules are applied at only two distinct times:

1. A limited set of language-specific rules (whitespace handling, hyphenation, and so forth) are applied during the word breaking portion of the population process.

2. The full set of language-specific rules, possibly including stemming and thesaurus expansions and replacements, are applied to your search phrase at query time.

Each full-text indexed column can only be designated with a single LCID. So how can you design a table to hold documents and content from multiple languages with different language-specific indexing rules and different character sets? One obvious approach is to create a separate table for every language. Listing 5-5 creates three separate tables, one each for English, Spanish, and German content. Note that we advise against using this method (for reasons we'll detail shortly), and these tables don't exist in the iFTS_Books database.

Listing 5-5. *Separate Tables for Each Language*

```
CREATE TABLE dbo.Book_EN
(
  Book_ID int NOT NULL PRIMARY KEY,
  Content varbinary(max),
  File_Ext nvarchar(4)
);
GO

CREATE TABLE dbo.Book_ES
(
  Book_ID int NOT NULL PRIMARY KEY,
  Content varbinary(max),
  File_Ext nvarchar(4)
);
GO

CREATE TABLE dbo.Book_DE
(
  Book_ID int NOT NULL PRIMARY KEY,
  Content varbinary(max),
  File_Ext nvarchar(4)
);
GO
```

With this method of breaking content up into separate language-specific tables, you can ensure that all content will be indexed properly according to the rules of the language, and that all queries for language-specific content will properly match up with the proper content. However, this method represents a logistical and maintenance nightmare. Maintaining content in all of these separate tables is a complex undertaking, and adding support for additional languages is overly complicated. Even querying can be daunting with this method of storing multilanguage content.

The next method essentially represents the same type of underlying architecture, but instead of creating language-specific tables, you would create language-specific columns in the same table. Using this method, your table would contain multiple varbinary(max) columns, each designated to hold content written in a different language. Listing 5-6 creates a denormalized dbo.Book_Denorm table that uses this method of storing multilanguage content. Again, we advise against this method of storing multilanguage data, and this table doesn't exist in the iFTS_Books database.

Listing 5-6. *Creating the Denormalized dbo.Book_Denorm Table*

```
CREATE TABLE dbo.Book_Denorm
(
  Book_ID int NOT NULL CONSTRAINT PK_Book_Denorm PRIMARY KEY,
  Content_DE varbinary(max),
  File_Ext_DE nvarchar(4),
  Content_EN varbinary(max),
  File_Ext_EN nvarchar(4),
  Content_ES varbinary(max),
  File_Ext_ES nvarchar(4)
);
GO
```

This method offers no improvement over the language-specific separate tables architecture. As with that design, using language-specific columns for content represents a less-than-optimal design. The problem again is that maintenance and administration are severely complicated by the fact that your indexed content is stored in multiple places. You also have to contend with multiple full-text indexes to index the same content, which can cause administrative headaches.

A better method, and the method we recommend, is to store an LCID with your content. This LCID can be used to narrow your full-text searches to only the content that's relevant to the language you're interested in. Listing 5-7 shows a simplified version of the CREATE TABLE statement for the dbo.Book table we've created in the iFTS_Books database. By "simplified," we mean to indicate that we've removed the FILESTREAM attribute and some additional columns that aren't relevant to demonstrating the concept of marking content with an LCID.

Listing 5-7. *Create Simplified dbo.Book Table*

```
CREATE TABLE dbo.Book
(
  Book_ID int NOT NULL CONSTRANT PK_Book PRIMARY KEY,
  Book_LCID int NOT NULL,
  Book_Content varbinary(max) NOT NULL
);
GO
```

Using this method, you can use iFTS to search the table in English. You can ensure that there's no mismatch between the English search phrase and the English-specific content in the full-text index by limiting the scope of your search to only that content marked with `Book_LCID = 1033`. Listing 5-8 is a simple query against the `dbo.Book` table, searching for the German word *gift* (English translation: *poison*). Seventeen hits are returned, as shown in Figure 5-6.

Listing 5-8. *Searching for the German Word "gift"*

```
SELECT
  Book_ID,
  Book_LCID
FROM dbo.Book
WHERE FREETEXT
(
  *,
  N'gift',
  LANGUAGE 1031
);
GO
```

Results

	Book_ID	Book_LCID
1	3	1033
2	5	1033
3	6	1033
4	8	1033
5	9	1033
6	10	1033
7	11	1033
8	13	1033
9	15	1033
10	19	1031
11	23	1031
12	26	1033
13	27	1033
14	28	1033
15	31	1033
16	32	1033
17	39	1033

Figure 5-6. *Results of search for German word "gift"*

You'll notice in the results shown in Figure 5-6 that several English language documents were returned. It's highly unlikely that the English language (LCID 1033) results for *gift* have anything to do with the German (LCID 1031) hits for *gift*. In order to improve the accuracy of results, we have to narrow the search down to only consider the German-language documents during the search. We do this in the `WHERE` clause, as shown in Listing 5-9. The results are shown in Figure 5-7.

Listing 5-9. *Restricting German Word Search to Only German Documents*

```
SELECT
  Book_ID,
  Book_LCID
FROM dbo.Book
WHERE FREETEXT
```

```
(
  *,
  N'gift',
  LANGUAGE 1031
)
AND Book_LCID = 1031;
GO
```

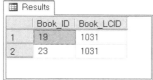

Figure 5-7. *Results of German word search against only German language content*

You can retrieve all content from the English and German content stored in the column that relates to the German word *gift* and the English equivalent word *poison* by unioning the results of two language-specific queries together. This is shown in Listing 5-10. Note that the individual queries use the language-specific words *gift* and *poison* to represent the same concept differently in each query. The results are shown in Figure 5-8.

Listing 5-10. *Combining the Results for an English and German Search in One Result Set*

```
SELECT
  Book_ID,
  Book_LCID
FROM dbo.Book
WHERE FREETEXT
(
  *,
  N'gift',
  LANGUAGE 1031
)
AND Book_LCID = 1031

UNION ALL

SELECT
  Book_ID,
  Book_LCID
FROM dbo.Book
WHERE FREETEXT
```

```
(
  *,
  N'poison',
  LANGUAGE 1033
)
AND Book_LCID = 1033;
GO
```

	Book_ID	Book_LCID
1	19	1031
2	23	1031
3	3	1033
4	5	1033
5	8	1033
6	10	1033
7	11	1033
8	13	1033
9	20	1033
10	26	1033
11	27	1033
12	31	1033
13	32	1033
14	39	1033

Figure 5-8. *Results of combined multilanguage result set*

Likewise, you can add more language-specific terms representing the same concept and union the results together into a single result set. The downside to storing all of your content in a single column is that, during the indexing process, the declared language of the column is the default language for all content stored in that column. This means that, unless your content is stored in a format such as HTML or XML that honors language-specific markup, the content will be broken into tokens using the default column language word breakers.

■Tip Note that you can override the default language for the column by storing language-aware content such as XML or Word documents in the column, as we described previously.

We recommend using a combination of storing LCIDs with your content and storing language-specific tags or markup in your content (when possible) in order to maximize the precision and accuracy of your results. By storing this additional metadata with your content, you can maximize your results and store all of your content in a single column, which greatly simplifies administration, maintenance, and querying over the alternatives.

Summary

There are several aspects that need to be considered when creating multilanguage full-text search solutions. In this chapter, we briefly discussed the history of written language and explored several of the issues that you'll face in implementing your own iFTS-based multi-language applications. We also talked about how iFTS handles these issues. Finally, we provided recommendations for multilanguage content storage and optimizing database design. In the next chapter, we'll consider the methods that SQL Server provides for storing, manipulating, managing, indexing, and retrieving large object (LOB) data.

CHAPTER 6

■ ■ ■

Indexing BLOBs

Now that we have all this useful information, it would be nice to be able to do something with it.

—Unix User's Manual

SQL Server 2008 continues the improved support for *large object (LOB)* data that was introduced in SQL Server 2005. This improvement is driven by Microsoft's vision for data as well as customer demand. When SQL Server 2000 was first released, it was estimated that all the digital data in the world totaled 1 petabyte (1 million terabytes). Estimates done in 2007 revised that figure to upward of 7 petabytes of digital data stored around the world. Today it appears that everyone has his own personal terabyte, much of it unstructured data. Documents today are born digitally, live digitally, and die digitally—they live their entire life inside a database and sometimes never have a paper representation.

It wasn't too long ago that data analysis always came up short. Essential data was often not recorded, not collected, not warehoused, not accessible, sometimes not recoverable, and all too often not kept (in other words, deleted). Information Technology (IT) has matured and there's been a realization that data, and the information that can be derived from it, are the currency of the kingdom. Business intelligence can now provide actionable insights into data that simply weren't possible before. Frequently digital data is stored in its native format in the database; with the most common format being XML. Today the challenge is not only storing and managing more data efficiently, but being able to search it and have the data reveal itself to the searcher.

The improved LOB data type support in SQL Server 2008 is centered around the new generation of LOB data types, including varchar(max), nvarchar(max), varbinary(max), and xml. SQL Server 2008 improves on *binary large object (BLOB)* data type support by providing FILESTREAM access for varbinary(max) data. SQL Server FILESTREAM allows you to store, manipulate, and stream BLOB data from an NTFS file system using T-SQL statements and the OpenSqlFilestream API. The real advantage to FILESTREAM is that you can not only store and manipulate the LOB data stored in your database using T-SQL commands, you can retrieve it directly from the file system using ADO.Net without having to read the binary data into the SQL Server cache. In case you missed it—you can access the varbinary data you stored in the database through the file system!

In this chapter, we'll discuss indexing varbinary(max) BLOB data, both with and without FILESTREAM, xml data, and character LOB data.

LOB Data

SQL Server's storage mechanisms have historically made storing LOB data an interesting (and frustrating) exercise. SQL Server stores data in 8KB pages and 64KB extents (composed of eight consecutive pages). In prior versions of SQL Server, the image, text, and ntext data types provided support for LOB data. Using these data types effectively, however, was kludgy at best. SQL Server 2008 supports the newer generation of easier-to-use varbinary(max), varchar(max), and nvarchar(max) data types (first introduced in SQL Server 2005) that replace the old LOB data types.

■ **Tip** The image, text, and ntext data types are deprecated and shouldn't be used for new development. Use varbinary(max), varchar(max), and nvarchar(max) instead.

While the non-LOB data types such as varchar(*n*) and varbinary(*n*) max out at 8,000 bytes of storage, the LOB data types in SQL Server 2008 allow you to store up to 2.1GB of data in a single variable or column instance. This is particularly useful when used in conjunction with iFTS to index large documents. The iFTS_Books database has several LOB data type columns that demonstrate a variety of LOB full-text indexing options:

- The dbo.Commentary table has a Commentary column defined as an nvarchar(max). This column contains additional commentary text describing the books in the database.

- The dbo.Commentary table also has an xml data type column called Article_Content that holds articles about books and book-related topics in XML format.

- The dbo.Book table Book_Content column is a varbinary(max) column with the FILESTREAM attribute. This column contains the actual content of each book stored in the database.

Character LOB Data

The varchar(max) and nvarchar(max) data) and nvarchar(max) data types are used to store character data. *Character large object (CLOB)* and *national character large object (NCLOB)* data consists of character data stored in varchar(max) and nvarchar(max) type columns, respectively. The Commentary column of the dbo.Commentary column stores NCLOB data in an nvarchar(max) column.

■ **Note** "National character" is the name given to internationalized character data by the ISO SQL Standard. SQL Server stores national character data as Unicode in the nchar and nvarchar data types.

You can use SELECT queries and DML statements to query and manipulate your CLOB and NCLOB data just like any other non-LOB data types. Internally, SQL Server uses Unicode to store nvarchar(max) data. You need to use nvarchar(max) to support non-ASCII character sets, including Chinese, Russian, Arabic, and Hindi, among many others. In other words, while Western alphabets can be represented fully using the 7-bit ASCII character set, Unicode can be used to represent non-Western alphabets. For non-Western alphabets, Unicode represents each character as a 16-bit (double-byte) code point. The Unicode system encapsulates all known alphabets.

■Note Although ASCII requires only 7 bits to represent characters, some collation settings may require use of the 8th bit in each byte to represent characters with accents or other diacritic marks.

Some restrictions apply to full-text indexing character or national character data in a varchar(max) or nvarchar(max) column, including the following:

- You can only use the plain text filter on a column, so you can't properly full-text index other document types such as word-processing documents and spreadsheets.

- You can only apply a single language/LCID to a column, and only the word-stemmer for that language will be applied to the column.

These are essentially the same restrictions as on non-LOB character type columns. The advantage to the varchar(max) and nvarchar(max) data types over non-LOB character data types is that each row can contain up to 2.1 billion bytes of data.

In the case of the Commentary column, the LCID of the column's full-text index is 1033 (English). This means that the word breaker and stemmer applied to the column will use English language rules to perform linguistic analysis when you perform a full-text search against the column. Consider the search query in Listing 6-1, which looks for inflected forms of the English word *go*. The results are shown in Figure 6-1.

Listing 6-1. *Full-text Query for "Go"*

```
SELECT
  Commentary_ID,
  Commentary
FROM dbo.Commentary
WHERE FREETEXT
(
  Commentary,
  N'go'
);
```

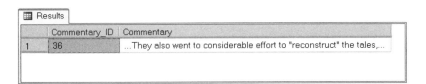

Figure 6-1. *Result of full-text query for "go"*

The row with `Commentary_ID` 36 is returned, since the `Commentary` column contains the word *went*, an inflected form of the word *go* in English.

XML LOB Data

The `dbo.Commentary` table also contains an `xml` data type column. Like the other LOB data types, the `xml` data type can hold up to 2.1GB of data. However, unlike the `varchar(max)` and `nvarchar(max)` data types, the `xml` data type's capacity is not directly related to the length of the character representation of the XML data. The `xml` data type uses an internal representation based on the XQuery/XPath Data Model (XDM), which tends to be generally more compact than `nvarchar`-based XML data representations. You can test this with a query like the one shown in Listing 6-2; results are shown in Figure 6-2.

■**Tip** The `xml` data type uses Unicode representations for character data and stores numeric and other data in compact binary representations.

Listing 6-2. *Comparing the Length of xml Data Type Columns and nvarchar(max) Representations*

```
SELECT
  Commentary_ID,
  DATALENGTH(Article_Content) AS XML_Length,
  DATALENGTH
  (
    CAST
    (
      Article_Content AS nvarchar(max)
    )
  ) AS Char_Length
FROM dbo.Commentary;
```

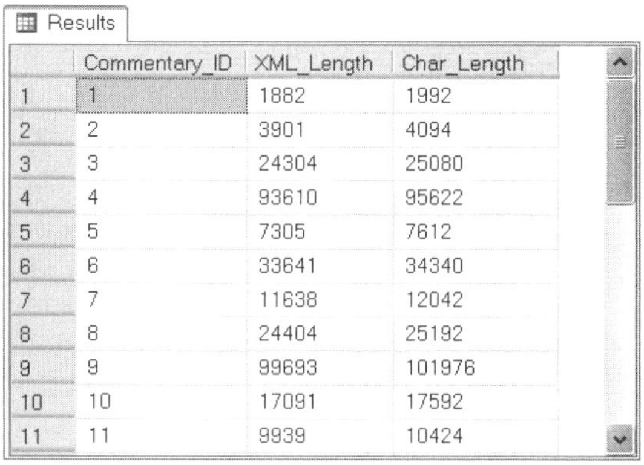

	Commentary_ID	XML_Length	Char_Length
1	1	1882	1992
2	2	3901	4094
3	3	24304	25080
4	4	93610	95622
5	5	7305	7612
6	6	33641	34340
7	7	11638	12042
8	8	24404	25192
9	9	99693	101976
10	10	17091	17592
11	11	9939	10424

Figure 6-2. *Comparing the lengths of xml data type and character-based representations*

An advantage of full-text indexing XML data is the XML word breaker, which respects `xml:lang` language identifier tags in your XML data. This means that you can store language-specific XML data in different rows of the same column, as we've done in the `Article_Content` column of the `dbo.Commentary` table. You can see the `xml:lang` attribute used on the root `<article>` tags of the `Article_Content` XML data with a simple query like the one in Listing 6-3. Results are shown in Figure 6-3.

Listing 6-3. *Viewing Article_Content XML Data in the dbo.Commentary Table*

```
SELECT
  Commentary_ID,
  Article_Content
FROM dbo.Commentary;
```

	Commentary_ID	Article_Content
21	27	`<article><source><name>Wikipedia</name><url>http://en.wi...`
22	28	`<article><source><name>Wikipedia</name><url>http://en.wi...`
23	29	`<article><source><name>Wikipedia</name><url>http://en.wi...`
24	30	`<article xml:lang="en"><source><name>Wikipedia</name><...`
25	31	`<article xml:lang="en"><source><name>Wikipedia</name><...`
26	32	`<article xml:lang="es"><source><name>Wikipedia</name><...`
27	33	`<article xml:lang="de"><source><name>Wikipedia</name><...`
28	36	`<article xml:lang="de"><source><name>Wikipedia</name><...`
29	38	`<article xml:lang="ja"><source><name>Wikipedia</name><u...`

Figure 6-3. *The xml:lang attribute was applied to the root level of many Article_Content XML entries.*

While you can store XML documents in `varbinary(max)` data type columns and full-text index and search them there, to take advantage of `xml` data type features (such as the built-in XQuery support), you must store your XML in `xml` data type columns.

The `xml:lang` attribute in the sample XML is assigned a two-character language code as defined by the Internet Assigned Numbers Authority (IANA). The IANA language registry is based on the ISO 639-2 standard for language representation codes. (You can see the complete language code registry at `http://www.iana.org/assignments/language-subtag-registry`.) The `xml:lang` attribute allows you to add to the language code, so that, for example, `en-US` would indicate that data is in US English, while `en-GB` indicates international English—English as it's written everywhere else in the world. We provide a table listing SQL Server 2008–supported `xml:lang` codes and their corresponding LCIDs in Chapter 5.

The main difference between how full-text indexes handle XML data and other data types is how the word breaker works. When you create a full-text index on an `xml` data type column, the XML word breaker disregards element tags and attributes, indexing only the data contained in the elements. So, if you ran a full-text search for the word *synthesised* against the column, iFTS would return no results, despite the fact that `Commentary_ID` 8 contains the following element in the `Article_Content` data:

```
<section id="Synthesised plot synopsis">
  . . .
</section>
```

Full-text querying the `xml` data type column is exactly like querying any other column. Listing 6-4 shows a full-text query for the word *city*, with partial results shown in Figure 6-4. Note that we've truncated the results significantly to clearly show examples of matching XML data in these results.

Listing 6-4. *Full-Text Querying XML Data for "city"*

```
SELECT
  Commentary_ID,
  Article_Content
FROM dbo.Commentary
WHERE FREETEXT
(
  Article_Content,
  N'city',
  LANGUAGE 1033
);
```

	Commentary_ID	Article_Content
1	4	...<para>...the first edition reading "he went into the city", where t...
2	7	...<para>...the siege of the city of Ilion, or Troy, by the Greeks (S...
3	8	...<para>...but also king of the city of Orchomenus in Boeotia (a ...
4	16	...<para>...sending one or more tornadoes into the city that caus...
5	19	...<para>...and Brutus and Cassius have to leave the city. </para>
6	26	...<para>Regional cults (cities are listed north to south):<list>in ...
7	28	...<para>... a city-port connected to Athens by the Long Walls. S...
8	30	...<para>Only 4 cities have more than 20,000 inhabitants: Zara...

Figure 6-4. *Results of full-text query for "city"*

You can also search for words in alternate languages against this column, as shown in Listing 6-5. The first query searches for the Spanish word *abogados* ("lawyers" in English), and the second query searches for the Japanese word 性質 ("character" or literally "characteristic quality" in English). The results are shown in Figure 6-5, with the XML data truncated to highlight the matches.

Listing 6-5. *Full-Text Query Against Non-English XML Data*

```
SELECT Commentary_ID, Article_Content
FROM dbo.Commentary
WHERE FREETEXT
(
  Article_Content,
  N'abogados',
  LANGUAGE 3082
);
```

```
SELECT
  Commentary_ID,
  Article_Content
FROM dbo.Commentary
WHERE FREETEXT
(
  Article_Content,
  N'性質',
  LANGUAGE 1041
);
```

	(No column nam...	(No column na...	(No column name)
1	Spanish	32	...\<para>...presidente John Adams. De profesión abogado, ocupó la preside...
2	Japanese	38	...\<para>...\<list>1. 巻: 平面図形の性質 2. 巻: 面積の変形(幾何的代数) 3. 巻: 円...

Figure 6-5. *Results of full-text queries against non-English XML data*

The xml:lang attribute doesn't restrict full-text searches to specific languages. With regard to full-text search, the xml:lang attribute applies the proper word breakers when populating a full-text index. If you perform a search for the word *Africa*, as shown in Listing 6-6, iFTS will locate it in both English and Spanish XML data. The results are shown in Figure 6-6, truncated to highlight the matching XML data.

Listing 6-6. *Searching for "Africa"*

```
SELECT
  Commentary_ID,
  Article_Content
FROM dbo.Commentary
WHERE FREETEXT
(
  Article_Content,
  N'Africa',
  LANGUAGE 1033
);
```

	Commentary_ID	Article_Content
1	31	...\<para>...In Africa, traditional medicine is used for 80% of prima...
2	32	...\<para>... repatriación de los esclavos negros al África.\</para>...

Figure 6-6. *Results of search for "Africa"*

EAST ASIAN LANGUAGE SUPPORT

In order to properly display East Asian language characters, such as the Japanese characters in Listing 6-5, you may need to install East Asian language support for your Windows OS installation. This option is available in the Control Panel, under Regional and Language Options. The following is a screenshot of the Regional and Language Options window from Windows XP; it's nearly identical on Windows Server 2003.

The option to Install files for East Asian languages is available under the Languages tab. Check this box and click OK to install the support files. You'll need the original installation CDs during the installation. Once you've installed East Asian language support, you may need to restart your computer.

East Asian language support must be installed to display East Asian character sets (Japanese, Chinese, and so on) in SSMS and other Windows applications. Without East Asian language support installed, Windows will display the characters of these languages as small empty squares on the screen.

Note that even though we specified language LCID 1033 (English) in the query, the results returned XML data that was marked with xml:lang attributes for both English (en) and Spanish (es). We covered how this works in greater detail in Chapter 5, but to briefly explain it here, search terms are stemmed in the chosen language, and then the full-text index is consulted to find matches. The full-text index doesn't store any language-specific metadata for the words that it stores.

Binary LOB Data

In addition to character and XML data, SQL Server allows you to create full-text indexes on BLOB data in the form of `varbinary(max)` columns. The `varbinary(max)` data type is intended to store binary data, which means that if you query the column directly, you'll be unable to read the data in the image column, as it's in binary format.

■**Tip** You can also create full-text indexes on BLOB data in `image` data type columns. However, the `image` data type is deprecated and should be avoided in future development work.

The `varbinary(max)` data type is important to iFTS, as you can store a variety of document types in this column and indicate the type of data stored in another column, referred to as the *type column*. The type column tells the iFTS indexer which filter to launch to extract text and property data from the `varbinary(max)` column.

When you index BLOB data, specifying the type column is mandatory. The type column is a character data type column that holds a set of predefined file extensions which associate your full-text indexed BLOB data to a specific filter. The type column is essentially a column containing the file extension your document would have if it were stored in the file system. The filters (also referred to as *iFilters* because of their dependence on the `IFilter` programming interface) were originally developed for Microsoft's Index Server product, a search server designed to index documents stored in the file system. Index Server identified document formats by looking at the file extension and then launching the correct filter, a model that was carried over to SQL Server full-text search.

If the contents of the image column contain OLE-structured storage documents, another filter may be launched. For example, if you store a TIFF image in an MS Word document, the Word filter will be used to extract the text data and properties in the document, while a TIFF filter will be used to run optical character recognition (OCR) software to extract any textual data that might be in the TIFF image.

You can store plain text documents, MS Word documents, XML fragments, PDF files, and JPEG images in a `varbinary(max)` data type column and the SQL FTS indexer will extract all text data from these documents. Note that only the NTFS properties of a JPEG image will be omitted by the NFTS file properties filter, and these properties won't be stored in the index.

■**Note** In the example given, the filter will also properly recognize dates, numbers, and currency figures, and will store them with additional metadata indicating the type of content. However, despite this additional metadata, you can still only query the data as text.

SQL Server 2008 iFTS can recognize 50 different document types, including those listed in Table 6-1. You can retrieve a full listing of document types supported by your SQL Server 2008 instance by querying the `sys.fulltext_document_types` catalog view.

Table 6-1. *Some Common iFTS BLOB File Formats*

Extension	Document Type	Language-Aware
.doc	MS Word Document	Yes
.html, .htm	HTML Document	Yes (`ms.locale META` tag)
.pdf	Adobe Acrobat PDF Document	Yes*
.ppt	MS PowerPoint Document	Yes
.rtf	Rich Text Document	No
.txt	Plain Text Document	No
.vsd	MS Visio Diagram	Yes*
.xls	MS Excel Spreadsheet	Yes
.xml	XML Document	Yes (`xml:lang` attribute)

* *The filters for these file formats aren't installed with SQL Server 2008 by default. We'll discuss where to obtain filters that support these file formats in Chapter 10.*

When you store an MS Word document in a `varbinary(max)` column, the full-text search engine uses the type column value of `.doc` to launch the MS Office filter to index the document content. Because it's a language-aware file type, the MS Office filter launches the appropriate word breakers for any languages marked in the document content.

MARKING LANGUAGE-SPECIFIC TEXT IN MS WORD

You can mark text as language-specific in MS Word documents by highlighting the appropriate text and selecting Tools ➤ Language ➤ Set Language. Other language-aware document types have different methods for marking language-specific text. By default Word will select the language that matches your operating system's Regional and Language Options configuration. If the computer you're creating your Word documents on has a different language setting than the language you want to create your document in, you'll have to select appropriate styles or create a language-specific template. Other language-aware document types have different methods for marking language-specific text. You'll have to check the documentation to determine the proper method for marking language-specific text.

The `dbo.Book` table in the sample database contains the full content of several books in BLOB format in the `Book_Content` column, which is declared as `varbinary(max)` with the FILESTREAM option. The `Book_File_Ext` column is the type column that contains the associated file extensions. If you query this table, you'll notice that the column contains MS Word, XML, plain text, PDF, and LaTeX documents. We don't recommend directly querying the Book_Content column, since it contains several very large documents. Querying this column directly could cause SSMS to become unresponsive as it tries to retrieve the large BLOB documents.

■Tip By default, SQL Server 2008 doesn't have filters for PDF and LaTeX documents. We'll discuss adding support for both of these file formats in detail in Chapter 10.

Querying the Book_Content column is the same as querying any other LOB data type column. Listing 6-7 queries the Book_Content column for references to *Yorick* (as in "Alas, poor Yorick! I knew him, Horatio . . ."). Results are shown in Figure 6-7.

Listing 6-7. *Searching for "Yorick"*

```
SELECT
  b.Book_ID,
  t.Title,
  t.Title_LCID,
  b.Book_File_Ext,
  b.Book_LCID
FROM dbo.Book b
INNER JOIN dbo.Book_Title bt
  ON b.Book_ID = bt.Book_ID
INNER JOIN dbo.Title t
  ON bt.Title_ID = t.Title_ID
WHERE FREETEXT
(
  b.Book_Content,
  N'Yorick'
)
AND t.Is_Primary_Title = 1;
```

	Book_ID	Title	Title_LCID	Book_File_Ext	Book_LCID
1	9	Hamlet	1033	.txt	1033
2	22	Hamlet	1033	.doc	1036

Figure 6-7. *Alas, Yorick has been found.*

As you can see in Figure 6-7, *Yorick* was located in two versions of the classic tale of *Hamlet* that we've stored in the database—the English plain text version (LCID 1033) and the French MS Word document version (LCID 1036).

FILESTREAM BLOB Data

The FILESTREAM option is new to SQL Server 2008. Everyone has an opinion on whether BLOBs belong in the file system or the database, with many options designed to try to find a middle ground between the two ideas. In the Microsoft Research paper "To BLOB or Not To BLOB: Large Object Storage in a Database or a Filesystem" (http://research.microsoft.com/research/pubs/view.aspx?msr_tr_id=MSR-TR-2006-45), Jim Gray and company made specific recommendations about when to store BLOB data in the database and when to store it in the file system.

Prior to SQL Server 2008, it was common to store BLOB data in the file system with only pointers (file paths) to the BLOB files maintained in the database. Typically, this involved creating a nested hierarchy of subfolders—which maximizes efficiencies of scale offered by the NFTS file format and optimizes throughput when enumerating large numbers of files in a directory. This was especially true in SQL Server 2000 and before, since the old-style image data type was extremely kludgy to work with.

Managing BLOB data in the file system can often be more efficient than storing it in the database. By default, Windows NTFS (NT File System) is designed to stream large quantities of BLOB data more efficiently than SQL Server, which itself excels at managing non-LOB data sets. In SQL Server 2005, the new varbinary(max) data type made managing BLOB data in SQL Server easier than was previously possible, but the difference in efficiency between SQL Server BLOB data management and NTFS BLOB streaming was still a significant factor for applications that had to store large quantities of BLOB data on the server.

On the down side, storing BLOB data in the file system introduced a new layer of custom-built abstraction into the mix. Storing data in the file system meant it was up to the database developer to create techniques to keep the file system and database file paths in sync. Whenever a file was deleted or a file name was changed on the file system, the database had to be updated, or if file information was changed in the database, the file stored in the file system had to be changed to reflect that. A lot of companies made a lot of money creating and selling document management systems that, at their core, performed this most basic of functions. On the flip side, disaster recovery, including the most basic backup and restore methodologies, is simplified greatly when BLOB data is stored in the database.

With the introduction of FILESTREAM functionality in SQL Server 2008, there's a new solution to this problem. Basically, SQL Server allows you to create a varbinary(max) column and decorate it with a FILESTREAM attribute. You can use standard T-SQL query and DML statements to manipulate the column like any other varbinary(max) column.

The difference is in how SQL Server manages your FILESTREAM data. Under the hood, SQL Server stores your FILESTREAM BLOBs in the file system, taking advantage of NTFS's content-streaming capabilities. You don't have to worry about keeping the contents of the file system and the database in sync; SQL Server handles that for you. Additionally, SQL Server takes advantage of NTFS's transactional capabilities during T-SQL DML statements, so you get file system transactions thrown in for free.

Efficiency Advantages

FILESTREAM can offer performance advantages over SQL Server's internal BLOB storage mechanisms. To demonstrate, we ran several rounds of DML statements and queries against two tables: one with a FILESTREAM-enabled varbinary(max) column and the second with a varbinary(max) column that's not FILESTREAM-enabled. We ran these tests on a Xeon 64-bit dual-processor (3GHz) server with 6GB of memory dedicated to the SQL Server instance. The results of our simple test on the table that's not FILESTREAM-enabled are shown in Figure 6-8.

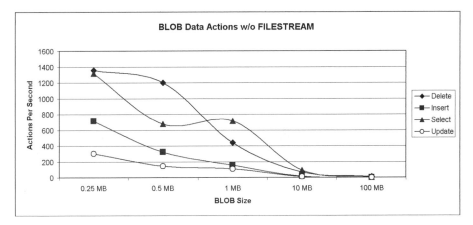

Figure 6-8. *Efficiency of BLOB data actions without FILESTREAM*

As you can see, the number of actions completed per second drops dramatically as the size of the BLOB data increases. At 0.25MB, we were able to complete approximately 1,200 SELECT queries per second against the table; at 100MB, that number dropped to less than 2 per second. We ran the same test against a FILESTREAM-enabled table and got the results shown in Figure 6-9.

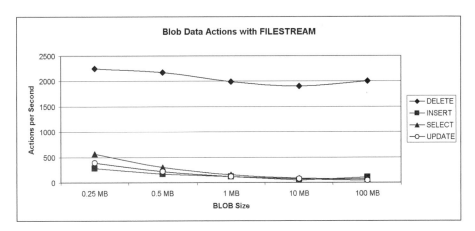

Figure 6-9. *Efficiency of BLOB data actions with FILESTREAM*

As you can see in this figure, the efficiency of most BLOB actions starts out slightly lower than the equivalent non-FILESTREAM actions for smaller files. As the BLOB sizes increase beyond 1MB, however, the FILESTREAM-enabled versions show improved efficiency over the non-FILESTREAM versions. In fact, the sweet spot in our tests appeared to be somewhere between 1MB and 10MB. Note also that DELETE operations on a FILESTREAM-enabled table are extremely fast, since the operation simply invokes operating system functionality to delete the underlying file. We agree with Microsoft's recommendation that FILESTREAM increases the efficiency of T-SQL access and manipulation for BLOBs greater than 1MB in size, and we strongly recommend FILESTREAM for storage of BLOBs larger than 10MB.

FILESTREAM Requirements

The first requirement for FILESTREAM access is NTFS. You can't create a FILESTREAM on an old FAT (File Allocation Table) file system. Next, you have to configure SQL Server to enable FILESTREAM functionality. You can use the SQL Server Configuration Manager utility to easily enable and configure FILESTREAM access.

To access the FILESTREAM configuration options, right-click on the SQL Server service in the Configuration Manager and select Properties from the pop-up context menu. In the Properties window, click on the FILESTREAM tab and select the appropriate options. In Figure 6-10, we've selected the following options:

1. The Enable FILESTREAM for Transact-SQL access option turns on FILESTREAM access and makes it available for T-SQL querying and DML access.

2. The Enable FILESTREAM for file I/O streaming access option exposes the FILESTREAM access for local streaming I/O.

3. When you choose the Enable FILESTREAM for file I/O streaming access option, you must choose a Windows share name that will be used to expose the FILESTREAM for streaming I/O.

4. Finally there's an option to Allow remote clients to have streaming access to FILESTREAM data. This option allows you to expose the FILESTREAM data to remote client connections.

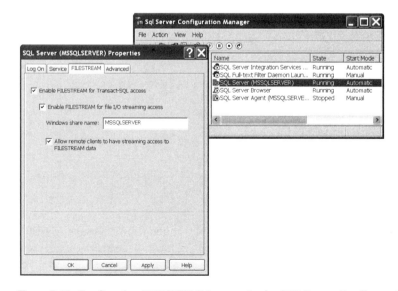

Figure 6-10. *Configuring FILESTREAM access in the SQL Server Configuration Manager*

After you enable FILESTREAM access in the SQL Server Configuration Manager, you need to set the access level in T-SQL using sp_configure, as shown in Listing 6-8.

Listing 6-8. *Setting FILESTREAM Access Level in T-SQL*

```
EXEC sp_configure 'filestream_access_level', 2;
GO
RECONFIGURE;
GO
```

You can use sp_configure to set the FILESTREAM access level to one of the levels shown in Table 6-2.

Table 6-2. *FILESTREAM Access Levels*

Level	Description
0	Disables FILESTREAM support for the SQL Server instance
1	Enables FILESTREAM access via T-SQL for the SQL Server instance
2	Enables FILESTREAM access via T-SQL and via the file system for the SQL Server instance

After you've enabled FILESTREAM access, you must create a FILESTREAM filegroup in which to store your data. You can do this with the CREATE DATABASE or ALTER DATABASE statements. Listing 6-9 shows the CREATE DATABASE statement used to create the iFTS_Books sample database, with the clause that creates the FILESTREAM filegroup in bold.

Listing 6-9. *Creating a Database with a FILESTREAM Filegroup*

```
CREATE DATABASE iFTS_Books
ON  PRIMARY
(
  NAME = N'iFTS_Books',
  FILENAME = N'C:\iFTS_Books\iFTS_Books_Data.mdf',
  SIZE = 43904KB,
  MAXSIZE = UNLIMITED,
  FILEGROWTH = 1024KB
),
FILEGROUP FileStreamGroup
CONTAINS FILESTREAM
DEFAULT
(
  NAME = N'iFTS_Books_FileStream',
  FILENAME = N'C:\iFTS_Books\iFTS_Books_FileStream'
)
```

```
LOG ON
(
  NAME = N'iFTS_Books_log',
  FILENAME = N'C:\iFTS_Books\iFTS_Books_Log.ldf',
  SIZE = 1024KB,
  MAXSIZE = 2048GB,
  FILEGROWTH = 10%
);
GO
```

In the CONTAINS FILESTREAM clause, the NAME is the logical name for the FILESTREAM and must be unique within the database. The FILENAME for a FILESTREAM is the path to the folder where FILESTREAM BLOB data will be stored. The path up to the last folder must exist prior to creation, and the last folder must not exist at creation time (it will be created automatically).

Once you've enabled FILESTREAM access on the SQL Server instance and created the FILESTREAM filegroup, you can create tables with FILESTREAM-enabled varbinary(max) columns. Listing 6-10 shows the CREATE TABLE statement for the dbo.Book table, which contains a FILESTREAM-enabled varbinary(max) column.

Listing 6-10. *CREATE TABLE Statement for FILESTREAM-Enabled dbo.Book Table*

```
CREATE TABLE dbo.Book
(
  Book_ID int NOT NULL,
  Book_GUID uniqueidentifier ROWGUIDCOL  NOT NULL,
  Book_LCID int NOT NULL,
  Book_Subject_ID tinyint NOT NULL,
  Book_Class_Code nchar(1),
  Book_Subclass_Code nvarchar(3) NOT NULL,
  Book_Content varbinary(max) FILESTREAM  NOT NULL,
  Book_File_Ext nvarchar(4) NOT NULL,
  Book_Image_Name nvarchar(100),
  Book_Image varbinary(max),
  Change_Track_Version timestamp,
  CONSTRAINT PK_Book PRIMARY KEY CLUSTERED
  (
    Book_ID ASC
  ),
  UNIQUE NONCLUSTERED
  (
    Book_GUID ASC
  )
);
GO
```

The Book_Content column of the dbo.Book table is a varbinary(max) column decorated with the FILESTREAM attribute. This means that any data that's stored in the column will automatically be stored on the NTFS file system and managed by SQL Server. A particular requirement of FILESTREAM-enabled tables is that they must contain a uniqueidentifier ROWGUIDCOL column with a unique constraint declared on it. The dbo.Book table declares the Book_GUID column, which has a unique constraint declared on it. Once you've created a FILESTREAM-enabled table, you can query and manipulate it using T-SQL just like any other table.

FILESTREAM AND 8.3 NAMES

For backward compatibility with older 16-bit applications, NTFS automatically creates 8.3-format file names. An 8.3 file name is simply a name with a maximum length of 12 characters: up to 8 characters for the main file name, a period, and an extension up to 3 characters in length.

The 8.3 file name creation and enumeration process can cause considerable performance degradation in a directory with thousands of files stored in it. Because of this, if you store a large number of documents (thousands of files) in a FILESTREAM-enabled varbinary(max) column, you may suffer performance problems due to 8.3 naming. To avoid or resolve this issue, simply turn off NTFS 8.3 name creation with the fsutil.exe command-line utility on Windows XP or Windows Server 2003. The fsutil.exe command looks like this:

```
fsutil.exe behavior set disable8dot3 1
```

For more information on disabling NTFS 8.3 naming, see Microsoft Knowledge Base article #121007 at http://support.microsoft.com.

T-SQL Access

As we discussed, once you've enabled FILESTREAM access on your SQL Server instance, you can query and manipulate your FILESTREAM-enabled columns using standard T-SQL query and DML statements. Listing 6-11 retrieves the plain text version of *Hamlet* in the database using a simple SELECT query, with partial results shown in Figure 6-11.

Listing 6-11. *Querying a FILESTREAM-Enabled Column*

```
SELECT
  b.Book_ID,
  CAST
  (
    b.Book_Content AS nvarchar(max)
  ) AS Book_Content
FROM dbo.Book b
WHERE b.Book_ID = 9;
```

Figure 6-11. *Plain text version of* Hamlet *queried from FILESTREAM-enabled column*

You can also issue UPDATE, DELETE, INSERT, and MERGE statements against the FILESTREAM-enabled column. The sample code in Listing 6-12 inserts Lincoln's Gettysburg Address into the dbo.Book table, queries it, and then deletes it to demonstrate running DML actions against the FILESTREAM-enabled Book_Content column. The results are shown in Figure 6-12.

Listing 6-12. *Performing DML Actions Against a FILESTREAM-Enabled Column*

```
INSERT INTO dbo.Book
(
  Book_ID,
  Book_GUID,
  Book_LCID,
  Book_Class_Code,
  Book_Subclass_Code,
  Book_Content,
  Book_File_Ext,
  Book_Image_Name,
  Book_Image
)
VALUES
(
  100,
  NEWID(),
  1033,
  N'E',
  N'E',
  CAST
  (
    N'Four score and seven years ago our fathers brought forth on this
    continent a new nation, conceived in Liberty, and dedicated to the
    proposition that all men are created equal.

    Now we are engaged in a great civil war, testing whether that nation,
    or any nation, so conceived and so dedicated, can long endure. We are
    met on a great battle-field of that war. We have come to dedicate a
    portion of that field, as a final resting place for those who here
    gave their lives that that nation might live. It is altogether
    fitting and proper that we should do this.

    But, in a larger sense, we cannot dedicate—we cannot consecrate—we
    cannot hallow—this ground. The brave men, living and dead, who
    struggled here, have consecrated it, far above our poor power to add
    or detract. The world will little note, nor long remember what we
    say here, but it can never forget what they did here. It is for us
    the living, rather, to be dedicated here to the unfinished work which
    they who fought here have thus far so nobly advanced. It is rather
```

```
  for us to be here dedicated to the great task remaining before us—
  that from these honored dead we take increased devotion to that cause
  for which they gave the last full measure of devotion—that we here
  highly resolve that these dead shall not have died in vain—that
  this nation, under God, shall have a new birth of freedom—and that
  government of the people, by the people, for the people, shall not
  perish from the earth.' AS varbinary(max)
 ),
 N'.txt',
 NULL,
 NULL
);
GO

SELECT
  Book_ID,
  CAST(Book_Content AS nvarchar(max)) AS Book_Content
FROM dbo.Book
WHERE Book_ID = 100;
GO

DELETE FROM dbo.Book
WHERE Book_ID = 100;
GO
```

Figure 6-12. *Result of DML action against a FILESTREAM-enabled column*

When you delete a row from a table that has a FILESTREAM-enabled column in it, or set the value of the column to NULL, the underlying file in the file system is deleted. You can also wrap DML statements that modify FILESTREAM data in an explicit T-SQL transaction. SQL Server ensures the durability of FILESTREAM BLOBs when the transaction is committed. If you roll back the transaction, the DML statements that affect the FILESTREAM BLOBs are rolled back as well.

Storage Considerations

Each instance of BLOB data that you store in a FILESTREAM-enabled column is physically stored as a file in the file system. Figure 6-13 shows the iFTS_Books database FILESTREAM files as viewed through Windows Explorer.

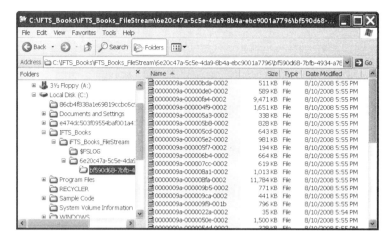

Figure 6-13. *FILESTREAM files stored in the file system*

Each file shown in Figure 6-13 represents a single FILESTREAM data BLOB stored in the dbo.Book table. If you've exposed your FILESTREAM data for file system access, SQL Server exposes the data via Windows file sharing. The FILESTREAM-enabled varbinary(max) column exposes the PathName() method to return the full logical path to the FILESTREAM files. This feature is useful if you're using the OpenSqlFilestream API to access FILESTREAM data from client applications. Listing 6-13 uses the PathName() method to retrieve the full path to the file containing the book *A Connecticut Yankee In King Arthur's Court,* with the result following. Note that the path returned by your SQL Server when running this sample may differ from the result shown here.

Listing 6-13. *Retrieving Full Path to* A Connecticut Yankee in King Arthur's Court

```
SELECT
  Book_Content.PathName()
FROM dbo.Book
WHERE Book_ID = 3;
```

```
\\SQL2008\MSSQLSERVER\v1\iFTS_Books\dbo\Book\Book_Content\E36D2F0D-➥
F690-4F34-A59D-738E22D2A0DC
```

Bear in mind that the files stored in the file system by FILESTREAM are not encrypted by SQL Server, even if you're using the SQL Server Transparent Data Encryption (TDE) option to encrypt your entire database. Also, you can't use the Write() method of the varbinary(max) data type to perform T-SQL–chunked updates to FILESTREAM data. Setting a FILESTREAM-enabled value to NULL deletes the underlying file from the file system.

OpenSqlFilestream API

As mentioned previously, one of the advantages of SQL Server 2008 FILESTREAM storage is the ability to stream data using NTFS. In fact, you can use the OpenSqlFilestream API to stream FILESTREAM data directly from the file system, bypassing SQL Server's cache and freeing up server resources for other processes. Although OpenSqlFilestream is a native Win32 API, the .NET Framework provides a managed wrapper in the form of the System.Data.SqlTypes.SqlFileStream class.

To demonstrate OpenSqlFilestream functionality on the client side, we created a simple C# application. Our application executes a full-text search query against the iFTS_Books sample database, displays a list of matching titles, and allows you to download and open any of the matching documents through the OpenSqlFilestream API. In this section, we'll highlight the code that pertains to retrieving FILESTREAM data from SQL Server.

■Note The full code listing is available in the sample downloads file, available at www.apress.com.

We'll begin our discussion of client-side FILESTREAM access by demonstrating the sample application in action. Then we'll highlight and describe the portions of code that are critical to using the OpenSqlFilestream API in your own code.

The sample application displays a simple Windows form that allows you to perform a full-text search against the iFTS_Books database by entering search terms in the Enter Search String text box and clicking the Search button. All titles that match the search criteria you enter are displayed in a DataGridView control once the search completes. Figure 6-14 shows the results of a full-text search for the word *fish*.

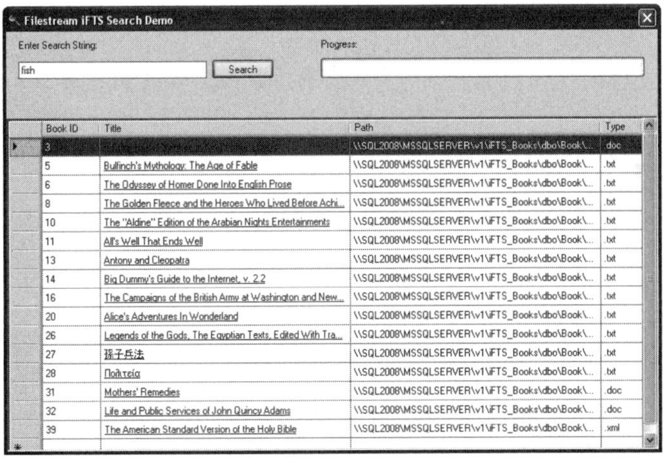

Figure 6-14. *Results of search for "fish"*

You can click on any of the hyperlinks in the Title column of the `DataGridView` to retrieve the document from the server via the OpenSqlFilestream API. Once the file is downloaded from the server and saved to the local file system, it is automatically opened, as shown in Figure 6-15.

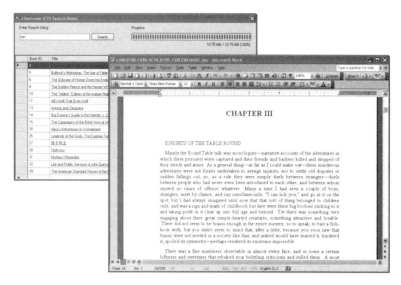

Figure 6-15. *Downloading and opening a file with the OpenSqlFilestream API*

The key `FILESTREAM` functionality of this application consists of three major operations:

1. Retrieving a pathname to the `FILESTREAM` file from SQL Server.

2. Getting a SQL Server `FILESTREAM` transaction context ID for the operation.

3. Using the OpenSqlFilestream API to stream the data back to the client via NTFS.

The first operation is performed by the query that's sent to SQL Server when you enter a search term and click Search. The query that is generated is shown in Listing 6-14.

Listing 6-14. *Full-Text Search Query Generated by Sample Application*

```
SELECT
  b.Book_ID,
  t.Title,
  b.Book_Content.PathName() AS FilePath,
  b.Book_File_Ext
FROM dbo.Book b
INNER JOIN dbo.Book_Title bt
  ON b.Book_ID = bt.Book_ID
INNER JOIN dbo.Title t
  ON bt.Title_ID = t.Title_ID
WHERE FREETEXT(Book_Content, @SearchString)
  AND t.Is_Primary_Title = 1;
```

The FilePath column uses the PathName() method of the FILESTREAM-enabled b.Book_Content column to return the logical UNC path to the FILESTREAM files for each matching title returned by the query. This fulfills the first requirement: retrieving the pathname for the FILESTREAM files.

Once you click on a hyperlink in the DataGridView, the application begins the process of downloading the file. We designed the GetFile method to perform this function asynchronously to keep the user interface (UI) responsive. The asynchronous nature of the sample code adds some additional complexity, but the basic requirements are the same whether your application is synchronous or asynchronous. The first step is to open a connection to SQL Server, begin a transaction, and retrieve a FILESTREAM transaction context with the GET_FILESTREAM_TRANSACTION_CONTEXT function. This function returns a varbinary(max) token that represents the context of the current FILESTREAM transaction. The varbinary result of this function maps to a .NET byte array. Listing 6-15 shows the portion of the GetFile method that gets the FILESTREAM transaction context.

Listing 6-15. *Getting a FILESTREAM Transaction Context*

```
// This method retrieves a file with the OpenSqlFileStream API
private void GetFile
(
  string filePath,
  string fileType
)
{

  ...

  try
  {
    ...

    // Create and open a new SQL connection. This is required because the
    // FILESTREAM requires a SQL Server transaction context, so we need
    // to create a transaction, which means we need an open connection
    sqlConnection = new SqlConnection
    (
      connectionString
    );
    sqlConnection.Open();

    // Create a SQL Server transaction context over the connection
    SqlTransaction sqlTransaction = sqlConnection.BeginTransaction
    (
      "fileStreamTx"
    );
```

```
  // Use the T-SQL GET_FILESTREAM_TRANSACTION_CONTEXT() function
  // to get the transaction context identifier from SQL Server. The
  // transaction context is returned as a varbinary value, which
  // maps to the .NET byte array.
  sqlCommand = new SqlCommand
  (
    "SELECT GET_FILESTREAM_TRANSACTION_CONTEXT();",
    sqlConnection,
    sqlTransaction
  );
  byte[] transactionContext = (byte[])sqlCommand.ExecuteScalar();

...

}
```

After the code retrieves a FILESTREAM transaction context from SQL Server, it uses the SqlFileStream class, which acts as a managed wrapper around the OpenSqlFileStream API, to retrieve the FILESTREAM data from SQL Server. The data is retrieved into a .NET byte array buffer in 4KB increments. As the data is buffered on the client, it's written back out to a file in the local file system using a .NET BinaryWriter. Listing 6-16 shows the portion of the GetFile method that's concerned with retrieving the actual data via the OpenSqlFilestream API.

Listing 6-16. *Retrieving a File with the OpenSqlFilestream API*

```
// This method retrieves a file with the OpenSqlFileStream API
private void GetFile
 (
  string filePath,
  string fileType
)
{

  ...

  // Here we use the managed SqlFileStream wrapper to retrieve the data
  sqlFileStream = new SqlFileStream
  (
    filePath,
    transactionContext,
    FileAccess.Read
  );

  // A 4KB buffer to hold the SqlFileStream data as it's retrieved
  byte [] buffer = new byte[4096];
```

```
// Progress status variables
long fileLength = sqlFileStream.Length;  // Length of data to retrieve
long totalBytesRead = 0;                 // Total bytes retrieved
int bytesBuffered = 0;                   // Bytes buffered currently

// Write the data back out to the local file system in a BinaryWriter
// as it's retrieved
binaryWriter = new BinaryWriter
(
  File.Open(destinationFileName, FileMode.Create)
  // Create/overwrite existing file of same name
);

// Keep going until the total bytes received is equal to the total
// bytes expected
while (totalBytesRead != fileLength)
{
  // Buffer 4 KB of data at a time, and write to output file as
  // soon as data is received
  bytesBuffered = sqlFileStream.Read(buffer, 0, 4096);
  binaryWriter.Write(buffer, 0, bytesBuffered);

  totalBytesRead += bytesBuffered;

  ...

}

...

  return;
}
```

Since this method is called asynchronously, there's some additional required code in the Callback method. In addition to cleaning up and disposing of SQL Server connectivity-related objects, the application needs to either commit or roll back the transaction created for the OpenSqlFilestream API. This is important, since failing to commit or roll back the transaction can result in server-side resource leaks. This method also calls another helper routine to open the file that was retrieved to the local file system, as shown in Listing 6-17.

Listing 6-17. *Callback Method Performs Cleanup*

```
private void Callback
(
  IAsyncResult iar
)
{
```

```
...

// Do all the cleanup

...

if (sqlCommand != null)
{
  if (sqlCommand.Transaction != null)
    sqlCommand.Transaction.Commit();
  sqlCommand.Dispose();
}

...

// Opens the file on the local file system
OpenFile(destinationFileName);
}
```

The rest of the program is support code designed to support asynchronous data retrieval and provide feedback to the user, in order to keep the UI responsive and improve the overall user experience.

Summary

In this chapter, we talked about how to full-text index LOB data in SQL Server 2008. In SQL Server 7.0 and 2000, full-text indexing LOB data presented several challenges that the new generation of LOB data types helps overcome. The varchar(max), nvarchar(max), varbinary(max), and xml data types collectively provide significant improvements over their deprecated SQL 2000 counterparts.

We also discussed SQL Server 2008's powerful new FILESTREAM feature, which leverages the power of NTFS to efficiently store and stream unstructured BLOB data from the file system. FILESTREAM functionality can provide a significant performance boost for manipulating and streaming large BLOB data (greater than 1MB in size). We discussed the performance benefits and demonstrated FILESTREAM-enabled column usage.

Finally, we demonstrated use of the OpenSqlFilestream API via the .NET SqlFileStream managed wrapper class. This API helps you improve client application performance and server efficiency by allowing you to access FILESTREAM data while keeping SQL Server resources free for use by other users and processes.

In the next chapter, we'll discuss iFTS stopwords and stoplists, which allow you to specify that iFTS should ignore specific words during the indexing process.

CHAPTER 7

■ ■ ■

Stoplists

Sick I am of idle words, past all reconciling, . . .

—George du Maurier

All versions of SQL Server that have supported full-text search have included an option to ignore certain words that are considered unimportant for search purposes. In SQL Server 2005 and earlier, this option was known as the *noise word* list. Noise word lists were language-specific text files stored in the file system. In SQL Server 2008, noise word lists have been replaced by *stoplists*, which are likewise composed of words, known as *stopwords*, that are unimportant for search. Unlike noise word lists, stoplists are stored in the database rather than in the file system. SQL Server 2008 also provides T-SQL language improvements designed to make stoplists more flexible than noise word lists and to facilitate and ease their management.

In SQL Server 2005 and prior versions, FTS utilized noise word lists to indicate words that should be ignored during full-text searches. These noise word lists were stored as plain text files under SQL Server's MSSQL\FTDATA directory with names like noiseXXX.txt, where the *XXX* indicates a three-letter language code such as ENU for U.S. English and JPN for Japanese. In prior versions of SQL Server, you were allowed a single noise word list per supported language.

SQL Server 2008 changes this with stoplists. Stoplists are stored in the database instead of the file system, and you can create as many stoplists as you like for any supported language. The only limitation is that you can assign only one stoplist to any given full-text index.

The reasons for creating or using a stoplist include the following:

- To prevent your full-text indexes from becoming bloated with unnecessary and unimportant words

- To improve the quality of full-text search results by eliminating unimportant word matches from the results

- To increase the efficiency of full-text searches by eliminating searching and stemming of irrelevant words

In this chapter we'll discuss the creation, management, and use of stoplists in SQL Server 2008.

System Stoplists

By default, SQL Server 2008 provides system stoplists for most languages that iFTS supports. Table 7-1 lists the default iFTS-supported languages that don't have a system stoplist.

Table 7-1. *Supported Languages Without a System Stoplist*

LCID	Language Name
1042	Korean
1066	Vietnamese
3076	Chinese (Hong Kong SAR, PRC)
4100	Chinese (Singapore)
5124	Chinese (Macau SAR)

In addition, there are a few languages that have a stoplist installed, but aren't supported by default in iFTS. These languages are listed in Table 7-2.

Table 7-2. *System Stoplists for Languages Not Supported by Default*

LCID	Language Name
1030	Danish
1045	Polish
1055	Turkish

The system stoplists include single-digit numbers, individual letters of the alphabet, and words that are considered generally uninformative for purposes of full-text search. The English (LCID 1033) stoplist, for instance, has 154 entries, including words such as *you*, *an*, *the*, and *our*. You can view the system stoplists by querying the sys.fulltext_system_stopwords catalog view. This view returns a column with the stopword entries from the system stoplists and a language_id column with the LCID of each entry. Listing 7-1 shows how to query the English language system stoplist, with partial results shown in Figure 7-1.

Listing 7-1. *Querying the English Language System Stoplist*

```
SELECT *
FROM sys.fulltext_system_stopwords
WHERE language_id = 1033;
```

You can specify that a full-text index use the system stoplist by adding the WITH STOPLIST = SYSTEM clause to your CREATE FULLTEXT INDEX or ALTER FULLTEXT INDEX statements. If you don't specify a stoplist when you create a full-text index, SQL Server defaults to the system stoplist.

■**Tip** If you don't want your full-text index to use a stoplist at all, use the WITH STOPLIST = OFF clause when you create it.

---

	stopword	language_id	
65	each	1033	
66	else	1033	
67	for	1033	
68	from	1033	
69	get	1033	
70	got	1033	
71	had	1033	
72	has	1033	
73	have	1033	

Figure 7-1. *Viewing the English language system stoplist*

Creating Custom Stoplists

You can create and manage custom stoplists in SQL Server 2008, using either the SSMS GUI or T-SQL statements. When you create a custom stoplist, you can either create an empty stoplist or base it on a system stoplist. To create a custom stoplist in the SSMS GUI, right-click on Storage ➤ Full Text Stoplists in the Object Explorer. Then select New Full-Text Stoplist... from the pop-up context menu, as shown in Figure 7-2.

Figure 7-2. *Creating a new full-text stoplist in SSMS*

The New Full-Text Stoplist window allows you to name your full-text stoplist, specify a database principal as the owner of the stoplist, and choose whether your stoplist will initially be empty or be populated from an existing stoplist. In Figure 7-3, we've created a custom stoplist named NoFish_Stoplist with dbo as the owner. The stoplist will be initially populated from the system stoplist.

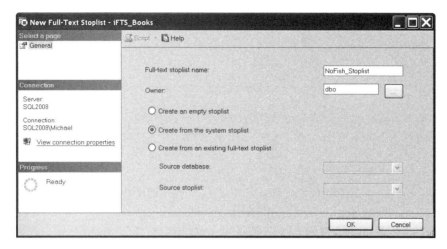

Figure 7-3. *Defining a custom stoplist in the New Full-Text Stoplist window*

After you've created a custom stoplist, you can add or remove stopwords from the stoplist by right-clicking the name of the stoplist in the Object Explorer and selecting Properties from the pop-up context menu, as shown in Figure 7-4.

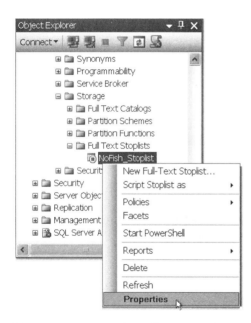

Figure 7-4. *Accessing the Full-Text Stoplist Properties window*

The Full-Text Stoplist Properties window allows you to perform the following stoplist management activities from the Action drop-down list:

- *Add stopword* allows you to add a stopword to the stoplist for a specific language.

- *Delete stopword* allows you to delete a stopword from the stoplist for a specific language.

- *Delete all stopwords* allows you to delete all stopwords from the stoplist for a specific language.

- *Clear stoplist* allows you to delete all stopwords from the stoplist for all languages.

In Figure 7-5, we demonstrate how to add the word *fish* to the NoFish_Stoplist.

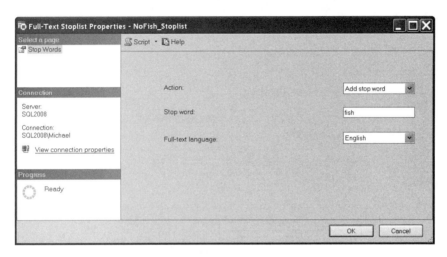

Figure 7-5. *Adding "fish" to a stoplist*

Once you've created a custom stoplist, you can use the SSMS Create Full-Text Index wizard to create a new full-text index that uses it. You can also assign it to an existing full-text index by right-clicking on the full-text indexed table and selecting Full-Text index ➤ Properties, as shown in Figure 7-6.

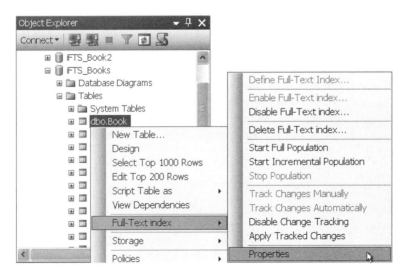

Figure 7-6. *Selecting Full-Text Index Properties*

In the Full-Text Index Properties window, you can assign a custom stoplist to the full-text index, as shown in Figure 7-7.

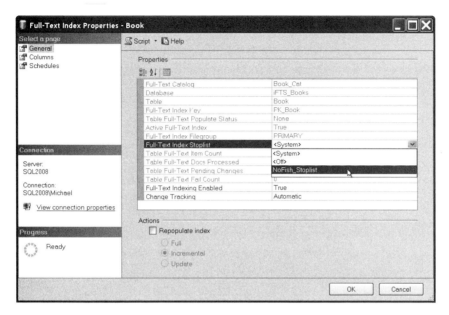

Figure 7-7. *Assigning a custom stoplist to an existing full-text index*

■**Caution** If your full-text index is set for automatic change tracking, changing the stoplist will kick off a full population.

Managing Stoplists

SQL Server 2008 provides three catalog views that are useful for retrieving the contents of system and custom stoplists. The sys.fulltext_stoplists catalog view returns a list of the names and IDs of all the custom stoplists in the current database. The sys.fulltext_system_stopwords catalog view returns a list of all the stopwords in the system stoplist, along with their associated languages. Listing 7-2 retrieves the full list of stopwords in the system stoplist in all languages. Partial results are shown in Figure 7-8.

Listing 7-2. *Retrieving All Stopwords from the System Stoplist*

```
SELECT *
FROM sys.fulltext_system_stopwords;
```

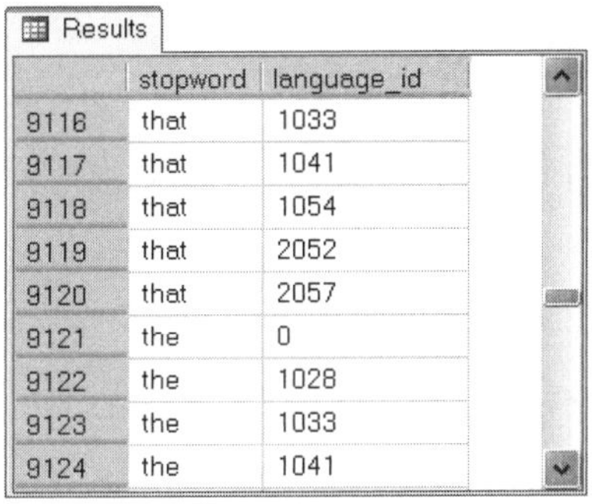

Results

	stopword	language_id
9116	that	1033
9117	that	1041
9118	that	1054
9119	that	2052
9120	that	2057
9121	the	0
9122	the	1028
9123	the	1033
9124	the	1041

Figure 7-8. *Stopwords in the system stoplist*

The sys.fulltext_stopwords catalog view is the custom stoplist equivalent of the sys.fulltext_system_stopwords catalog view. The sys.fulltext_stopwords view returns all stopwords in all custom stoplists, for all languages, in the current database. Let's create a simple scalar user-defined function (UDF) that performs a function similar to the OBJECT_ID system function for custom stoplists. This function will help support retrieval of stoplists by name and provide by-name capability for stoplist dynamic management functions (DMFs), which we'll describe in upcoming chapters. The dbo.Stoplist_ID function, shown in Listing 7-3, accepts a custom stoplist name and returns the ID for that stoplist.

Listing 7-3. *UDF to Return a Stoplist ID by Name*

```
CREATE FUNCTION dbo.Stoplist_ID
(
  @name sysname
)
RETURNS int
AS
BEGIN
  RETURN
  (
    SELECT stoplist_id
    FROM sys.fulltext_stoplists
    WHERE name = @name
  );
END;
```

In Listing 7-4, we use the dbo.Stoplist_ID function with the sys.fulltext_stopwords catalog view to return the stopwords in the NoFish_Stoplist. Partial results are shown in Figure 7-9. We'll use the dbo.Stoplist_ID function again in Chapter 9 to simplify the process of passing a stoplist ID to full-text search DMFs that accept it as a parameter.

Listing 7-4. *Viewing the Stopwords in the NoFish_Stoplist Custom Stoplist*

```
USE iFTS_Books;
GO
SELECT *
FROM sys.fulltext_stopwords
WHERE stoplist_id = dbo.Stoplist_ID(N'NoFish_Stoplist');
```

	stoplist_id	stopword	language	language_id
3506	6	fiquemos	Brazilian	1046
3507	6	fiques	Brazilian	1046
3508	6	fish	English	1033
3509	6	fixe	French	1036
3510	6	fixus	Dutch	1043
3511	6	fiz	Brazilian	1046
3512	6	fizemos	Brazilian	1046
3513	6	fizer	Brazilian	1046
3514	6	fizera	Brazilian	1046

Figure 7-9. *Stopwords in a custom stoplist*

You might need to script your custom stoplist creation and management actions. SQL Server provides a variety of T-SQL statements to administer stoplists, including statements to create, drop, and modify stoplists, as well as additional clauses on the CREATE FULLTEXT INDEX and ALTER FULLTEXT INDEX statements that let you assign stoplists to new or existing full-text indexes, respectively. Listing 7-5 uses T-SQL statements to create the NoFish_Stoplist, add the word *fish* to it, and assign it to the existing full-text index on the dbo.Book table.

Listing 7-5. *Creating a Custom Stoplist and Assigning It to a Full-Text Index*

```
USE iFTS_Books;
GO

CREATE FULLTEXT STOPLIST NoFish_Stoplist
FROM SYSTEM STOPLIST
AUTHORIZATION dbo;

ALTER FULLTEXT STOPLIST NoFish_Stoplist
ADD 'fish' LANGUAGE 1033;

ALTER FULLTEXT INDEX ON dbo.Book
SET STOPLIST = NoFish_Stoplist;
```

In Listing 7-5, we created a stoplist based on the system stoplist. With the CREATE FULLTEXT STOPLIST statement, you can also specify that a stoplist be created empty or populated from another existing stoplist.

We used the ALTER FULLTEXT STOPLIST statement to add the stopword *fish* to the stoplist. The ALTER FULLTEXT STOPLIST statement also allows you to drop individual stopwords, all stopwords for a specific language, or all stopwords for all languages from your stoplist with its DROP clause.

Finally, we used the ALTER FULLTEXT INDEX statement's SET STOPLIST clause to set the stoplist for the full-text index on the dbo.Book table to NoFish_Stoplist.

■**Tip** Stopwords are limited to a maximum token length of 64 characters.

Adding individual stopwords to a stoplist can be a tedious process, since you have to issue a separate ALTER FULLTEXT STOPLIST statement for each stopword. We've created the dbo.Add_Stopwords stored procedure in Listing 7-6 to make it easier to add multiple stopwords to a custom stoplist with a single statement. Note that this procedure already exists in the iFTS_Books sample database.

Listing 7-6. *The dbo.Add_Stopwords Procedure*

```
USE iFTS_Books;
GO

CREATE PROCEDURE dbo.Add_Stopwords
(
  @stoplist sysname,
  @words nvarchar(max),
  @lcid int = 1033
)
AS
BEGIN
  SET @words = N',' + REPLACE(@words, N';', N'') + N',';

  CREATE TABLE #Stopwords
  (
    Word nvarchar(64)
  );

  WITH Numbers (n)
  AS
  (
    SELECT 1

    UNION ALL

    SELECT n + 1
    FROM Numbers
    WHERE n < LEN(@words)
```

```
)
INSERT INTO #Stopwords (Word)
SELECT
  SUBSTRING
  (
    @words,
    n + 1,
    CHARINDEX(N',', @words, n + 1) - n - 1
  )
FROM Numbers
WHERE SUBSTRING(@words, n, 1) = N','
AND n < LEN(@words)
OPTION (MAXRECURSION 0);

DECLARE Stopword_Cursor CURSOR
FORWARD_ONLY READ_ONLY
FOR
SELECT LTRIM(RTRIM(Word)) AS Word
FROM #Stopwords
WHERE LEN(Word) > 0;

OPEN Stopword_Cursor;

DECLARE @sql nvarchar(400),
  @word nvarchar(64);

FETCH NEXT
FROM StopWord_Cursor
INTO @word;

WHILE @@FETCH_STATUS = 0
BEGIN

  IF NOT EXISTS
  (
    SELECT 1
    FROM sys.fulltext_stopwords fsw
    WHERE fsw.stoplist_id = dbo.Stoplist_ID(@stoplist)
      AND fsw.stopword = @word
      AND fsw.language_id = @lcid
  )
  BEGIN

    SET @sql = N'ALTER FULLTEXT STOPLIST ' +
      QUOTENAME(@stoplist) +
      N' ADD ' + QUOTENAME(@word, '''') +
      N' LANGUAGE ' + CAST(@lcid AS nvarchar(4)) + ';';
```

```
    EXEC (@sql);

  END;

  FETCH NEXT
  FROM StopWord_Cursor
  INTO @word;

  END;

  CLOSE StopWord_Cursor;

  DEALLOCATE StopWord_Cursor;

END;
GO
```

The dbo.Add_Stopwords stored procedure accepts three parameters: the name of the stoplist you want to modify, a comma-delimited list of stopwords to add to the stoplist, and an LCID code (the default is 1033 [English]). The procedure uses a CTE and the built-in T-SQL string manipulation functions to split the comma-delimited list into separate words that are inserted into a temporary table:

```
SET @words = N',' + REPLACE(@words, N';', N'') + N',';

CREATE TABLE #Stopwords
(
  Word nvarchar(64)
);

WITH Numbers (n)
AS
(
  SELECT 1

  UNION ALL

  SELECT n + 1
  FROM Numbers
  WHERE n < LEN(@words)
)
INSERT INTO #Stopwords (Word)
SELECT
  SUBSTRING
  (
    @words,
    n + 1,
    CHARINDEX(N',', @words, n + 1) - n - 1
  )
```

```
FROM Numbers
WHERE SUBSTRING(@words, n, 1) = N','
AND n < LEN(@words)
OPTION (MAXRECURSION 0);
```

Once all the stopwords are in the temporary table, the procedure uses a cursor to iterate the rows, and uses the `sys.fulltext_stopwords` catalog view to see if the stopword already exists in the custom stoplist. If the word doesn't already exist, the stored procedure creates a dynamic SQL `ALTER FULLTEXT STOPLIST` statement for each word. Each dynamic SQL statement is executed as it's created:

```
DECLARE Stopword_Cursor CURSOR
FORWARD_ONLY READ_ONLY
FOR
SELECT LTRIM(RTRIM(Word)) AS Word
FROM #Stopwords
WHERE LEN(Word) > 0;

OPEN Stopword_Cursor;

DECLARE @sql nvarchar(400),
  @word nvarchar(64);

FETCH NEXT
FROM StopWord_Cursor
INTO @word;

WHILE @@FETCH_STATUS = 0
BEGIN

  IF NOT EXISTS
  (
    SELECT 1
    FROM sys.fulltext_stopwords fsw
    WHERE fsw.stoplist_id = dbo.Stoplist_ID(@stoplist)
      AND fsw.stopword = @word
      AND fsw.language_id = @lcid
  )
  BEGIN

    SET @sql = N'ALTER FULLTEXT STOPLIST ' +
      QUOTENAME(@stoplist) +
      N' ADD ' + QUOTENAME(@word, '''') +
      N' LANGUAGE ' + CAST(@lcid AS nvarchar(4)) + ';';

    EXEC (@sql);

  END;
```

```
FETCH NEXT
FROM StopWord_Cursor
INTO @word;

END;

CLOSE StopWord_Cursor;

DEALLOCATE StopWord_Cursor;
```

We've also included some simple protections against SQL injection in this code, removing semicolon characters from the comma-delimited list of words and using the QUOTENAME function to quote both the stoplist name and the stopwords. Listing 7-7 uses the dbo.Add_Stopwords procedure to add multiple words to the NoFish_Stoplist at once.

Listing 7-7. *Using dbo.Add_Stopwords to Add Multiple Stopwords to a Stoplist*

```
EXEC dbo.Add_Stopwords 'NoFish_Stoplist', 'monkey,banana,catfish', 1033;
```

You can also create simple convenience functions like this one to remove multiple stopwords in a given language from the stoplist, or even to add and remove multiple stopwords from multiple languages on the stoplist.

Upgrading Noise Word Lists to Stoplists

When you upgrade a full-text catalog from a SQL Server 2005 database, SQL Server doesn't upgrade your old noise word lists automatically. It will copy the noise word lists to the MSSQL\FTData\FTNoiseThesaurusBak subdirectory under your SQL Server 2008 installation directory, but that's about it. If you only used the default system noise word lists in SQL Server 2005, you won't need to upgrade your old noise word lists, since the SQL Server 2008 system stoplists have equivalent content.

If you customized your old noise word lists, however, you'll need to create a custom stoplist and import the old noise words into the stoplist. SQL Server doesn't provide a standard utility to perform this function, but it's easy enough to create one with the OPENROWSET rowset provider. Listing 7-8 is a stored procedure we created for the purpose of upgrading old noise word lists. The dbo.Upgrade_Noisewords procedure creates a custom stoplist and imports your noise word files into it. The procedure accepts three parameters:

1. @Stoplist: This is the name of the stoplist you want to import your noise words into. If a stoplist with this name doesn't exist, it's created for you automatically.

2. @Path: The full path to the directory containing the old noise word files.

3. @LCID: The LCID of the noise word file you wish to import. If you specify a valid LCID, such as 1033 for English, the corresponding noise word file (in this case noiseENU.txt) is imported. If you set this parameter to NULL, all supported noise word files are imported.

Listing 7-8. *Procedure to Upgrade Existing Noise Word Lists to Stoplists*

```sql
CREATE PROCEDURE dbo.Upgrade_Noisewords
(
  @Stoplist sysname,
  @Path nvarchar(2000),
  @LCID int
)
AS
BEGIN

  -- First create a temp table that maps noise word file three-letter
  -- codes to the proper LCIDs

  CREATE TABLE #ThreeLetterCode
  (
    Code nvarchar(3) NOT NULL PRIMARY KEY,
    LCID int NOT NULL
  );

  INSERT INTO #ThreeLetterCode
  (
    Code,
    LCID
  )
  VALUES (N'CHS', 2052), (N'CHT', 1028), (N'DAN', 1030), (N'DEU', 1031),
         (N'ENG', 2057), (N'ENU', 1033), (N'ESN', 3082), (N'FRA', 1036),
         (N'ITA', 1040), (N'JPN', 1041), (N'KOR', 1042), (N'NEU', 0),
         (N'NLD', 1043), (N'PLK', 1045), (N'PTB', 1046), (N'PTS', 2070),
         (N'RUS', 1049), (N'SVE', 1053), (N'THA', 1054), (N'TRK', 1055);

  -- Next see if a stoplist with the specified name exists.
  -- If not, create it with dynamic SQL

  DECLARE @Sql nvarchar(2000);

  IF NOT EXISTS
  (
    SELECT 1
    FROM sys.fulltext_stoplists
    WHERE name = @Stoplist
  )
  BEGIN

    SET @Sql = N'CREATE FULLTEXT STOPLIST ' +
      QUOTENAME(@Stoplist) + N';';
```

```
  EXEC (@sql);

END;

-- Declare a cursor that iterates the possible three-letter codes we
-- previously stored in the temp table. The inner join to the
-- sys.fulltext_languages catalog view ensures we only try to import
-- noise word lists for languages supported on this instance

DECLARE File_Cursor CURSOR
FORWARD_ONLY READ_ONLY
FOR
SELECT
  tlc.Code,
  tlc.LCID
FROM #ThreeLetterCode tlc
INNER JOIN sys.fulltext_languages fl
  ON tlc.LCID = fl.LCID
WHERE tlc.LCID = COALESCE(@LCID, tlc.LCID);

-- Open the cursor and iterate the three-letter codes, importing the
-- files and adding them to the stoplist

OPEN File_Cursor;

DECLARE @Code nvarchar(3),
  @Language int;

FETCH NEXT
FROM File_Cursor
INTO
  @Code,
  @Language;

WHILE @@FETCH_STATUS = 0
BEGIN

  -- The file is initially imported as a binary file since some of the
  -- files can be Unicode while others might not

  DECLARE @BinFile varbinary(max),
    @Words nvarchar(max);

  -- OPENROWSET is used to import the file as a BLOB

  SELECT @Sql = N'SELECT @BinFile = BulkColumn ' +
    N'FROM OPENROWSET(BULK ' +
```

```
      QUOTENAME(@Path + N'\noise' + @Code + N'.txt', '''') +
      N', SINGLE_BLOB) AS x;';

EXEC dbo.sp_executesql @Sql,
  N'@BinFile varbinary(max) OUTPUT',
  @BinFile = @BinFile OUTPUT;

-- If the BLOB has the byte order mark (0xFFFE) at the start, it will
-- be cast to nvarchar(max), otherwise varchar(max). The varchar(max)
-- is then implicitly cast to nvarchar(max)

SET @Words = CASE SUBSTRING(@BinFile, 1, 2)
    WHEN 0xFFFE THEN CAST(@BinFile AS nvarchar(max))
    ELSE CAST(@BinFile AS varchar(max))
  END;

-- This series of nested REPLACE functions removes carriage returns,
-- line feeds, extra spaces, and the "?about" that occurs in some files.
-- It also replaces spaces with commas to create a comma-separated list.

SELECT @Words = REPLACE
(
  REPLACE
  (
    REPLACE
    (
      REPLACE
      (
        REPLACE(@Words, 0x0a, N' '), 0x0d, N' '
      ), N'  ', N' '
    ), N' ', N','
  ), N'?about,', N''
);

-- The dbo.Add_Stopwords procedure adds the comma-separated list of
-- stopwords to the stoplist

EXEC dbo.Add_Stopwords @Stoplist,
  @Words,
  @Language;

FETCH NEXT
FROM File_Cursor
INTO
  @Code,
  @Language;
```

```
    END;

    CLOSE File_Cursor;

    DEALLOCATE File_Cursor;

END;
GO
```

The procedure identifies which files need to be loaded and uses a cursor to iterate the list. It then loads each noise word file from a predetermined list as a varbinary(max) BLOB via the OPENROWSET function.

If the BLOB that gets loaded in starts with the Unicode byte order mark (BOM), 0xFFFE, it's converted to an nvarchar(max). If the file isn't Unicode, it's first converted to varchar(max) and subsequently converted to nvarchar(max) via an implicit conversion.

Each file is then "parsed" with a series of nested REPLACE function calls. The REPLACE functions eliminate carriage returns and line feeds, double spaces, and the "?isabout" entry that occurs in some noise word files. The procedure then converts all single spaces to commas, creating a comma-delimited list of noise words.

After each file is converted to a comma-delimited list, the procedure calls the dbo.Add_StopWords procedure to add the noise words to your stoplist. Listing 7-9 calls dbo.Upgrade_Noisewords to import a SQL Server 2005 English noise word file to a SQL Server 2008 stoplist named English_Stopwords.

Listing 7-9. *Upgrading an English Noise Word File to a Stoplist*

```
EXEC dbo.Upgrade_Noisewords N'English_Stopwords',
  N'C:\iFTS_Books\NoiseWords',
  1033;
```

Stoplist Behavior

SQL Server iFTS stoplists behave in some interesting and noteworthy ways in relation to your full-text indexes and queries. In this section, we'll discuss how stoplists and the stopwords they contain are used to shrink the overall size of the full-text index and make query processing more efficient.

Stoplists and Indexing

When you create or populate a full-text index, SQL Server uses the stoplist associated with the index to ignore instances of the stopwords during full-text indexing. Basically, iFTS won't index any stopwords it encounters during the indexing process. SQL Server will only ignore exact matches of the stopwords, however. Going back to our example from earlier in the chapter, we added the word *fish* to a custom stoplist named NoFish_Stoplist. After assigning the NoFish_Stoplist custom stoplist to the dbo.Book table, you can use the sys.dm_fts_index_keywords_by_document DMF to verify that *fish* wasn't included in the full-text index. (We'll discuss this and other full-text DMFs in detail in Chapter 9.) Listing 7-10 retrieves the full-text-indexed words that begin with the first four characters *fish*, with partial results shown in Figure 7-10.

■**Note**   As we mentioned previously, when you change the stoplist assigned to a full-text index that has automatic change tracking turned on, SQL Server kicks off a full population. There may be a delay between when you change the stoplist assignment and when SQL Server completes the full population.

Listing 7-10. *Retrieving Words from the Full-Text Index with the Prefix "fish"*

```
SELECT *
FROM sys.dm_fts_index_keywords_by_document
(
  DB_ID(),
  OBJECT_ID('dbo.Book')
)
WHERE display_term LIKE N'fish%';
```

	keyword	display_term	column_id	document_id	occurrence_count
34	0x0066006900730068006500730	fishes	6	26	1
35	0x0066006900730068006500730	fishes	6	31	1
36	0x0066006900730068006500730	fishes	6	39	27
37	0x0066006900730068006500730	fishes	6	101	2
38	0x0066006900730068006500730	fishes	6	102	2
39	0x0066006900730068006500730	fishes	6	103	2
40	0x0066006900730068006500730	fishes	6	104	2
41	0x0066006900730068006500730	fishes	6	105	2
42	0x0066006900730068006500730	fishes	6	106	2

Figure 7-10. *Viewing indexed words with the prefix "fish" after adding a custom stoplist*

After applying the custom stoplist to the dbo.Book table, the word *fish* no longer appears in the full-text index; however, note that inflectional forms of the word *fish* (such as *fishes*, *fished*, and *fishing*) are still indexed by iFTS.

Stoplists and Queries

When you define a stoplist and assign it to your full-text index as we've done in this chapter, queries for exact words (such as CONTAINS predicate queries without the FORMSOF predicate) against the full-text index will result in no matches being found. You can see this by executing a simple iFTS CONTAINS query, as shown in Listing 7-11. The query returns no matching rows, since the custom stoplist containing the word *fish* is assigned to the full-text index on the dbo.Book table.

Listing 7-11. *Simple CONTAINS Query for "fish"*

```
SELECT Book_Id
FROM dbo.Book
WHERE CONTAINS (*, '"fish"');
```

If, however, you perform a generational term search for the word *fish,* SQL Server will match inflectional terms of the word. Listing 7-12 uses `FREETEXT` to perform a generational term search and returns the IDs of books that contain inflectional forms of the word *fish.* Partial results are shown in Figure 7-11.

Listing 7-12. *Searching for Inflectional Forms of "fish"*

```
SELECT Book_ID
FROM dbo.Book
WHERE FREETEXT(*, 'fish');
```

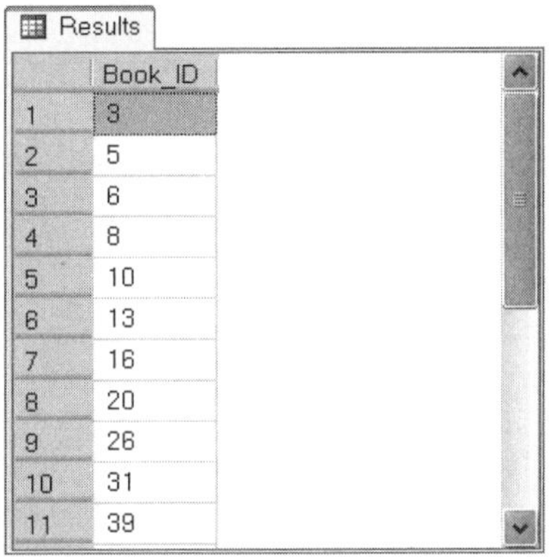

	Book_ID
1	3
2	5
3	6
4	8
5	10
6	13
7	16
8	20
9	26
10	31
11	39

Figure 7-11. *Results of generational term query for the word* fish*, with stoplist*

One of the interesting aspects of the interaction between the stoplist and the generational search terms is that stopwords aren't stripped from your full-text search predicates. Instead, your full-text search terms are first stemmed to find thesaurus and inflectional forms. Once the stemming is complete, the exact match form of the stopword is marked for exclusion from the search. Listing 7-13 uses the `sys.dm_fts_parser` DMF to show the inflectional forms that SQL Server generates against `NoFish_Stoplist` for this generational term query. The results are shown in Figure 7-12.

Tip We'll discuss the `sys.dm_fts_parser` DMF in detail in Chapter 9. This useful function provides some insight into how SQL Server stems words during a search. It also provides information about which words iFTS will try to match and which it will ignore.

Listing 7-13. *Viewing Inflectional Forms of the Word* Fish *Against the Stoplist*

```
SELECT *
FROM sys.dm_fts_parser
(
  N'FORMSOF(INFLECTIONAL, fish)',
```

```
1033,
dbo.Stoplist_ID(N'NoFish_Stoplist'),
1
);
```

	keyword	group_id	phrase...	occurrence	special_term	display_term	expansion_type	source_term
1	0x00660089007300680065007З	1	0	1	Exact Match	fishes	2	fish
2	0x0066008900730068006500640	1	0	1	Exact Match	fished	2	fish
3	0x0066008900730068006900 6E0067	1	0	1	Exact Match	fishing	2	fish
4	0x0066006900730068	1	0	1	Noise Word	fish	0	fish

Figure 7-12. *Inflectional forms generated by the word "fish," against a stoplist*

Note that, despite the word *fish* being in the NoFish_Stoplist custom stoplist, the stemmer still generates the inflectional forms *fishes*, *fished*, and *fishing*. Note also in the special_term column that Exact Match is indicated for each of these words. The word *fish*, however, is marked as a Noise Word, indicating that it won't be matched during the search.

■**Note** We're not sure why the iFTS team chose to use the term *Noise Word* in this DMF to describe what they now call *stopwords*. This particular DMF is subject to change, however, and perhaps this disconnect will be addressed in a future release.

Summary

In prior versions of SQL Server, noise word files gave us a means to exclude certain words from full-text indexes and subsequent full-text searches. In SQL Server 2008, these noise word files, formerly stored in the file system, have been replaced with stoplists that are stored in the database. You can create and manage custom stoplists using standard T-SQL CREATE, ALTER, and DROP FULLTEXT STOPLIST DDL statements. Stoplists provide several benefits, including less bloated full-text indexes, more efficient full-text search queries, and the ability to specifically exclude words that you deem unnecessary for your full-text searches.

In this chapter, we talked about how to create and manage stoplists, and how to upgrade your existing noise word files to SQL Server 2008 stoplists. We provided procedures to simplify the tasks of adding multiple stopwords to your stoplists and upgrading your existing noise word lists. We also discussed the effects of stoplists and stopwords on your full-text indexes and full-text search queries.

In the next chapter, we'll continue the discussion of iFTS support for generational terms as we introduce full-text thesauruses.

CHAPTER 8

■ ■ ■

Thesauruses

What's another word for thesaurus?

—Steven Wright

SQL Server provides powerful full-text search thesauruses that can be used for customizing searches for relevant text. Using thesauruses, you can define two types of custom pattern-based rules:

- *Expansions* that can automatically expand the scope of your searches to include additional relevant search terms.

- *Replacements* that substitute your search terms with other specified terms.

Thesaurus files are language-specific and can be modified to suit your specific needs. In this chapter, we'll discuss thesaurus management, options, and improvements to thesaurus functionality in SQL Server 2008.

Thesaurus Files

SQL Server uses language-specific XML thesaurus files stored in the file system. These files are stored in the `MSSQL\FTData` subdirectory under the SQL Server installation directory. Each thesaurus is named using the format `ts<language>.xml`, where `<language>` is a three-character language code or *global* for the global thesaurus. Figure 8-1 shows a partial listing of the contents of the `MSSQL\FTData` directory.

THESAURUSES IN THE DATABASE

One of the ultimate goals of the iFTS team is to move thesaurus files out of the file system and into the database, in much the same way that noise words have been moved into the database in the form of stoplists. Unfortunately for us, time constraints kept the iFTS team from incorporating this into SQL Server 2008. We can expect thesaurus files to be incorporated completely into the database in a future release.

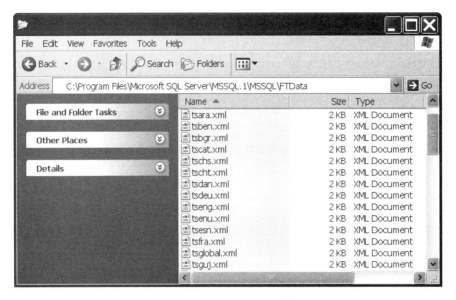

Figure 8-1. *XML thesaurus files in MSSQL\FTData subdirectory*

The thesaurus files for SQL Server 2008 follow the format shown in Listing 8-1.

Listing 8-1. *Sample Thesaurus File*

```
<XML ID = "Microsoft Search Thesaurus">
  <thesaurus xmlns = "x-schema:tsSchema.xml">

    <diacritics_sensitive>0</diacritics_sensitive>

    <expansion>
      <sub>aqua</sub>
      <sub>azure</sub>
      <sub>aquamarine</sub>
      <sub>indigo</sub>
      <sub>teal</sub>
      <sub>cobalt</sub>
      <sub>navy</sub>
      <sub>blue</sub>
    </expansion>

    <replacement>
      <pat>fl</pat>
      <pat>fla</pat>
      <pat>flor</pat>
      <sub>florida</sub>
    </replacement>
```

```
    <expansion>
      <sub>skirmish</sub>
      <sub>scuffle</sub>
      <sub>battle</sub>
      <sub>fight</sub>
    </replacement>

  </thesaurus>
</XML>
```

The `<diacritics_sensitive>` element accepts a value of 0 or 1 indicating whether the words in the thesaurus should be sensitive to accent marks and other diacritical marks. A value of 0 makes the thesaurus insensitive to diacritical marks, while a value of 1 turns diacritic sensitivity on. When diacritic sensitivity is turned off, the thesaurus treats words such as *resume* and *resumé* as equivalent. It will also treat the same word with other accent marks as equivalent, so that if you accented the first *é* in *résumé* it would be treated as equivalent to both *resumé* and *resume*.

The `<expansion>` element defines an expansion set, which will expand your search to include all of the terms in the expansion set when any of the terms is included in your search. The `<replacement>` element defines a replacement set that automatically replaces any matching terms in your query with a single substitution term. The individual terms defined in the thesaurus are limited to 512 characters each (which should be more than enough in most situations). We'll discuss both expansion sets and replacement sets in greater detail later in the chapter.

Editing and Loading Thesaurus Files

The default thesaurus files that are installed with SQL Server 2008 show the structure of the file with a few simple `<expansion>` and `<replacement>` elements, but the contents of the sample files are commented out with the XML comment node delimiters (`<!--` and `-->`). Because the contents are commented out, the default thesaurus files have no effect on your full-text search queries. The default contents of the English language (LCID 1033) thesaurus file, `tsenu.xml`, are shown in Listing 8-2.

■**Tip** If you decide to edit the sample thesaurus files, be sure to remove the XML `<!--` and `-->` comment node delimiters or your changes will have no effect.

Listing 8-2. *Default tsenu.xml Thesaurus File*

```
<XML ID = "Microsoft Search Thesaurus">
  <!--
    Commented out (SQL Server 2008)

    <thesaurus xmlns = "x-schema:tsSchema.xml">
      <diacritics_sensitive>0</diacritics_sensitive>
      <expansion>
```

```
        <sub>Internet Explorer</sub>
        <sub>IE</sub>
        <sub>IE5</sub>
    </expansion>
    <replacement>
        <pat>NT5</pat>
        <pat>W2K</pat>
        <sub>Windows 2000</sub>
    </replacement>
    <expansion>
        <sub>run</sub>
        <sub>jog</sub>
    </expansion>
</thesaurus>

-->
</XML>
```

The root `<XML>` element has an `ID` attribute that is set to *Microsoft Search Thesaurus*. The `ID` attribute is not mandatory, and doesn't appear to affect the functionality of the thesaurus files if you change it to another value or remove it altogether.

■**Note** The `<XML>` root element is poorly named. According to the World Wide Web Consortium (W3C) XML recommendation, no elements should have a name that begins with the letters "*XML*" (in that order, in any upper- or lowercased combination). There are no plans to make the thesaurus files compliant with this requirement of the standard at this time.

The `<thesaurus>` element sits below the `<XML>` root element and acts as a container for the diacritic sensitivity setting and the expansion and replacement sets. The `<thesaurus>` element must have its XML namespace set to `x-schema:tsSchema.xml`. This is mandatory—not setting the XML namespace for this element, or setting it to an incorrect URI, will result in your thesaurus file being ignored and having no effect on your queries.

You can edit XML thesaurus files using a simple text editor such as Notepad or a more specialized XML editor such as Altova XMLSpy.

■**Caution** The authors ran into problems saving thesaurus files with an older version of the TextPad editor. Specifically, TextPad didn't save the Unicode byte order mark at the beginning of the file, which caused problems at load time. This issue appears to be resolved in newer versions of TextPad.

When you save your thesaurus files to the MSSQL\FTData subdirectory, make sure you save it with a name following the ts<*language*>.xml convention. Also, the thesaurus files must be saved in Unicode format with the byte order mark. The byte order mark should be automatically added to the file by your editor when you save it in Unicode format.

■**Tip** During the upgrade process, existing thesaurus files are copied to the MSSQL\FTData\ FTNoiseThesaurusBak subdirectory of your SQL Server installation directory. You can simply copy your existing SQL Server 2005 thesaurus files from this subdirectory to the MSSQL\FTData subdirectory to start using them with SQL Server 2008.

After you've edited and saved your custom thesaurus files, you can reload them using the new system stored procedure sys.sp_fulltext_load_thesaurus_file. This procedure accepts up to two parameters:

- A mandatory int LCID parameter indicating which file should be loaded. The LCID is mapped to a language-specific thesaurus file; for instance, LCID 1033 is mapped to the English language thesaurus file tsenu.xml.

- An optional bit parameter indicating whether the thesaurus file should be loaded if it has been previously loaded. If you set this parameter to 0 (the default), the thesaurus file is reloaded whether it was previously loaded or not. A value of 1 will cause the thesaurus file to be loaded only if it wasn't previously loaded. Note that this second optional parameter is currently undocumented in BOL, but it is detected by SSMS Intellisense.

This new procedure is very useful, particularly when modifying and testing thesaurus files. In prior versions of SQL Server, a change to a thesaurus file required the full-text search service to be restarted in order to pick up the changes. Debugging a thesaurus file was a time-consuming process. The new sys.sp_fulltext_load_thesaurus_file procedure eliminates the need to restart any services. As soon as you execute this procedure, the file is loaded and SQL Server automatically picks up the changes. Listing 8-3 loads the English language thesaurus file into SQL Server. Note that only members of the serveradmin fixed server role or the system administrator can execute this procedure.

Listing 8-3. *Loading the English Language Thesaurus File*

```
EXEC sys.sp_fulltext_load_thesaurus_file 1033;
```

You can modify which XML file is used by changing the entry in HKEY_LOCAL_MACHINE\ SOFTWARE\Microsoft\Microsoft SQL Server\MSSQL10.MSSQLSERVER\MSSearch\ Language*XXX*, where *XXX* is your language.

THESAURUS CACHING

When SQL Server 2008 loads thesaurus files, it caches them in internal tables in the `tempdb` database. SQL Server uses lazy caching, meaning that the query engine checks to see whether the correct thesaurus has been loaded the first time it's needed, at query time. If the correct thesaurus isn't loaded yet, SQL Server automatically loads it. You can override this behavior in SQL Server 2008 by using the `sys.sp_fulltext_load_thesaurus_file` procedure to load your thesaurus files on demand.

One notable change from SQL Server 2005 thesaurus files is that the former `tsneu.xml` file (neutral language thesaurus file) has been renamed `tsglobal.xml` (global thesaurus file). To load the global thesaurus file, specify LCID 0 when you execute the `sys.sp_fulltext_load_thesaurus_file` procedure. We'll discuss how the global thesaurus file acts in concert with the language-specific local thesaurus files later in this chapter.

Unfortunately, SQL Server 2008 doesn't offer much in the way of error reporting when there's a problem with your thesaurus files. It will report errors in the following three situations:

- If the thesaurus file isn't a well-formed XML document, you'll receive an error message indicating that the file can't be loaded.

- If the thesaurus file for the LCID you specify doesn't exist, you'll likewise receive an error message indicating that the file can't be loaded.

- If the thesaurus file duplicates one or more phrases in expansion or replacement sections, you'll receive an informational warning that the duplicate rule "causes ambiguity" and "hence the phrase will be ignored."

When ambiguous rules are encountered, expansion rules take precedence over replacement rules. Consider the ambiguous thesaurus in Listing 8-4, which contains multiple rules for the term *fl*.

Listing 8-4. *Ambiguous Thesaurus File*

```xml
<XML ID="Microsoft Search Thesaurus">
  <thesaurus xmlns="x-schema:tsSchema.xml">
    <diacritics_sensitive>0</diacritics_sensitive>
    <replacement>
      <pat>fl</pat>
      <pat>fla</pat>
      <sub>florida</sub>
    </replacement>
    <expansion>
      <sub>fl</sub>
      <sub>floor</sub>
    </expansion>
    <expansion>
```

```
      <sub>fl</sub>
      <sub>fluid</sub>
    </expansion>
  </thesaurus>
</XML>
```

The thesaurus in Listing 8-4 contains one replacement rule and two expansion rules for the term *fl*. The expansion rules take precedence over the replacement rule, so the replacement rule is ignored. The two expansion rules can be indicated using the form *E(fl, floor)* and *E(fl, fluid)*. In this format, the *E* indicates that the rule is an expansion rule. The expansion terms are shown as a list in parentheses. Any of the terms will be expanded to all of the terms in the list. Of the two expansion rules, the one that's defined first, *E(fl, floor)*, is used; the other rule is ignored. When you try to load an ambiguous thesaurus file like the one shown in Listing 8-4, SQL Server returns only a generic warning message like the following; it's up to you to manually locate and fix the offending rules:

```
Informational: Ignoring duplicate thesaurus rule 'fl' while loading thesaurus
file for LCID 0. A duplicate thesaurus phrase was encountered in either the
<sub> section of an expansion rule or the <pat> section of a replacement rule.
This causes an ambiguity and hence this phrase will be ignored.
```

In almost every other instance of problems with your thesaurus files, including incorrect element names or failure to use the correct Uniform Resource Indicator (URI) for the `<thesaurus>` element namespace, attempting to load and use your thesaurus file will fail silently. We've created the `dbo.Validate_Thesaurus_File` procedure to load and validate your thesaurus files against rules similar to the ones SQL Server 2008 applies when loading your thesaurus files. Simply pass this procedure the full pathname to a thesaurus file and it will validate the thesaurus file for you. The full source listing for the `dbo.Validate_Thesaurus_File` procedure is available in the sample code download for this book. Because the listing is lengthy, we're not going to reproduce it in its entirety. Instead we'll discuss the types of errors it catches and show an example of usage here.

▓**Tip** Complete code listings for this procedure, and other code found throughout this book, is available at `www.apress.com` in the Downloads section.

One of the goals of the `dbo.Validate_Thesaurus_File` procedure was to give complete information about the types of errors and problems in thesaurus files that cause them not to load/work properly. The `dbo.Validate_Thesaurus_File` procedure can capture the following types of errors:

- File format (non-Unicode with byte order mark) errors

- Well-formedness errors (for example, multiple root elements)

- Thesaurus files with no `<XML>` root element

- Improper XML namespace on <thesaurus> element

- Invalid values in <diacritics_sensitive> element

- Ambiguous expansion and replacement rules

The procedure also gives you useful warnings about other thesaurus file content that might load with no errors, but could cause unexpected results. In addition, the procedure attempts to tell you where it encounters errors in the XML file by numbering your elements (in XML document order). Listing 8-5 demonstrates a call to dbo.Validate_Thesaurus_File to validate the tsglobal.xml global thesaurus file.

Listing 8-5. *Validating the tsglobal.xml Global Thesaurus File*

```
EXEC dbo.Validate_Thesaurus_File N'C:\Program Files\Microsoft SQL➥
  Server\MSSQL10.MSSQLSERVER\MSSQL\FTData\tsglobal.xml';
```

The following are the results, after we introduced some problems into our tsglobal.xml file:

```
WARNING: The <diacritics_sensitive> element #1 under <thesaurus> element #1
is defined under the namespace URI "wrong-schema" but the namespace URI needs
to be "x-schema:tsSchema.xml". The thesaurus file should load properly, but
this element may be ignored resulting in unexpected query results.
WARNING: Ambiguous term found: [Term = "fl": <thesaurus> #1, <expansion>
#1]. Your thesaurus file should load properly, but some ambiguous rules will
be ignored.
WARNING: Ambiguous term found: [Term = "fl": <thesaurus> #1, <expansion>
#4]. Your thesaurus file should load properly, but some ambiguous rules will
be ignored.
WARNING: Ambiguous term found: [Term = "fl": <thesaurus> #1, <replacement>
#1]. Your thesaurus file should load properly, but some ambiguous rules will
be ignored.
WARNING: Ambiguous term found: [Term = "fla": <thesaurus> #1, <expansion>
#3]. Your thesaurus file should load properly, but some ambiguous rules will
be ignored.
WARNING: Ambiguous term found: [Term = "fla": <thesaurus> #1, <replacement>
#2]. Your thesaurus file should load properly, but some ambiguous rules will
be ignored.
Total Error Count = 0
Total Warning Count = 6
```

We hope this procedure will come in handy for troubleshooting iFTS thesaurus file problems.

■**Tip** Because SQL Server 2008 uses the `xml` data type to load and parse your thesaurus file content, it will throw an exception if your XML thesaurus file is not well-formed. Mismatched and improperly nested tags, for instance, will raise an exception.

Expansion Sets

An expansion set in the thesaurus file is defined by `<sub>` tags contained within an `<expansion>` tag. If any of the words contained in the `<sub>` tags are encountered, your search is automatically expanded to include all other words defined in the expansion set. You can include as many expansion sets as you want in a SQL Server 2008 XML thesaurus file, but each expansion set word is limited to 512 Unicode characters. Through expansion sets, you gain the ability to search for multiple synonyms of any given search term, as shown in Figure 8-2.

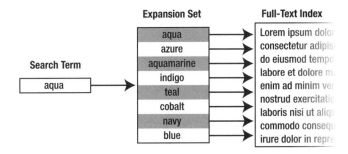

Figure 8-2. *Logical view of expansion set operation*

In the previous example in Listing 8-1, we included an expansion set with several synonyms for the word *blue*:

```
<expansion>
  <sub>aqua</sub>
  <sub>azure</sub>
  <sub>aquamarine</sub>
  <sub>indigo</sub>
  <sub>teal</sub>
  <sub>cobalt</sub>
  <sub>navy</sub>
  <sub>blue</sub>
</expansion>
```

With this expansion set, performing a search for any of the synonyms (the word *aqua*, for instance) results in your search being automatically broadened to include all of the words in the expansion set. Consider the CONTAINS query in Listing 8-6.

Listing 8-6. *CONTAINS Query with Thesaurus Expansion*

```
SELECT Book_ID
FROM dbo.Book
WHERE CONTAINS
(
  Book_Content,
  N'FORMSOF(THESAURUS, aqua)'
);
```

With the expansion set we defined earlier in this section, this query is internally expanded to the equivalent query in Listing 8-7.

Listing 8-7. *CONTAINS Query After Thesaurus Expansion*

```
SELECT Book_ID
FROM dbo.Book
WHERE CONTAINS
(
  Book_Content,
  N'"aqua" OR "azure" OR "aquamarine" OR "indigo" OR "teal" OR "cobalt"➥
    "navy" OR "blue"'
);
```

This automatic expansion can be verified with the new sys.dm_fts_parser DMF, using a query like the one in Listing 8-8. The results are shown in Figure 8-3.

Listing 8-8. *Verifying Thesaurus Expansions with sys.dm_fts_parser*

```
SELECT *
FROM sys.dm_fts_parser
(
  N'FORMSOF(THESAURUS, aqua)',
  1033,
  null,
  0
);
```

	keyword	group_id	phrase_id	occurrence	special_term	display_term	expansion_type	source_term
1	0x006100...	1	0	1	Exact Match	aqua	0	aqua
2	0x006100...	1	2	1	Exact Match	azure	4	aqua
3	0x006100...	1	3	1	Exact Match	aquamarine	4	aqua
4	0x006900...	1	4	1	Exact Match	indigo	4	aqua
5	0x007400...	1	5	1	Exact Match	teal	4	aqua
6	0x006300...	1	6	1	Exact Match	cobalt	4	aqua
7	0x006E00...	1	7	1	Exact Match	navy	4	aqua
8	0x006200...	1	8	1	Exact Match	blue	4	aqua

Figure 8-3. *Viewing the thesaurus expansions for the search term aqua*

Replacement Sets

Replacement sets provide an alternative to expansion sets. Like expansion sets, replacement sets are defined using XML in the thesaurus files. Replacement sets also have the same 512-character limitation on terms. You can define replacement sets with `<pat>` and `<sub>` tags contained within a `<replacement>` tag. Though they're defined in the same thesaurus files, replacement sets behave differently from expansion sets. While expansion sets automatically expand your search to include every search term in the set, replacement sets simply replace your search term with another search term per your definition. Where expansion sets are commonly used to define synonyms for words, replacement sets are useful for redefining acronyms and abbreviations in your searches. Replacement sets operate on search terms in the manner shown in Figure 8-4.

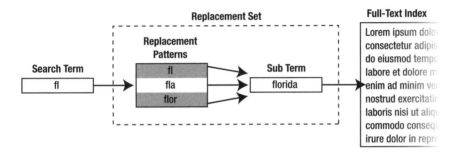

Figure 8-4. *Logical view of replacement set operation*

In Listing 8-1, we created the replacement set shown in Figure 8-4, replacing various search term abbreviations for Florida with the word *florida*, as shown:

```
<replacement>
  <pat>fl</pat>
  <pat>fla</pat>
  <pat>flor</pat>
  <sub>florida</sub>
</replacement>
```

With this replacement set, performing a search for any of the defined abbreviations results in a search for the word *florida*. Note that the original search term is completely replaced in the search, so that the original search term is not included in the final search. Listing 8-9 shows a simple CONTAINS query with thesaurus replacement.

Listing 8-9. *CONTAINS Query with Thesaurus Replacement*

```
SELECT Book_ID
FROM dbo.Book
WHERE CONTAINS
(
  Book_Content,
  N'FORMSOF(THESAURUS, fl)'
);
```

The replacement set we defined earlier in this section replaces the search term *fl* with the replacement term *florida*, resulting in SQL Server treating the query as the equivalent shown in Listing 8-10. Note that the query in Listing 8-10 is simply a representative query; it shows how SQL Server evaluates the thesaurus-replacement query in Listing 8-9 with the previously defined replacement rules in place.

Listing 8-10. *CONTAINS Query After Thesaurus Replacement*

```
SELECT Book_ID
FROM dbo.Book
WHERE CONTAINS
(
  Book_Content,
  N'"florida"'
);
```

As with expansion sets, you can verify replacement set activity with the sys.dm_fts_parser DMF, as shown in Listing 8-11. The results are shown in Figure 8-5.

Listing 8-11. *Verifying Thesaurus Replacements with sys.dm_fts_parser*

```
SELECT *
FROM sys.dm_fts_parser
(
  N'FORMSOF(THESAURUS, fl)',
  1033,
  NULL,
  0
);
```

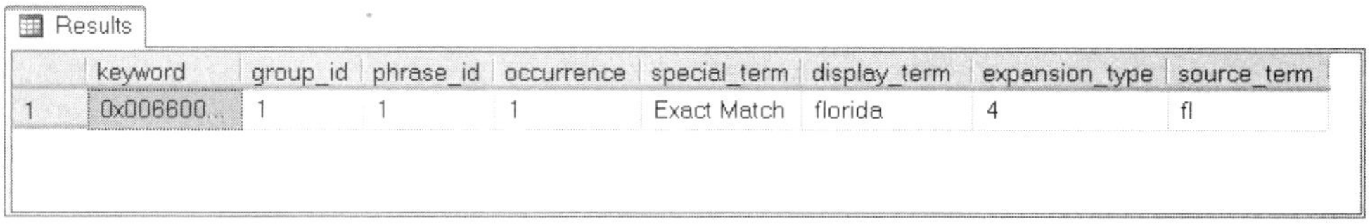

	keyword	group_id	phrase_id	occurrence	special_term	display_term	expansion_type	source_term
1	0x008600...	1	1	1	Exact Match	florida	4	fl

Figure 8-5. *Viewing thesaurus replacement for the search term "fl"*

Global and Local Thesauruses

SQL Server 2005 had the neutral language thesaurus (tsneu.xml), which was used when you specified an LCID of 0. SQL Server 2008 replaces the neutral language thesaurus with the global thesaurus (tsglobal.xml). Like the neutral language thesaurus, the global thesaurus is used when you specify an LCID of 0. Unlike the neutral language thesaurus, the global thesaurus now works in tandem with local language thesauruses no matter which language you specify in your query. When you specify a full-text search with thesaurus expansion, the global thesaurus is consulted in addition to the local language thesaurus, regardless of which language you indicate. As an example, consider the following replacement rule as a global thesaurus entry:

```
<replacement>
  <pat>ca</pat>
  <sub>california</sub>
</replacement>
```

This replacement rule in the global thesaurus can be indicated using the form: $R(ca \rightarrow california)$. In this format. the R indicates a replacement rule, and the term to the right of the arrow in parentheses replace the term (or terms) to the left of the arrow. This particular rule causes the search term *ca* to be replaced with the term *california*. When added to the global thesaurus, this replacement rule is applied no matter what language you're using to search. In addition to the global thesaurus, the local thesaurus for the specified search language is also consulted by iFTS. If the global thesaurus and the local language thesaurus for the language specified in the query contain overlapping rules, the local thesaurus rules take precedence over the global thesaurus. Consider if the following replacement rule were placed in the English language thesaurus (`tsenu.xml`):

```
<replacement>
  <pat>ca</pat>
  <sub>canada</sub>
</replacement>
```

This replacement rule can be indicated using the form $R(ca \rightarrow canada)$. Even if the conflicting replacement rule for the search term *ca*, $R(ca \rightarrow california)$, is defined in the global thesaurus, the local replacement rule $R(ca \rightarrow canada)$ takes precedence and will be used by the full-text query engine.

A Practical Example

As a practical example of full-text thesaurus usage, we've implemented a simple thesaurus that accounts for "oddities" in the works of William "The Bard" Shakespeare. Shakespeare's works were written in Early Modern English, quite different from English in its current incarnations. Because of this, there are a lot of differences in spelling that we would consider anomalous in Modern English. Many words have extraneous *e*'s at the end, for example.

Another issue with Shakespeare's works is in the typography of the age. Many commonly used words in printing were prepacked into clichés, or entire words contained on single slugs of metal. Because printing press letters were expensive, printers often ran out of certain letters and clichés during print runs. Rather than spending money on additional sets of letters, it was a common practice of the time to substitute similar-looking letters for one another. Probably the most common example is the substitution of the letter *u* for the letter *v*, and vice versa. Shakespeare's original printed works are full of such substitutions, and many scholars prefer the faithful reproduction of these "canonical errors." Consider the following lines from *The Tragedie of Hamlet*:

> **Fran.** *Nay answer me: Stand & vnfold your selfe*

> **Bar.** *Long liue the King*

> **Fran.** *Barnardo?*

> **Bar.** *He*

> **Fran.** *You come most carefully vpon your houre*

With this in mind, we've introduced some Shakespearean texts in the iFTS_Books database that are reproduced with these types of canonical errors. Our thesaurus example will convert some of these spelling anomalies to their modern equivalents. The following thesaurus entries represent a sample from our Shakespearean English thesaurus (LCID 1033):

```
<expansion>
  <sub>appeare</sub>
  <sub>appear</sub>
</expansion>
<expansion>
  <sub>approue</sub>
  <sub>approve</sub>
</expansion>
<expansion>
  <sub>beleefe</sub>
  <sub>belief</sub>
</expansion>
<expansion>
  <sub>Faiery</sub>
  <sub>Faire</sub>
  <sub>Fairy</sub>
</expansion>
<expansion>
  <sub>haue</sub>
  <sub>have</sub>
</expansion>
```

This thesaurus uses expansion rules to accommodate archaic spellings of words such as *E*(*belief, beleefe*) and canonical typographical anomalies such as *E*(*upon, vpon*). With this thesaurus loaded, searches for the modern spellings of these words will also locate the archaic spellings, and vice versa. We've included a larger Shakespearean thesaurus in the sample download files for this book under the \Shakespeare subdirectory.

In addition to accounting for archaic language spellings and anomalies, thesaurus files are useful for expanding modern abbreviations and acronyms, and for retrieving matches for words that are synonymous with your search term. All of this can be used to make your database searches more intelligent and increase overall recall.

Translation

You can also use the thesaurus as a simple translator. With simple replacement rules, you can easily translate commonly used foreign words into the target language in much the same way that the previous example converted archaic English words into modern English. Consider the following sample thesaurus entries that replace Latin words with their English equivalents:

```
<replacement>
   <pat>octoginta</pat>
   <sub>eighty</sub>
</replacement>
<replacement>
   <pat>irrito</pat>
   <sub>provoke</sub>
   <sub>annoy</sub>
   <sub>excite</sub>
   <sub>stimulate</sub>
   <sub>aggravate</sub>
</replacement>
```

Because replacement rules are used in this example, the original Latin word is lost in the search, but the equivalent English terms are used to fulfill the search. You can use expansion and rules to widen your searches to include alternative methods of representing words as well. Consider the following expansion rules, which expand searches on Chinese words to automatically include both pinyin and English equivalents:

PINYIN: "SPELL-SOUND"

Pinyin literally means "spell-sound." It's a system of Romanization, where Chinese words are represented using Latin alphabet characters. Each syllable of a Chinese word has a tone, or pitch movement, which is important to the meaning of the word. As an example, the Chinese word "ma" can refer to either a mother or a horse, depending on the tone used. Pinyin makes extensive use of diacritical marks to differentiate the tone of syllables.

```
<expansion>
  <sub> 國際象棋 </sub>
  <sub>guójìxiàngqí</sub>
  <sub>chess</sub>
</expansion>
<expansion>
  <sub> 馬 </sub>
  <sub>mǎ</sub>
  <sub>knight</sub>
</expansion>
<expansion>
  <sub> 兵 </sub>
```

```
    <sub>bīng</sub>
    <sub>pawn</sub>
</expansion>
```

Using these sample thesaurus entries, you can search for chess-related terms using Traditional Chinese words or their pinyin or English equivalents. A search for any of these terms will be automatically expanded to include the alternate versions of the same group when thesaurus expansion is used. Refer to Chapter 5 for a detailed discussion of multilingual searches.

Word Bags

Thesauruses can also be used to expand a search using words that aren't necessarily synonyms, but might be closely related to the search term. This might be useful in applications where you want to automatically expand a search to include associated documents or products. For instance, when a user searches for *pancakes*, you might want to return related results that include associated products such as *syrup*. Consider the following sample thesaurus that expands selected product searches:

```
<expansion>
    <sub>pancakes</sub>
    <sub>syrup</sub>
    <sub>bacon</sub>
    <sub>eggs</sub>
</expansion>
<expansion>
    <sub>ham</sub>
    <sub>cheese</sub>
    <sub>bread</sub>
    <sub>lettuce</sub>
    <sub>tomato</sub>
</expansion>
```

This type of expansion is useful when you're attempting to make intelligent guesses at what a user really wants when she types in a given search term, or for applications in which you want to try to upsell products based on the user's current area of interest (as determined by her search terms).

Additional Considerations

There are additional considerations that you need to take into account when you define your full-text thesauruses, such as case sensitivity, accent sensitivity, nonrecursion, and other aspects. Let's discuss these aspects of full-text thesaurus creation.

Accent and Case Sensitivity

As we mentioned previously, the <diacritics_sensitive> element in your thesaurus files defines your thesaurus's sensitivity to diacritical marks, including accent marks. Your thesaurus's diacritics sensitivity setting should be set in sync with your full-text catalog's accent sensitivity setting. If your full-text catalog is using accent insensitivity, your thesaurus should have <diacritics_sensitive> set to 0; if your full-text catalog is accent sensitive, the thesaurus <diacritics_sensitive> setting should be 1. A mismatch between your full-text catalog's accent sensitivity and the thesaurus's <diacritics_sensitive> setting can result in accented search terms in your query not being matched by accented terms in your full-text index. A mismatch in accent sensitivity settings will also cause accented expansions and replacements to cause missed search matches.

The full-text thesaurus is always treated as case insensitive, regardless of your database collation settings. Even in a case-sensitive database, a full-text search for the capitalized search term *TV* will match a thesaurus rule for the lowercase term *tv*.

Nonrecursion

Thesaurus definitions are nonrecursive, meaning that one rule doesn't recursively invoke additional rules. Consider the following sample thesaurus replacement rules:

```
<replacement>
  <pat>fl</pat>
  <sub>fla</sub>
</replacement>

<replacement>
  <pat>fla</pat>
  <sub>florida</sub>
</replacement>
```

In this example, the rule $R(fl \rightarrow fla)$ replaces the search term *fl* with the search term *fla*. There's an additional rule, $R(fla \rightarrow florida)$, which is not invoked by the previous replacement rule. Listing 8-12 verifies this thesaurus rule application with the sys.dm_fts_parser DMF. As you can see in Figure 8-6, the search term *fl* is replaced with *fla*, but the replacement rule for *fla* is not invoked.

Listing 8-12. *Verifying Thesaurus Expansion with sys.dm_fts_parser*

```
SELECT
  special_term,
  display_term,
  expansion_type,
  source_term
FROM sys.dm_fts_parser
(
  N'FORMSOF(THESAURUS, "fl")',
  1033,
  NULL,
  0
);
```

	special_term	display_term	expansion_type	source_term
1	Exact Match	fla	4	fl

Figure 8-6. *Viewing thesaurus replacement rule*

Overlapping Rules

As we discussed previously in this chapter, ambiguous replacement and expansion rules in a thesaurus are dealt with at load time. However, it's possible to have overlapping rules that aren't considered ambiguous by the full-text search engine. An overlapping rule is one where some search terms are shared between the <pat> elements of replacement rules and the <sub> elements of expansion rules. In the following example, for instance, the rule $R(fl\ oz \rightarrow fluid\ ounces)$ overlaps with the rule $R(fl \rightarrow florida)$, because they have the search term *fl* in common:

```
<replacement>
  <pat>fl oz</pat>
  <sub>fluid ounces</sub>
</replacement>

<replacement>
  <pat>fl</pat>
  <sub>fla</sub>
</replacement>
```

If you perform a search for terms that have overlapping rules, the longest matching rule wins. In this instance, a search for *16 fl oz* will trigger the *fl oz* replacement rule, while a search for *fl state* will trigger the *fl* rule. If two overlapping replacement rules happen to have the same length, the first one in the thesaurus is used.

Stoplists

Full-text thesaurus entries take precedence over stopwords contained in stoplists. Consider the sample thesaurus entries from the previous section, for instance. These entries specify two replacement rules: $R(fl\ oz \rightarrow fluid\ ounces)$ and $R(fl \rightarrow fla)$. If you added the search term *fl* to your stoplist, these two rules that contain that search term will still be applied. Only after your thesaurus replacements and expansions are applied does the stoplist come into play, since stopwords aren't stored in the full-text index. It's a good idea to not put stopwords in <sub> entries of replacement rules, since they'll find no match in the full-text index. Stopwords in the <sub> entries of expansion rules will also find no matches in the full-text index, but they may be used as the point of entry for expansion to include other terms in the search.

General Recommendations

Microsoft makes some general recommendations regarding thesaurus files, including the following:

- Avoid using special characters in your thesaurus entries to avoid unexpected word breaker behavior.

- Thesaurus entries can't be empty strings or composed of strings of special characters that can be converted to empty strings by the word breaker.

In addition, when loading a full-text index with the sys.sp_fulltext_load_thesaurus_file procedure, the full-text thesaurus is loaded into a SQL Server xml data type instance. This has two implications:

1. There's an upper limit of 2.1GB of storage for any given thesaurus file. Since the file is being loaded into an xml data type instance, however, the actual XML file could be larger. As a practical matter, though, a large thesaurus file (greater than 10MB) could take a considerable amount of time to load and parse.

2. The XML thesaurus file has to follow most of the rules for well-formedness. The element tags must be properly nested, special characters must be properly entitized (converted to XML entities such as > for the > character), attribute values quoted, and so on. We say the thesaurus file has to follow *most* of the rules for well-formedness because it technically doesn't have to have a single root element, but subsequent root-level elements after the first <XML> element are ignored.

Summary

SQL Server 2008 full-text search thesauruses allow you to expand user search terms to include search term synonyms and replacements. Although the ultimate goal of the iFTS team is to integrate thesauruses into the database, in much the same way that they've integrated stoplists, time constraints prevented it for this release. For now, we have to manage thesauruses as XML files in the file system. Even so, SQL Server 2008 provides the new sys.sp_fulltext_thesaurus_file procedure to load thesaurus files on demand without the service restart required in previous releases.

We discussed expansion and replacement rules in thesaurus files and how they affect your queries. We talked about the new global thesaurus files and how they work in tandem with your local language-specific thesaurus files. We also addressed some of the issues you need to keep in mind when designing your thesauruses, such as accent sensitivity and overlapping rules.

In the next chapter, we'll continue the discussion of new iFTS features available through SQL Server 2008's catalog views and dynamic management views and functions.

CHAPTER 9

■■■

iFTS Dynamic Management Views and Functions

What is written clearly is not worth much, it's the transparency that counts.

—Louis-Ferdinand Celine

Historically speaking, transparency hasn't been a strong suit of SQL Server FTS. The problem was that there were no tools available to lay out the inner workings of the FTS engine. This was partially due to the fact that the FTS engine was a completely separate service from the SQL Server service. FTS has long been treated as an opaque "black box"—you push data through it and expect the results to come out in the proper form on the other end.

However, as many people have found over the years, despite the best intentions and planning, what you get out of the black box is not necessarily what you expect. Simply put, the black box paradigm is not an adequate model for developers and administrators trying to optimize and troubleshoot FTS problems.

SQL Server 2008 provides several new dynamic management views (DMVs), dynamic management functions (DMFs), catalog views, and other methods of retrieving iFTS-specific state information and metadata. The new DMVs and DMFs, in particular, provide insight into the inner workings of iFTS. You can now query your full-text indexes and see exactly what SQL Server has come up with after word-breaking your documents. Or you can see what SQL Server sees after it parses a full-text search query.

These features bring an unprecedented level of transparency and insight to iFTS, and will make troubleshooting, debugging, optimizing, and studying the internal details of iFTS easier than ever. In this chapter, we'll discuss the new transparency provided by these features and explore how you can use them in your own development and administration work.

DMVs and DMFs

The list of exciting new iFTS features in SQL Server 2008 includes several DMVs and DMFs that provide insight into the inner workings of iFTS. Among these are DMFs that show the result of word and phrase parsing and stemming, index population, and iFTS memory usage. In this section, we'll discuss these DMVs and DMFs.

Looking Inside the Full-Text Index

SQL Server 2008 provides two new DMFs that provide a view into your populated full-text indexes. We used these DMFs back in Chapter 4 to demonstrate hit highlighting; we'll explore them in greater detail here. The `sys.dm_fts_index_keywords` DMF accepts a database ID and a table object ID, returning the contents of the full-text index in relational format. This DMF returns the following four columns:

- `keyword` is an internal hexadecimal representation of the indexed keyword used by iFTS.

- `display_term` is a human readable representation of the indexed keyword.

- `column_id` is the ID of the source column for the indexed keyword.

- `document_count` is the number of documents (rows) containing the indexed keyword.

Listing 9-1 uses the `sys.dm_fts_index_keywords` DMF to retrieve the full-text index entries for the dbo.Book table. The results are returned in decreasing order of occurrence, as shown in Figure 9-1.

Listing 9-1. *Retrieving dbo.Book Full-Text Index Entries in Decreasing Order of Occurrence*

```
SELECT *
FROM sys.dm_fts_index_keywords
(
  DB_ID(N'iFTS_Books'),
  OBJECT_ID(N'dbo.Book')
)
ORDER BY document_count DESC;
```

The `sys.dm_fts_index_keywords_by_document` DMF also accepts a database ID and table object ID. This DMF is similar in functionality to the `sys.dm_fts_index_keywords` DMF, except that it provides a greater level of granularity by indicating the document IDs in which the indexed keywords were found. The `sys.dm_fts_index_keywords_by_document` DMF returns all of the columns returned by `sys.dm_fts_index_keywords`, with two exceptions:

- `document_id` is an additional column containing the ID of the document (or row) in which the indexed keyword was found.

- `occurrence_count` replaces the `document_count` column and indicates how many times the indexed keyword was found in the current document (or row).

Results

	keyword	display_term	column_id	document_count
1	0x006E006F0074	not	6	82
2	0x007300680061006C006C	shall	6	67
3	0x006F006E0065	one	6	60
4	0x006D0061006E	man	6	57
5	0x006D00610079	may	6	54
6	0x007300680065	she	6	54
7	0x00750070006F006E	upon	6	54
8	0x006400610079	day	6	52
9	0x0070006C006100630065	place	6	52
10	0x00740068006F0075	thou	6	52
11	0x0067006F0064	god	6	51
12	0x006D0065006E	men	6	51

Figure 9-1. *Contents of dbo.Book full-text index (partial)*

This DMF can be used to determine, for instance, how many indexed keywords your individual documents (or rows) contain. Listing 9-2 demonstrates this, with results shown in Figure 9-2.

Listing 9-2. *Retrieving the Number of Indexed Keywords per Document*

```
SELECT
  document_id,
  SUM(occurrence_count) AS keywords_per_document
FROM sys.dm_fts_index_keywords_by_document
(
  DB_ID(N'iFTS_Books'),
  OBJECT_ID(N'dbo.Book')
)
GROUP BY document_id
ORDER BY SUM(occurrence_count) DESC;
```

Results

	document_id	keywords_per_document
1	39	381115
2	31	273806
3	10	247070
4	5	74618
5	7	72667
6	6	70914
7	32	58114
8	28	51500
9	22	51037
10	3	49693
11	16	42061

Figure 9-2. *Partial list of number of keywords per document*

These two DMFs are useful in situations where you need to peek under the hood to see exactly what iFTS has indexed. Useful scenarios include simple applications like the hit high-lighter in Chapter 4, or when testing custom filters like the one we'll develop in Chapter 10.

Parsing Text

In previous versions of SQL Server, there was no easy way to test FTS's parsing and stemming functionality. While you could make educated guesses and assumptions about exactly what the parser and stemmers were producing, and you could test the results they produced, actually doing so could result in a lot of hard-to-find issues. SQL Server 2008 provides the sys.dm_fts_parser DMF to bring clarity to this situation, allowing you to see exactly what the parser and stemmer are producing for any given search query string. This DMF accepts a query string, LCID, stoplist ID, and accent-sensitivity indicator as parameters. It returns several columns:

- keyword is the internal hexadecimal representation of a keyword returned by the word breaker.

- group_id is an ID that indicates the logical group in the search query from which the keyword was extracted.

- phrase_id is an ID that indicates groupings of alternative forms of compound words; the compound word *data-base* is broken into two groups, with group 1 containing the words *data* and *base*, while group 2 contains the word *data-base*.

- occurrence is a positional indicator that returns the order of each term in the parsing result; in the phrase *all good things*, the word *all* has occurrence ID 1, *good* has ID 2, and *things* is assigned ID 3.

- special_term gives some additional characteristics about the term, including whether the keyword is an exact match, noise word, end of sentence, end of paragraph, or end of chapter.

- display_term is the human-readable form of the keyword as produced by the word breaker and stemmer.

- expansion_type tells you whether the keyword is an exact keyword from the search query (type 0), or the result of inflectional expansion (type 2) or thesaurus expansion/replacement (type 4).

- source_term is the source term or phrase from which the keyword was extracted or generated.

The query string that you pass into this DMF can be a CONTAINS style query, which we described in Chapter 3. You can also use the FORMSOF(FREETEXT, ...) option to perform FREETEXT-style inflectional form generation and thesaurus expansions and replacement. Listing 9-3 uses sys.dm_fts_parser to parse a FREETEXT-style query using the English language (LCID 1033), the default stoplist, and no accent sensitivity. The results are shown in Figure 9-3.

Listing 9-3. *Inflectional-Style Parsing with sys.dm_fts_parser*

```
SELECT *
FROM sys.dm_fts_parser
(
  N'FORMSOF(INFLECTIONAL, "a penny saved")',
  1033,
  NULL,
  0
);
```

	keyword	group_id	phrase_id	occurrence	special_term	display_term	expansion_type	source_term
1	0x0061	1	0	1	Exact Match	a	0	a penny saved
2	0x00700...	1	0	2	Exact Match	pence	2	a penny saved
3	0x00700...	1	0	2	Exact Match	pennies	2	a penny saved
4	0x00700...	1	0	2	Exact Match	penny	0	a penny saved
5	0x00730...	1	0	3	Exact Match	save	2	a penny saved
6	0x00730...	1	0	3	Exact Match	saves	2	a penny saved
7	0x00730...	1	0	3	Exact Match	saving	2	a penny saved
8	0x00730...	1	0	3	Exact Match	saved	0	a penny saved

Figure 9-3. *Results of sys.dm_fts_parser query parsing*

We demonstrated use of sys.dm_fts_parser in the hit-highlighter example in Chapter 4. This DMF is also useful for debugging custom filters, word breakers, and stemmers.

Accessing Full-Text Index Entries

One of the most significant new advances in iFTS is the ability to store full-text indexes directly in the database. This improvement also makes it easier to access the contents of the full-text indexes via normal SQL queries. The sys.dm_fts_index_keywords DMF accepts a database ID and object ID for a table, and retrieves the contents of the full-text index for that table. The columns returned by this DMF include the following:

- keyword is the hexadecimal representation of the indexed keyword used internally by iFTS.
- display_term is the human-readable indexed keyword.
- column_id is the ID of the column from which the indexed keyword was sourced.
- document_count is a count of the number of documents (or rows) in which the keyword was found in the source table.

Listing 9-4 shows the DMF in action, accessing the full-text index entries from the dbo.Book table. Partial results are shown in Figure 9-4.

Listing 9-4. *Accessing Full-Text Index Entries for the dbo.Book Table*

```
SELECT *
FROM sys.dm_fts_index_keywords
(
  DB_ID(N'iFTS_Books'),
  OBJECT_ID(N'dbo.Book')
);
```

	keyword	display_term	column_id	document_count	
11729	0x0062006C006F0077006500720073	blowers	6	2	
11730	0x0062006C006F007700650073	blowes	6	2	
11731	0x0062006C006F0077006500740068	bloweth	6	3	
11732	0x0062006C006F00770069006E0067	blowing	6	14	
11733	0x0062006C006F0077006E	blown	6	18	
11734	0x0062006C006F0077006E0065	blowne	6	1	
11735	0x0062006C006F00770073	blows	6	22	
11736	0x0062006C00750063006800650072	blucher	6	1	
11737	0x0062006C0075006400670065006F006E	bludgeon	6	1	
11738	0x0062006C00750065	blue	6	27	
11739	0x0062006C007500650064	blued	6	1	
11740	0x0062006C007500650069006E0067	blueing	6	2	

Figure 9-4. *Partial listing of keyword entries in dbo.Book full-text index*

The sys.dm_fts_index_keywords_by_document DMF is similar to the sys.dm_fts_index_keywords DMF, in that it returns full-text index entries for a given table. The sys.dm_fts_index_keywords_by_document DMF, however, gives you a greater level of granularity by returning information about full-text index entries on a per-document basis. The sys.dm_fts_index_keywords_by_document DMF returns the keyword, display_term, and column_id columns that are returned by the sys.dm_fts_index_keywords DMF. The sys.dm_fts_index_keywords_by_document DMF returns an additional document_id column with the ID of the document from which the keyword was sourced, and adds an additional occurrence_count column that tells you how many times the keyword appears in the given document. Listing 9-5 shows this DMF in action, with partial results shown in Figure 9-5.

Listing 9-5. *Accessing Full-Text Index Entries on a Per-Document Basis*

```
SELECT *
FROM sys.dm_fts_index_keywords_by_document
(
  DB_ID(N'iFTS_Books'),
  OBJECT_ID(N'dbo.Book')
);
```

	keyword	display_term	column_id	document_id	occurrence_count
23675	0x0062006C006F0077006500720073	blowers	6	11	1
23676	0x0062006C006F0077006500720073	blowers	6	31	1
23677	0x0062006C006F007700650073	blowes	6	9	2
23678	0x0062006C006F007700650073	blowes	6	25	2
23679	0x0062006C006F0077006500740068	bloweth	6	39	4
23680	0x0062006C006F00770069006E0067	blowing	6	3	2
23681	0x0062006C006F00770069006E0067	blowing	6	5	2
23682	0x0062006C006F00770069006E0067	blowing	6	6	2
23683	0x0062006C006F00770069006E0067	blowing	6	8	1
23684	0x0062006C006F00770069006E0067	blowing	6	10	1
23685	0x0062006C006F00770069006E0067	blowing	6	11	1
23686	0x0062006C006F00770069006E0067	blowing	6	16	1

Figure 9-5. *Full-text entries per document for the dbo.Book table*

Retrieving Population Information

SQL Server 2008 provides additional information about one of the most important processes in iFTS: the population process. You can use four of the new DMVs to gather information about full-text index populations currently in progress. This information can be used to diagnose and troubleshoot full-text index population slowness and other issues related to memory pressure and resource problems on the server. You can also use these DMVs for more mundane administrative tasks related to monitoring full-text index population.

The diagram in Figure 9-6 shows the relationships of the new full-text index population DMVs and a few iFTS-specific catalog views. The iFTS-specific DMVs provide point-in-time population information and don't retain historical information about populations.

■**Note** We'll discuss IFTS-specific catalog views in the "Catalog Views" section of this chapter.

The first iFTS-specific population DMV is the sys.dm_fts_active_catalogs DMV. This DMV allows you to list all of the active full-text catalogs that are currently undergoing some population activity on the server. Listing 9-6 queries the sys.dm_fts_active_catalogs DMV and returns the list of catalogs currently being populated on my local server, as shown in Figure 9-7. Note that your results will vary. This DMV returns status information and counts of various population specific items, such as the number of threads currently working on a full-text catalog and the number of full-text indexes being populated, among others.

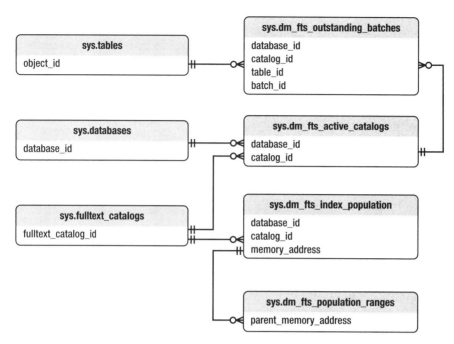

Figure 9-6. *iFTS-specific population DMVs and their relationships*

Listing 9-6. *Querying sys.dm_fts_active_catalogs*

```
SELECT
  fc.name AS catalog_name,
  d.name AS database_name,
  ac.name,
  CASE ac.is_paused
    WHEN 1 THEN N'Yes'
    ELSE N'No'
    END AS is_paused,
  CASE ac.status
    WHEN 0 THEN N'Initializing'
    WHEN 1 THEN N'Ready'
    WHEN 2 THEN N'Paused'
    WHEN 3 THEN N'Temporary error'
    WHEN 4 THEN N'Remount needed'
    WHEN 5 THEN N'Shutdown'
    WHEN 6 THEN N'Quiesced for backup'
    WHEN 7 THEN N'Backup is done through catalog'
    WHEN 8 THEN N'Catalog is corrupt'
    ELSE N'Unknown'
    END AS status,
```

```
    ac.status_description,
    ac.worker_count,
    ac.active_fts_index_count,
    ac.auto_population_count,
    ac.manual_population_count,
    ac.full_incremental_population_count,
    ac.row_count_in_thousands,
    CASE ac.is_importing
      WHEN 1 THEN N'Yes'
      ELSE N'No'
      END AS is_importing
FROM sys.dm_fts_active_catalogs ac
INNER JOIN sys.fulltext_catalogs fc
  ON ac.catalog_id = fc.fulltext_catalog_id
INNER JOIN sys.databases d
  ON ac.database_id = d.database_id;
```

	catalog...	database_...	name	is_paused	status	status_desc...	worker...	active...	auto...	manual...	full...	row...	is_importing
1	Book_Cat	iFTS_Books	Book_Cat	No	Ready	AVAILABLE	0	12	0	0	12	0	No

Figure 9-7. *Catalogs currently undergoing population activity*

The sys.dm_fts_outstanding_batches DMV gives you information about all outstanding population batches, or set of rows being populated, for each full-text catalog. This is useful for troubleshooting population issues and determining resource usage. Listing 9-7 returns a count of the number of outstanding batches in full-text catalogs currently being populated. The results are shown in Figure 9-8. Note again that your results may vary from those shown; if there are no currently outstanding batches, the DMV returns no rows.

Listing 9-7. *Retrieving the Number of Full-Text Index Population Batches*

```
SELECT
  OBJECT_NAME(ob.table_id) AS table_name,
  fc.name AS catalog_name,
  COUNT(*) AS outstanding_batches
FROM sys.dm_fts_outstanding_batches ob
INNER JOIN sys.fulltext_catalogs fc
  ON ob.catalog_id = fc.fulltext_catalog_id
INNER JOIN sys.databases d
  ON ob.database_id = d.database_id
GROUP BY
  ob.table_id,
  fc.name;
```

	table_name	catalog_name	outstanding_batches
1	Commentary	Book_Cat	1
2	Contributor_Birth_Place	Book_Cat	1
3	Contributor_Information	Book_Cat	1
4	Contributor_Name	Book_Cat	1
5	Contributor_Role	Book_Cat	1
6	LoC_Class	Book_Cat	1
7	LoC_Subclass	Book_Cat	1
8	Title	Book_Cat	1
9	Book	Book_Cat	2

Figure 9-8. *Counts of outstanding full-text index population batches*

As you can see in Figure 9-8, there are currently 10 batches outstanding in the current population process. These numbers will change throughout the population batches, as currently outstanding batches are finished and new batches are started.

The sys.dm_fts_index_populations DMV is useful for retrieving information about the currently running index population, including the number of parallelized ranges that have been created and completed for the current population. Listing 9-8 returns the population status during a catalog rebuild. Results are shown in Figure 9-9. Once again, your results will vary.

Listing 9-8. *Listing Populations Currently in Progress*

```
SELECT
    fc.name AS catalog_name,
    d.name AS database_name,
    ip.population_type,
    ip.population_type_description,
    SUM(ip.range_count) AS ranges,
    SUM(ip.completed_range_count) AS completed_ranges
FROM sys.dm_fts_index_population ip
INNER JOIN sys.fulltext_catalogs fc
    ON ip.catalog_id = fc.fulltext_catalog_id
INNER JOIN sys.databases d
    ON ip.database_id = d.database_id
GROUP BY
    fc.name,
    d.name,
    ip.population_type,
    ip.population_type_description;
```

	catalog_name	database_name	population_type	population_type_description	ranges	completed_ranges
1	Book_Cat	iFTS_Books	1	FULL	2	0
2	Book_Cat	iFTS_Books	4	AUTO	11	11

Figure 9-9. *Populations in progress during a catalog rebuild*

The sys.dm_fts_population_ranges DMV returns even greater detail concerning the current population process. Specifically, this DMV returns addresses of memory buffers, session ID information, the number of rows processed, retry status, and an error count. All of this information is particularly useful for deep troubleshooting of specific problems, such as failure to complete the population process. Listing 9-9 uses sys.dm_fts_population_ranges to retrieve this troubleshooting information. Figure 9-10 shows partial results of this query. Once again, you can expect your results to vary, and rows are returned only when a full-text population is in progress.

Listing 9-9. *Retrieving Additional Troubleshooting Information with sys.dm_fts_population_ranges*

```
SELECT *
FROM sys.dm_fts_population_ranges;
```

	memory_address	parent_memory_address	is_retry	session_id	processed_row_count	error_count
1	0x0A636B00	0x04460608	0	27	0	0
2	0x04EFE040	0x04460608	0	32	0	0
3	0x04EFECD0	0x044615C0	0	34	0	0
4	0x0A8E8040	0x044615C0	0	35	0	0
5	0x0886ECD0	0x08DFE690	0	0	0	0
6	0x08876040	0x08DFE690	0	0	0	0
7	0x0A8E8BE0	0x08DFF648	0	33	0	0
8	0x0886E040	0x08DFF648	0	23	0	0
9	0x08876CD0	0x0A906690	0	0	0	0
10	0x09168040	0x0A906690	0	0	0	0
11	0x09168CD0	0x0A907648	0	0	0	0
12	0x0A59A040	0x0A907648	0	0	0	0
13	0x0A59ACD0	0x0A596690	0	0	0	0
14	0x0887A040	0x0A596690	0	0	0	0

Figure 9-10. *Partial result of additional iFTS troubleshooting information*

Services and Memory Usage

SQL Server 2008 provides additional DMVs that retrieve information about memory buffers currently in use by the full-text crawl process and the activity of the full-text daemon hosts on the server instance. Listing 9-10 uses the sys.dm_fts_hosts DMV to retrieve information about full-text daemon hosts on the current instance, with results shown in Figure 9-11. The IDs returned by this DMV will be different for each machine.

Listing 9-10. *Retrieving Full-Text Daemon Host Information*

```
SELECT *
FROM sys.dm_fts_fdhosts;
```

	fdhost_id	fdhost_name	fdhost_process_id	fdhost_type	max_thread	batch_count
1	7	MSSQL10.MSSQLSERVERA5f9...	2832	MultiThreaded	2	0

Figure 9-11. *Full-text deamon host information*

The sys.dm_fts_memory_pools DMV returns information about shared memory pools available to the Full-Text Gatherer component. These memory pools represent the memory available for the full-text crawl and full-text crawl range processes. Listing 9-11 retrieves the memory pool information. Results are shown in Figure 9-12. As you probably expect by now from these DMVs, your results will vary from those shown depending on full-text population activity on your server.

Listing 9-11. *Retrieving Full-Text Gatherer Shared Memory Pool Information*

```
SELECT *
FROM sys.dm_fts_memory_pools;
```

	pool_id	buffer_size	min_buffer_limit	max_buffer_limit	buffer_count
1	0	262144	0	100	13
2	1	1048576	0	100	0

Figure 9-12. *Available Full-Text Gatherer memory pools*

Closely related to sys.dm_fts_memory_pools, the sys.dm_fts_memory_buffers DMV returns information about the memory buffers that compose the Full-Text Gatherer's shared memory pools. This DMV allows you to see the amount of memory currently in use during the population process. Listing 9-12 retrieves information about memory buffers currently in use during the population process. Figure 9-13 shows the results. Once more, you can expect your results to be different from those shown here, depending on your full-text index population activity. You can use this information to troubleshoot population issues related to memory pressure.

Listing 9-12. *Retrieving Population Process Memory Buffer Information*

```
SELECT *
FROM sys.dm_fts_memory_buffers;
```

	pool_id	memory_address	name	is_free	row_count	bytes_used	percent_used	
1	0	0x0CE24110	Global\OSMMSSQL10.MSSQLS...	0	0	632	0	
2	0	0x0BE28040	Global\OSMMSSQL10.MSSQLS...	0	0	632	0	
3	0	0x0CDE2848	Global\OSMMSSQL10.MSSQLS...	0	0	632	0	
4	0	0x0D980C68	Global\OSMMSSQL10.MSSQLS...	0	0	632	0	
5	0	0x0D981B80	Global\OSMMSSQL10.MSSQLS...	0	0	632	0	
6	0	0x0BF8E848	Global\OSMMSSQL10.MSSQLS...	0	0	632	0	
7	0	0x0BF39050	Global\OSMMSSQL10.MSSQLS...	0	0	632	0	
8	0	0x0CF72CE0	Global\OSMMSSQL10.MSSQLS...	0	0	632	0	
9	0	0x0D7C8848	Global\OSMMSSQL10.MSSQLS...	0	0	632	0	
10	0	0x0BFFA400	Global\OSMMSSQL10.MSSQLS...	0	0	632	0	
11	0	0x0BFFA040	Global\OSMMSSQL10.MSSQLS...	0	0	632	0	

Figure 9-13. *Viewing memory buffer information during a full-text index population*

Catalog Views

Whereas DMVs provide server state information for a specific point in time, catalog views
return metadata about server instances, databases, and database objects. The database engine
uses this metadata internally to manage server instances and databases, and to fulfill queries
and other requests. While SQL Server can use any number of various data structures to store
this data internally, catalog views are designed to allow you to access it via T-SQL in read-only
tabular data structures. SQL Server 2008 provides several iFTS-specific catalog views that
provide information about full-text catalogs, indexes, and stoplists required by iFTS. We'll look
at these iFTS-specific catalog views in this section.

Listing Full-Text Catalogs

The sys.fulltext_catalogs catalog view returns a single row for each full-text catalog in
the current database. The information returned includes the ID of the catalog, the name of the
catalog, the accent sensitivity setting, whether the catalog is the default catalog, and the database principal defined as the catalog owner.

■**Caution** In addition, the sys.fulltext_catalogs catalog view also returns the ID of the filegroup
where the catalog was created, the ID of the full-text file associated with the catalog, and the file system path
of where the catalog was created. These columns are deprecated and will be removed in a future version of
SQL Server; avoid using them in future work.

Listing 9-13 retrieves the list of full-text catalogs in the current database. The results are
shown in Figure 9-14.

Listing 9-13. *Retrieving the List of Full-Text Catalogs*

```
SELECT
  fulltext_catalog_id,
  name,
  is_default,
  is_accent_sensitivity_on,
  principal_id,
  is_importing
FROM sys.fulltext_catalogs;
```

	fulltext_catalog_id	name	is_default	is_accent_sensitivity_on	principal_id	is_importing
1	5	Book_Cat	1	0	1	0

Figure 9-14. *All full-text catalogs in the iFTS_Books database*

Retrieving Full-Text Index Metadata

SQL Server 2008 provides several iFTS-specific catalog views that allow you to peek under the hood to enumerate your full-text indexes and the related tables, columns, and relational indexes. We've used some of these catalog views in previous examples, but we'll explain them in greater detail in this section.

The first catalog view, sys.fulltext_indexes, returns a single row for each full-text index in the current database. The information reported includes the ID of the table to which the full-text index belongs, the catalog ID, the ID of the stoplist associated with the full-text index, and change tracking and current full-text index crawl status. Listing 9-14 uses the sys.fulltext_indexes catalog view to retrieve the full-text index information for the current database. The results are shown in Figure 9-15.

■**Tip** When joining to the sys.fulltext_stoplists catalog view, an outer join is necessary, since the default SYSTEM stoplist doesn't have an entry in the catalog view.

Listing 9-14. *Retrieving Full-Text Index Information*

```
SELECT
  t.name AS table_name,
  c.name AS catalog_name,
  i.unique_index_id,
  CASE i.is_enabled
    WHEN 1 THEN N'Yes'
    ELSE N'No'
    END AS is_enabled,
```

```
    i.change_tracking_state_desc AS change_tracking,
    CASE i.has_crawl_completed
      WHEN 1 THEN N'Yes'
      ELSE N'No'
      END AS crawl_complete,
    COALESCE(s.name, N'**SYSTEM**') AS stoplist_name
FROM sys.fulltext_indexes i
INNER JOIN sys.tables t
  ON i.object_id = t.object_id
INNER JOIN sys.fulltext_catalogs c
  ON i.fulltext_catalog_id = c.fulltext_catalog_id
LEFT JOIN sys.fulltext_stoplists s
  ON i.stoplist_id = s.stoplist_id;
```

	table_name	catalog_name	unique_index_id	is_enabled	change_tracking	crawl_complete	stoplist_name
1	Commentary	Book_Cat	1	Yes	AUTO	Yes	**SYSTEM**
2	Contributor_Birth_Place	Book_Cat	1	Yes	AUTO	Yes	**SYSTEM**
3	Contributor_Information	Book_Cat	1	Yes	AUTO	Yes	**SYSTEM**
4	Contributor_Name	Book_Cat	2	Yes	AUTO	Yes	**SYSTEM**
5	Contributor_Role	Book_Cat	1	Yes	AUTO	Yes	**SYSTEM**
6	LoC_Class	Book_Cat	1	Yes	AUTO	Yes	**SYSTEM**
7	LoC_Subclass	Book_Cat	2	Yes	AUTO	Yes	**SYSTEM**
8	Subject	Book_Cat	1	Yes	AUTO	Yes	**SYSTEM**
9	Title	Book_Cat	1	Yes	AUTO	Yes	**SYSTEM**
10	Book	Book_Cat	1	Yes	AUTO	Yes	**SYSTEM**

Figure 9-15. *Full-text index information for iFTS_Books database*

The sys.fulltext_index_catalog_usages catalog view returns only a few columns. The data returned by the catalog view represents the full-text catalog to full-text index mappings, and the full-text index to relational index usages. Listing 9-15 retrieves all of this mapping information from the catalog view and joins the results to other relevant catalog views in order to display the information in human-readable format. Results are shown in Figure 9-16.

Listing 9-15. *Retrieving Full-Text Index to Relational Index Relationships*

```
SELECT      .
  t.name AS table_name,
  c.name AS catalog_name,
  i.name AS index_name,
  i.type_desc
FROM sys.fulltext_index_catalog_usages icu
INNER JOIN sys.tables t
  ON icu.object_id = t.object_id
INNER JOIN sys.fulltext_catalogs c
  ON icu.fulltext_catalog_id = c.fulltext_catalog_id
INNER JOIN sys.indexes i
  ON icu.object_id = i.object_id
  AND icu.index_id = i.index_id;
```

	table_name	catalog_na...	index_name	type_desc
1	Commentary	Book_Cat	PK_Commentary	CLUSTERED
2	Contributor_Birth_Place	Book_Cat	PK_Contributor_Birth_Place	CLUSTERED
3	Contributor_Information	Book_Cat	PK_Contributor_Information	CLUSTERED
4	Contributor_Name	Book_Cat	UQ_Contributor_Name	NONCLUSTERED
5	Contributor_Role	Book_Cat	PK_Contributor_Role	CLUSTERED
6	LoC_Class	Book_Cat	PK_LoC_Class	CLUSTERED
7	LoC_Subclass	Book_Cat	UQ_LoC_SubClass	NONCLUSTERED
8	xyz	Book_Cat	PK__xyz__3BD019961EC48A19	CLUSTERED
9	Subject	Book_Cat	PK_Subject	CLUSTERED
10	Title	Book_Cat	PK_Title	CLUSTERED
11	Test1	Book_Cat	PK__Test1__3213E83F3C54ED00	CLUSTERED
12	Book	Book_Cat	PK_Book	CLUSTERED

Figure 9-16. *IFTS relational index usage*

While the sys.fulltext_index_catalog_usages catalog view gives you a picture of the relational indexes used by the full-text indexes, the sys.fulltext_index_columns catalog view provides insight into the actual relational columns being indexed by the full-text indexes. You can join the rows returned by the sys.fulltext_index_columns to the sys.columns catalog view in order to retrieve column metadata for each full-text index. This information is particularly useful for administrative tasks such as scripting full-text index DML statements or displaying the relationships between full-text indexes and relational columns in a GUI application. Listing 9-16 retrieves the column information for all the full-text indexes in the iFTS_Books database, with results shown in Figure 9-17.

Listing 9-16. *Retrieving Full-Text Index Column Information*

```
SELECT
    t.name AS table_name,
    c.name AS column_name,
    c.column_id,
    ic.language_id
FROM sys.fulltext_index_columns ic
INNER JOIN sys.tables t
    ON ic.object_id = t.object_id
INNER JOIN sys.columns c
    ON ic.object_id = c.object_id
    AND ic.column_id = c.column_id
ORDER BY
    t.name,
    c.name,
    c.column_id;
```

	table_name	column_name	column_id	language_id
1	Book	Book_Content	6	1033
2	Commentary	Article_Content	3	1033
3	Commentary	Commentary	2	1033
4	Contributor_Birth_Place	Birth_City	2	1033
5	Contributor_Birth_Place	Birth_Country	4	1033
6	Contributor_Birth_Place	Birth_State	3	1033
7	Contributor_Information	Information	2	1033
8	Contributor_Name	First_Name	5	1033
9	Contributor_Name	Last_Name	4	1033
10	Contributor_Name	Middle_Name	6	1033
11	Contributor_Role	Contributor_Role_Description	2	1033
12	LoC_Class	Class_Description	2	1033
13	LoC_Subclass	Subclass_Description	4	1033
14	Subject	Subject_Description	2	1033
15	Title	Title	4	1033

Figure 9-17. *Full-text index column information*

Full-text indexes are stored in inverted index structures known as *fragments*. You can use the sys.fulltext_index_fragments catalog view to look at the fragments currently in use. By querying this catalog view for *queryable fragments*, you can determine whether an index reorganization or rebuild will help performance. A queryable fragment is one that has a status of 4 (*Closed. Ready for query*) or 6 (*Being used for merge input and ready for query*). If your query returns a large number of fragments for a given index, a reorganization can help improve query performance. Listing 9-17 demonstrates this by querying for all queryable fragments in the current database, with results shown in Figure 9-18. Your results will vary from those shown in Figure 9-18, depending on the number and size of queryable fragments in your database.

Listing 9-17. *Returning the Number of Queryable Fragments*

```
SELECT *
FROM sys.fulltext_index_fragments
WHERE status IN (4, 6);
```

	table_id	fragment_id	fragment_object_id	timestamp	status	data_size	row_count
1	101575400	16	1840725610	0x000000000000575A	4	847221	13339
2	165575628	16	1776725382	0x0000000000005753	4	2009	35
3	229575856	16	1808725496	0x0000000000005755	4	21615	378
4	293576084	16	1792725439	0x0000000000005757	4	4812	85
5	341576255	16	1824725553	0x0000000000005759	4	587	10
6	437576597	16	1872725724	0x000000000000575E	4	712	12
7	469576711	16	1856725667	0x000000000000575C	4	2282	39
8	484196775	11	1888725781	0x000000000000575F	4	295	6
9	549576996	16	1904725838	0x0000000000005761	4	4988	85
10	581577110	20	1936725952	0x0000000000005763	4	9498	171
11	980198542	15	1920725895	0x0000000000005765	4	367	4
12	2105058535	92	13243102	0x0000000000005797	4	10146501	105292

Figure 9-18. *List of queryable fragments in the iFTS_Books database*

Revealing Stoplists

Like full-text indexes, stoplists are stored in the database by SQL Server 2008. There are three new catalog views that provide insight into the contents of the system stoplist and user stoplists. The `sys.fulltext_system_stopwords` catalog view allows you to view the default system stopword entries. Listing 9-18 lists all of the stopwords in the English (LCID 1033) system stoplist, with partial results shown in Figure 9-19.

Listing 9-18. *Listing English (LCID 1033) System Stoplist Information*

```
SELECT *
FROM sys.fulltext_system_stopwords
WHERE language_id = 1033;
```

	stopword	language_id
62	did	1033
63	do	1033
64	does	1033
65	each	1033
66	else	1033
67	for	1033
68	from	1033
69	get	1033
70	got	1033
71	had	1033
72	has	1033
73	have	1033

Figure 9-19. *Partial English system stoplist*

The `sys.fulltext_stoplists` catalog view returns a list of user-defined stoplists. Note that the default system stoplists aren't included in the results of this catalog view. Listing 9-19 retrieves the list of user-defined stoplists, with the result shown in Figure 9-20. Your results may vary from those shown, depending on how many user-defined stoplists you've created in your database.

■**Tip** To get the results like those shown in Figure 9-20, you need to create a user-defined stoplist like the `NoFish_Stoplist` we created in Chapter 7.

Listing 9-19. *Retrieving the Names of All User-Defined Stoplists*

```
SELECT *
FROM sys.fulltext_stoplists;
```

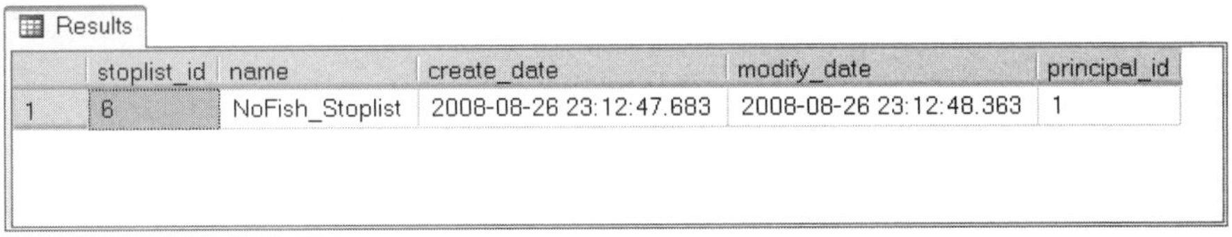

	stoplist_id	name	create_date	modify_date	principal_id
1	6	NoFish_Stoplist	2008-08-26 23:12:47.683	2008-08-26 23:12:48.363	1

Figure 9-20. *User-defined stoplists listing*

The `sys.fulltext_stopwords` catalog view returns a list of stopwords that comprise the user-defined full-text stoplists. You can join `sys.fulltext_stopwords` to the `sys.fulltext_stoplists` catalog view in order to retrieve the contents of user-defined stoplists by name. Listing 9-20 shows how to retrieve the contents of the `NoFish_Stoplist` in this way, with partial results shown in Figure 9-21.

Listing 9-20. *Retrieving the Contents of a User-Defined Stoplist*

```
SELECT sw.*
FROM sys.fulltext_stoplists sl
INNER JOIN sys.fulltext_stopwords sw
  ON sl.stoplist_id = sw.stoplist_id
WHERE sl.name = N'NoFish_Stoplist'
  AND sw.language_id = 1033;
```

Results

	stoplist_id	stopword	language	language_id
63	6	do	English	1033
64	6	does	English	1033
65	6	each	English	1033
66	6	else	English	1033
67	6	fish	English	1033
68	6	for	English	1033
69	6	from	English	1033
70	6	get	English	1033

Figure 9-21. *English (LCID 1033) user-defined stoplist entries*

Viewing Supported Languages and Document Types

SQL Server 2008 provides two additional iFTS-specific catalog views that return information about supported languages and document types. The `sys.fulltext_languages` catalog view retrieves all iFTS supported languages on an instance of SQL Server. Listing 9-21 returns a list of all supported languages for a SQL Server instance, with partial results shown in Figure 9-22.

Listing 9-21. *Retrieving List of iFTS-Supported Languages*

```
SELECT *
FROM sys.fulltext_languages
ORDER BY name;
```

Results

	lcid	name
8	5124	Chinese (Macau SAR)
9	4100	Chinese (Singapore)
10	1050	Croatian
11	1043	Dutch
12	1033	English
13	1036	French
14	1031	German
15	1095	Gujarati
16	1037	Hebrew
17	1081	Hindi
18	1039	Icelandic

Figure 9-22. *List of iFTS-supported languages*

■ **Tip** The `iFTS_Books` database includes a table called `dbo.XML_Lang_Code` that maps a number of LCID codes to XML language (`xml:lang` attribute) codes.

You can also return a list of supported document types on an instance of SQL Server with the `sys.fulltext_document_types` catalog view. This is particularly useful after installing new filter components, to ensure that they've been properly registered with your SQL Server instance. Listing 9-22 queries the sys.fulltext_document_types catalog view, with partial results shown in Figure 9-23.

Listing 9-22. *Retrieving a List of Supported iFTS Document Types*

```
SELECT *
FROM sys.fulltext_document_types;
```

	document_type	class_id	path	version	manufacturer
1	.ascx	E0CA5340-4534-11CF-B952-00AA0051FE20	C:\Program Files\...	12.0.6828.0	Microsoft Corporation
2	.asm	C7310720-AC80-11D1-8DF3-00C04FB6EF4F	C:\Program Files\...	12.0.6828.0	Microsoft Corporation
3	.asp	E0CA5340-4534-11CF-B952-00AA0051FE20	C:\Program Files\...	12.0.6828.0	Microsoft Corporation
4	.aspx	E0CA5340-4534-11CF-B952-00AA0051FE20	C:\Program Files\...	12.0.6828.0	Microsoft Corporation
5	.bat	C7310720-AC80-11D1-8DF3-00C04FB6EF4F	C:\Program Files\...	12.0.6828.0	Microsoft Corporation
6	.c	C7310720-AC80-11D1-8DF3-00C04FB6EF4F	C:\Program Files\...	12.0.6828.0	Microsoft Corporation
7	.cmd	C7310720-AC80-11D1-8DF3-00C04FB6EF4F	C:\Program Files\...	12.0.6828.0	Microsoft Corporation
8	.cpp	C7310720-AC80-11D1-8DF3-00C04FB6EF4F	C:\Program Files\...	12.0.6828.0	Microsoft Corporation
9	.cxx	C7310720-AC80-11D1-8DF3-00C04FB6EF4F	C:\Program Files\...	12.0.6828.0	Microsoft Corporation
10	.def	C7310720-AC80-11D1-8DF3-00C04FB6EF4F	C:\Program Files\...	12.0.6828.0	Microsoft Corporation
11	.dic	C7310720-AC80-11D1-8DF3-00C04FB6EF4F	C:\Program Files\...	12.0.6828.0	Microsoft Corporation

Figure 9-23. *List of supported iFTS document types*

Summary

SQL Server 2008 iFTS integration with the SQL query engine provides significant advantages over prior versions of FTS. In addition to the performance, administration, flexibility, and management benefits, this tighter integration with the database provides several opportunities for greater transparency into the inner workings of iFTS. In prior releases of SQL Server, FTS was somewhat of a black box, and full-text search administration and querying in general was somewhat of an arcane black art.

Microsoft has taken advantage of SQL Server 2008's new iFTS architecture by providing us with several iFTS-specific DMFs, DMVs, and catalog views. These new system functions and views provide more insight into the inner workings of iFTS than prior releases of SQL Server. This new transparency demystifies full-text search, making it easier to understand, query, administer, fine-tune, and troubleshoot. In this chapter, we discussed these new tools and the insight they can provide into the inner workings of your iFTS implementations.

In the next chapter, we'll discuss IFTS filters, including commercially developed filters and custom filter design and development.

CHAPTER 10

Filters

The wise ones fashioned speech with their thought, sifting it as grain is sifted through a sieve.

— Buddha

In the first chapter, we introduced the interrelated components that enable SQL Server iFTS functionality. In this chapter, we'll explore filter components in detail and provide an overview of other components, including the gatherer and protocol handlers, word breakers, and stemmers. We'll discuss the different types of filters available for use with SQL Server 2008 iFTS, including standard filters that come with SQL Server 2008 and third-party filters. We'll also show you how to create your own custom filters.

Introducing Filters

Filters are responsible for parsing data and returning chunks of content text and name/value property pairs. For purposes of security and stability, filters are run outside of the SQL Server process space. They're managed by the *filter daemon* process, which is kicked off by the *gatherer*, which is the component responsible for managing full-text index population, during the indexing process. Where the protocol handler is data source–specific (in the case of iFTS, the protocol handler is specific to SQL Server), filters are content-specific; that is, each filter handles specific content formats. Regular character content in SQL Server is indexed using the built-in plain text filter, `xml` data type content is indexed using the XML filter, and `varbinary(max)` content is filtered based on a corresponding file extension stored in a file type column.

Note We discussed filtering `xml` and `varbinary(max)` content in Chapter 6.

Standard Filters

SQL Server 2008 comes with several standard filters, supporting more than 50 different types of file content out of the box. Table 10-1 is a short listing of some of the more commonly used standard filters and the file types they support.

Table 10-1. *Standard SQL Server 2008 Filters*

Filter Name	File Extension	Description
Plain text filter	.TXT	Plain ASCII and Unicode text filter, no special handling or markup
Office document filter	.DOC, .XLS, .PPS	Microsoft Office documents
HTML filter	.HTM, .HTML	HTML documents
XML filter	.XML	XML documents

In addition to the standard filters, Microsoft provides the Microsoft Filter Pack for free download at http://download.microsoft.com. This filter pack works with several Microsoft products, including SQL Server 2008, and provides built-in support for indexing Microsoft Office 2007 documents (.DOCX, .XLSX, and so on), Visio documents (.VSD, .VSDX), and even compressed Zip files (.ZIP).

Third-Party Filters

If the standard filters don't cover all the content types that you need to index, there are a variety of third-party filters available to fill the void. Filters are available from several different vendors, including the following:

- Adobe PDF filters are available from www.adobe.com and www.foxitsoftware.com.

- An AutoCAD DWG filter is available at www.dwgifilter.com.

- A WordPerfect filter is available at www.corel.com.

There are several web sites that compile listings of available filters and filter developers; some filters are available for free while others can be bought commercially. A sample of these sites include Hilary Cotter's www.indexserverfaq.com site, the Document Locator site at www.documentlocator.com/Support/IFilters, and the iFilterShop site at www.ifiltershop.com.

We've included sample PDF content in the iFTS_Books database to demonstrate the installation and use of a free third-party filter. Though Adobe offers older versions of its PDF filter for separate download from the Adobe web site, the newest versions of the Adobe PDF filter are downloaded and installed as part of Acrobat Reader. To demonstrate third-party filter functionality, we downloaded and installed Acrobat Reader 9.0. To install the Adobe PDF filter and index PDF content, perform the following steps:

1. Download and install Adobe Acrobat Reader from www.adobe.com. Follow the wizard prompts as necessary.

2. The Adobe PDF filter is not exclusive to SQL Server. You install it and treat it like an operating system (OS) resource. You need to set your SQL Server full-text service to load OS resources with the following statement:

```
EXEC sys.sp_fulltext_service 'load_os_resources', 1;
GO
```

3. In prior versions of SQL Server, installing a new FTS filter required a restart of the full-text service. In SQL Server 2008, no restart is required; you just need to execute the following statement to update the SQL Server full-text service with the new filter:

```
EXEC sys.sp_fulltext_service 'update_languages', NULL;
```

4. Finally, you can verify the installation and registration with SQL Server iFTS by executing the following query (partial results are shown in Figure 10-1):

```
SELECT
  document_type,
  class_id,
  path
FROM sys.fulltext_document_types
WHERE document_type = N'.pdf';
```

	document_ty...	class_id	path
1	.pdf	4C904448-74A9-11D0-AF6E-00C04FD8DC02	C:\Program Files\Adobe\PDF IFilter 6.0\PDFFILT.dll

Figure 10-1. *Verifying installation and registration of the Adobe PDF filter*

■**Caution** Prior versions of the Adobe PDF filter were designed and developed as *apartment threaded*, which can cause performance and other issues when running in the multithreaded SQL iFTS environment. We recommend using the newer versions of the Adobe PDF filter when possible.

After installing the Adobe PDF filter, your full-text indexes will automatically update if you have them set for automatic change tracking. Otherwise, you'll need to kick off a full population manually.

Custom Filters

If you need to filter content for which the standard filters won't work and there are no available third-party filters, you can create a custom filter to index your content. Custom filter creation is made possible through the magic of the Component Object Model (COM). Successfully implementing a custom filter requires knowledge of a wide range of unmanaged coding technologies, including the following:

- C++ and object-oriented programming for Windows

- Development for COM interfaces and COM DLL component registration

- Multithreaded programming techniques

In addition, knowledge of memory management techniques in unmanaged code is essential to filter development. Knowledge of standard libraries such as the Microsoft Foundation Class (MFC) library, Active Template Library (ATL), and Standard Template Library (STL) is extremely useful for filter development.

Custom Filter Development

Windows exposes several interfaces for designing your own custom full-text search components, including the `IFilter` interface, which is the basis for filters. In this section, we'll create a simple custom filter to index the content of LaTeX documents.

■Tip Full-text search filters are often called *iFilters* because they're created based on the `IFilter` interface.

LaTeX (usually pronounced "LAY-tek") is a superset of Donald Knuth's TeX (pronounced "tek") typesetting system. TeX was originally designed as a markup system for the production of high-quality typesetting in documents. LaTeX was built on top of TeX to abstract away some of the more mundane tasks required to create TeX documents. A simple LaTeX document is shown in Listing 10-1.

Listing 10-1. *Simple LaTeX Document*

```
%%%%%%%%%%%%%%%%%%%%%%%%%%%%%%%%%%%%%%%%%%%%%%%%%%%%%%%%%%%%%%%%%%%%%%%%%%%%%%%%%
%
% Comments always begin with a % sign
% Everything after the % sign on the current line is ignored
%
%%%%%%%%%%%%%%%%%%%%%%%%%%%%%%%%%%%%%%%%%%%%%%%%%%%%%%%%%%%%%%%%%%%%%%%%%%%%%%%%%
\documentclass[12pt]{article}    % here we set up some document metadata
\title{Simple \LaTeX{} Document}
\author{Michael Coles and Hilary Cotter}
\date{July 19, 2008}

\begin{document}                 % let the document begin!
\maketitle

\LaTeX{} documents are created from plain text documents with special
typesetting markup included. In fact we created this sample document in
\textbf{notepad}.

\section{Why Use \LaTeX{}?}

\LaTeX{} is used extensively in the world of academic publishing because of its
ability to perfectly typeset technical information like the formula for the area
```

of a circle: $a = \pi r^2$ or the length of the hypotenuse of a right triangle
$c = \sqrt{a^2 + b^2}$.

\section{The \LaTeX{} Filter}

When creating a filter for \LaTeX{} we need to keep in mind that there are
several typesetting tags and additional markup that need to be taken into
consideration. \LaTeX{} recognizes over 5,000 special markup tags and symbols;
we will consider only a few of these for our filter sample.

\section{Acknowledgments}

Big thanks to Dr. Knuth and the folks at The \LaTeX{} Project
(\emph{http://www.latex-project.org}).

\section{The End}
Good bye!

\end{document}

After rendering this document with a LaTeX typesetting program, we get the result shown
in Figure 10-2.

Filter Interfaces

Now that we've given a brief overview of what LaTeX is and what it does, we'll look at the interfaces we need to implement to design a simple filter for LaTeX content. We've chosen to use
the sample plain text filter for simple content, which is included as part of the Windows 2003
Platform Software Development Kit (SDK), as a starting point for our example LaTeX filter.
We'll begin the design phase with a discussion of COM interfaces that the filter must implement.

■**Tip** The Windows 2003 Platform SDK includes a few different examples of source code for custom filters,
and is available for download from www.microsoft.com. We recommend downloading the Platform SDK
and familiarizing yourself with the source code before you undertake a new custom filter project.

Filters implement the IFilter interface and one or more of the IPersistFile, IPersistStream,
and IPersistStorage interfaces. Each filter DLL must also contain a COM class factory derived
from the IClassFactory interface. In addition, the filter DLL must export four functions—
DllRegisterServer, DllUnregisterServer, DllGetClassObject, and DllCanUnloadNow—as shown
in Figure 10-3.

Simple LATEX Document

Michael Coles and Hilary Cotter

July 19, 2008

LATEX documents are created from plain text documents with special typesetting markup included. In fact we created this sample document in notepad.

1   Why Use LATEX?

LATEX is used extensively in the world of academic publishing because of its ability to perfectly typeset technical information like the formula for the area of a circle: $a = \pi r^2$ or the length of the hypotenuse of a right triangle $c = \sqrt{a^2 + b^2}$.

2   The LATEX Filter

When creating a filter for LATEX we need to keep in mind that there are several typesetting tags and additional markup that need to be taken into consideration. LATEX recognizes over 5,000 special markup tags and symbols; we will consider only a few of these for our filter sample.

3   Acknowledgments

Big thanks to Dr. Knuth and the folks at The LATEX Project (*http://www.latex-project.org*).

1

Figure 10-2. *A rendered sample LaTeX document*

The IClassFactory, IFilter, IPersistFile, IPersistStream, and IPersistStorage interfaces all inherit from the COM IUnknown interface. IUnknown provides the following three virtual methods that must be implemented by the user:

- IUnknown::QueryInterface, which returns pointers to supported interfaces

- IUnknown::AddRef, which increments the reference count for the class

- IUnknown::Release, which decrements the reference count for the class

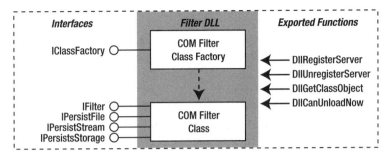

Figure 10-3. *Filter DLL classes, interfaces, and exported functions*

Every COM class must maintain a count of the number of current references to the interface pointer. When the reference count drops to 0, the memory for the interface is released.

The IClassFactory interface implements the following two additional methods for the creation and management of objects:

- IClassFactory::CreateInstance, which creates an uninitialized object

- IClassFactory::LockServer, which locks the object server in memory to enhance performance

In addition to IUnknown, the IPersist* interfaces also inherit from the IPersist interface. IPersist implements only a single method, IPersist::GetClassID, which returns a class identifier (CLSID) of the object. The IPersist* interfaces require that you implement methods to load and save data, as well as to check for changes to your source data during processing. In our sample, we'll be implementing the IPersistFile interface, which requires implementation of the following methods:

- IPersistFile::Load, which opens the specified file and initializes an object from the file's contents

- IPersistFile::Save, which saves the object to the specified file

- IPersistFile::SaveCompleted, which informs the object that it's safe to write to its file

- IPersistFile::IsDirty, which checks to see if the data in the file has changed since it was last saved

- IPersistFile::GetCurFile, which retrieves the path to the current file

Since we're creating a filter specifically for the SQL Server iFTS, we'll create nonfunctional stubs for many of the IPersistFile methods; the only method we're really concerned with for SQL Server iFTS is the IPersistFile::Load method.

The IFilter interface is where the real action happens. IFilter provides methods to initialize a filtering session, read chunks of data from the data source, and return text and values from the chunks of data. The IFilter interface requires implementation of the following five methods:

- IFilter::Init, which initializes a filtering session

- IFilter::GetChunk, which positions the filter at the beginning of the first, or subsequent, chunk of data

- IFilter::GetText, which retrieves text from the current data chunk

- IFilter::GetValue, which retrieves a value from the current data chunk

- IFilter::BindRegion, which is reserved for future use

Custom Filter Design

The design for the LaTeX filter is relatively simple. We simply open up the data source, read the data one chunk at a time, and parse the data, returning one line of textual data at a time. This is shown in simplified form as a flowchart in Figure 10-4.

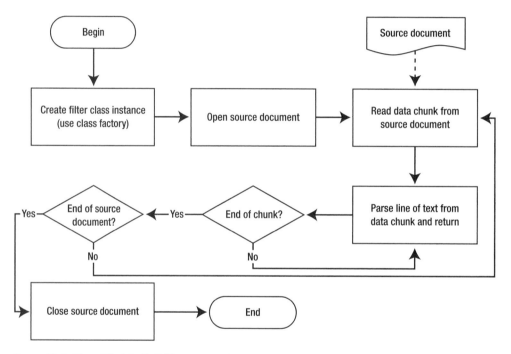

Figure 10-4. *Simplified LaTeX filter processing*

We say the design is relatively simple in this case because the data is simple plain text with textual markup. The textual data also has a natural break for pieces of text—the line break. All of this simplifies processing to the point of a basic nested loop. The outer loop of this process retrieves chunks of data from the source file and places them in a buffer. The inner loop returns single lines of data from the chunk buffer. The actual implementation is slightly more complex, since markup and some other details need to be properly handled, but overall the majority of the filter's functionality can be described with this simple processing model.

Our LaTeX filter implementation is based on the simple filter example provided in the Windows 2003 Platform SDK. The simple filter example grabs chunks of data from the source document and returns each chunk as text. The Platform SDK simple filter doesn't account for line breaks, comments, or markup—all of which must be accounted for in the LaTeX filter. The items we'll consider in the sample LaTeX filter include the following:

- The % character indicates the start of a comment. All characters after the % will be ignored, up to the end of the current line.

- The \ character indicates the start of a markup tag. There are two types of tags we'll consider: tags that have additional information in trailing braces ({}) and tags that don't have trailing braces. For this example, we won't be doing anything special with markup tags other than consuming and disposing of their content. In a more complex filter, however, you might want to grab the content of specific markup tags and return it as name/value property pairs.

- The carriage return (0x0d) and line feed (0x0a) characters both indicate an end-of-line condition. The end-of-line condition requires special handling, since comments and some tags can end with the end of a line of text.

The filter implementation requires two classes to be implemented: the filter class factory and the filter class, which we'll describe in the sections following. We'll implement this filter in C++ and compile to native code based on the Microsoft filter team's recommendations. Although .NET-based filter components are being tested in various forms, the filter team has recommended that filters be developed using C++/COM and compiled to native code.

Filter Class Factory

The CTeXFilterCF class is the LaTeX filter class factory. The sole purpose of this class factory is to build instances of the CTeXFilter class. The header file for this class is shown in Listing 10-2.

Listing 10-2. *CTeXFilterCF Header File*

```
class CTeXFilterCF : public IClassFactory
{
public:

  virtual SCODE STDMETHODCALLTYPE QueryInterface
  (
    REFIID riid,
    void ** ppvObject
  );
  virtual ULONG STDMETHODCALLTYPE AddRef();
  virtual ULONG STDMETHODCALLTYPE Release();
  virtual  SCODE STDMETHODCALLTYPE  CreateInstance
  (
    IUnknown * pUnkOuter,
    REFIID riid, void  ** ppvObject
  );
  virtual  SCODE STDMETHODCALLTYPE  LockServer
  (
    BOOL fLock
  );

private:
```

```
friend SCODE STDMETHODCALLTYPE DllGetClassObject
(
  REFCLSID   cid,
  REFIID     iid,
  void **    ppvObj
);
CTeXFilterCF();
~CTeXFilterCF();
long InstanceCount;
};
```

As you can see by the header declarations, the CTeXFilterCF class factory implements all of the IClassFactory interface methods. The CTeXFilterCF::CreateInstance method, shown in Listing 10-3, is the main method of this class. CreateInstance instantiates a new instance of the CTeXFilter class to filter content.

■**Tip** Using standard COM protocol, a successful COM operation returns the S_OK code and a failure returns an E_*error* code. You'll notice the use of these return codes in many of the COM-based methods.

Listing 10-3. *CTeXFilterCF::CreateInstance Class*

```
SCODE STDMETHODCALLTYPE CTeXFilterCF::CreateInstance
(
  IUnknown * pUnkOuter,
  REFIID riid,
  void ** ppvObject
)
{
  CTeXFilter *pIUnk = 0;

  if (0 != pUnkOuter)
    return CLASS_E_NOAGGREGATION;

  pIUnk = new CTeXFilter();

  if (0 != pIUnk)
  {
    if (SUCCEEDED(pIUnk->QueryInterface(riid, ppvObject)))
    {
      // Release extra refcount from QueryInterface
```

```
    pIUnk->Release();
  }
  else
  {
    delete pIUnk;
    return E_UNEXPECTED;
  }
}
else
  return E_OUTOFMEMORY;

return S_OK;
}
```

The CTeXFilterCF::AddRef and CTeXFilterCF::Release methods are important as well. These two COM methods maintain the reference count, removing the interface from memory when the reference count reaches 0. Listing 10-4 shows the AddRef and Release methods. These methods use the InterlockedIncrement and InterlockedDecrement functions to synchronize multithreaded access to the InstanceCount variable.

Listing 10-4. *CTeXFilterCF::AddRef and CTeXFilterCF::Release Methods*

```
ULONG STDMETHODCALLTYPE CTeXFilterCF::AddRef()
{
  return InterlockedIncrement(&InstanceCount);
}

ULONG STDMETHODCALLTYPE CTeXFilterCF::Release()
{
  ULONG Tmp = InterlockedDecrement(&InstanceCount);

  if (Tmp == 0)
    delete this;

  return Tmp;
}
```

The CTeXFilterCF::QueryInterface method is the implementation of the COM QueryInterface method, as required by the IUnknown interface. This method returns pointers to interfaces supported by this class. Listing 10-5 shows the implementation of QueryInterface.

Listing 10-5. *CTeXFilterCF::QueryInterface Method*

```
SCODE STDMETHODCALLTYPE CTeXFilterCF::QueryInterface
(
  REFIID riid,
  void ** ppvObject
)
```

```
{
  IUnknown *pUnkTemp;

  if (IID_IClassFactory == riid)
    pUnkTemp = (IUnknown *)(IClassFactory *)this;
  else if (IID_IUnknown == riid)
    pUnkTemp = (IUnknown *)this;
  else
  {
    *ppvObject = NULL;
    return E_NOINTERFACE;
  }

  *ppvObject = (void  *)pUnkTemp;
  pUnkTemp->AddRef();

  return S_OK;
}
```

The DllCanUnloadNow method informs SQL Server whether the filter DLL can be unloaded. To conserve memory, SQL Server will automatically unload the filter DLL if it hasn't been used for an extended period of time. Listing 10-6 shows the DllCanUnloadNow method.

Listing 10-6. *DllCanUnloadNow Method*

```
extern "C" SCODE STDMETHODCALLTYPE DllCanUnloadNow
(
  void
)
{
  if (0 >= InstanceCount)
    return S_OK;
  else
    return S_FALSE;
}
```

The DllMain method is the DLL entry point method, called when the DLL is initially loaded or unloaded. Listing 10-7 is the DllMain method exposed by the filter DLL.

Listing 10-7. *DllMain Method*

```
extern "C" BOOL WINAPI DllMain
(
  HINSTANCE hInstance,
  DWORD fdwReason,
  LPVOID lpvReserved
)
```

```
{
  if (DLL_PROCESS_ATTACH == fdwReason)
    DisableThreadLibraryCalls(hInstance);

  return TRUE;
}
```

The DllGetClassObject method is a method that COM calls internally to load and create an instance of the COM object. You won't call this method directly, but it's used by the COM CoLoadLibrary function, which is called in turn by the COM CoGetClassObject function. Listing 10-8 is the DllGetClassObject method.

Listing 10-8. *DllGetClassObject Method*

```
extern "C" SCODE STDMETHODCALLTYPE DllGetClassObject
(
  REFCLSID cid,
  REFIID iid,
  void ** ppvObj
)
{
  IUnknown *pResult = 0;

  if (CLSID_CTeXFilter == cid)
    pResult = (IUnknown *)new CTeXFilterCF;
  else
    return CLASS_E_CLASSNOTAVAILABLE;

  if (0 != pResult)
  {
    If (SUCCEEDED(pResult->QueryInterface(iid, ppvObj)))
      // Release extra refcount from QueryInterface
      pResult->Release();
    else
    {
      delete pResult;
      return E_UNEXPECTED;
    }
  }
  else
    return E_OUTOFMEMORY;

  return S_OK;
}
```

Filter Class

The filter class factory, CTeXFilterCF, creates instances of the filter class, CTeXFilter. The CTeXFilter class performs the actual filtering we discussed previously. This class implements both the standard COM IUnknown management methods and additional methods to perform the following three main filtering functions:

1. Open the source data for reading.

2. Read the source data in chunks.

3. Process the chunks, handling comments and markup tags, returning one line at a time.

The first step to implementing the filter is to define a CLSID for the filter class. The CLSID can be generated from the command line with the GUIDGEN utility, which is located in the bin subdirectory of the Platform SDK. Figure 10-5 shows the GUIDGEN utility in action.

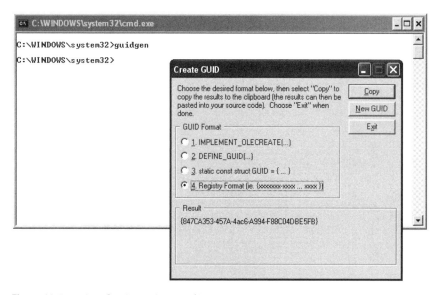

Figure 10-5. *Using the GUIDGEN utility to generate a CLSID*

The CLSID is added to the registry during installation so the OS can locate and create instances of the CTeXFilter class as needed. The CLSID we generated for the CTeXFilter class is {6fc40ad8-8657-4429-a816-abef6974b763}. Listing 10-9 defines the CLSID as a GUID constant.

Listing 10-9. *Defining the CLSID As a Constant*

```
// CTeXFilter Class ID
// {6fc40ad8-8657-4429-a816-abef6974b763}
GUID const CLSID_CTeXFilter =
```

```
{
  0x6fc40ad8,
  0x8657,
  0x4429,
  {0xa8, 0x16, 0xab, 0xef, 0x69, 0x74, 0xb7, 0x63}
};
```

The CTeXFilter class implements both the IFilter and IPersistFile interfaces. Apart from the COM interface methods, the CTeXFilter class implements several methods and flags required to process the source data. The flags exposed include end-of-line and end-of-buffer indicators, among others. Listing 10-10 shows the header for the CTeXFilter class.

Listing 10-10. *CTeXFilter Class Header*

```
// CTeXFilter filter class
class CTeXFilter :
  public IFilter,
  public IPersistFile
{
public:

  virtual  SCODE STDMETHODCALLTYPE  QueryInterface
  (
    REFIID riid,
    void ** ppvObject
  );
  virtual  ULONG STDMETHODCALLTYPE  AddRef();
  virtual  ULONG STDMETHODCALLTYPE  Release();

  virtual  SCODE STDMETHODCALLTYPE  Init
  (
    ULONG grfFlags,
    ULONG cAttributes,
    FULLPROPSPEC const * aAttributes,
    ULONG * pFlags
  );
  virtual  SCODE STDMETHODCALLTYPE  GetChunk
  (
    STAT_CHUNK * pStat
  );
  virtual  SCODE STDMETHODCALLTYPE  GetText
  (
    ULONG * pcwcBuffer,
    WCHAR * awcBuffer
  );
  virtual  SCODE STDMETHODCALLTYPE  GetValue
```

```
  (
    PROPVARIANT ** ppPropValue
  );
  virtual  SCODE STDMETHODCALLTYPE  BindRegion
  (
    FILTERREGION origPos,
    REFIID riid,
    void ** ppunk
  );

  virtual  SCODE STDMETHODCALLTYPE  GetClassID
  (
    CLSID * pClassID
  );
  virtual  SCODE STDMETHODCALLTYPE  IsDirty();
  virtual  SCODE STDMETHODCALLTYPE  Load
  (
    LPCWSTR pszFileName,
    DWORD dwMode
  );
  virtual  SCODE STDMETHODCALLTYPE  Save
  (
    LPCWSTR pszFileName,
    BOOL fRemember
  );
  virtual  SCODE STDMETHODCALLTYPE  SaveCompleted
  (
    LPCWSTR pszFileName
  );
  virtual  SCODE STDMETHODCALLTYPE  GetCurFile
  (
    LPWSTR  * ppszFileName
  );

private:
  friend class CTeXFilterCF; // Class Factory

  CTeXFilter();              // Ctor
  ~CTeXFilter();             // Dtor

  bool CTeXFilter::Eob() { return _Eob; }; // Return end of block flag
  bool CTeXFilter::Eol() { return _Eol; }; // Return end of line flag

  // Convert Code Page to Wide Character
  SCODE CTeXFilter::ConvertCP2Wide
```

```
(
  char * SourceBuffer,
  ULONG CodePage,
  ULONG BufferLength
);

WCHAR CTeXFilter::GetChar(); // Get a character from the buffer

// Unget a character from the buffer
void CTeXFilter::UngetChar(WCHAR Wch)
{
  UngotChar = Wch;
  UngetPending = true;
};

void CTeXFilter::GetMarkup();  // Get markup from the buffer
void CTeXFilter::DoMarkup();   // Do markup
void CTeXFilter::EatLine();    // Eat remaining characters on the current line
void CTeXFilter::EatBraces();  // Eat everything within the nested braces
                               // following, including the braces

bool In_Markup_Flag;     // Currently within markup flag
std::wstring Markup_Tag; // Markup tag
int BraceLevel;          // Brace nesting level flag
HANDLE FileHandle;       // Handle to the input file
long Refs;               // Reference count
WCHAR * FileName;        // Name of input file to filter
ULONG ChunkID;           // Current chunk id
ULONG CodePage;          // Current default codepage
bool Contents_Req_Flag;  // Contents requested flag
bool _Eof;               // End of file flag
WCHAR * Chunk_Buffer;    // Chunk buffer
WCHAR * CurrentChar;     // Current character pointer
ULONG Chunk_Length;      // Length of current chunk
ULONG Chunk_Read_Pos;    // Read position within current chunk
bool UngetPending;       // Unget character pending flag
WCHAR UngotChar;         // Ungot character
bool In_Comment_Flag;    // Currently within a comment flag
bool _Eol;               // End of line flag
bool _Eob;               // End of block flag
};
```

The CTeXFilter class exposes the CTeXFilter::Init method to initialize an instance of the class. The Init method opens the source document, sets appropriate flags, and prepares to read the source data in chunks. Listing 10-11 shows the CTeXFilter::Init method.

Listing 10-11. *CTeXFilter::Init Method*

```
SCODE STDMETHODCALLTYPE CTeXFilter::Init
(
  ULONG grfFlags,
  ULONG cAttributes,
  FULLPROPSPEC const * aAttributes,
  ULONG * pFlags
)
{
  // Ignore flags for text canonicalization (text is unformatted)
  // Check for proper attributes request and recognize only "contents"

  if (0 < cAttributes)
  {
    ULONG ulNumAttr;

    if (0 == aAttributes)
      return E_INVALIDARG;

    for (ulNumAttr = 0; ulNumAttr < cAttributes; ulNumAttr++)
    {
      if (guidStorage == aAttributes[ulNumAttr].guidPropSet &&
        PID_STG_CONTENTS == aAttributes[ulNumAttr].psProperty.propid)
        break;
    }

    if (ulNumAttr < cAttributes)
      _Contents_Req_Flag = true;
    else
      _Contents_Req_Flag = false;
  }
  else if (0 == grfFlags ||
    (grfFlags & IFILTER_INIT_APPLY_INDEX_ATTRIBUTES))
    _Contents_Req_Flag = true;
  else
    _Contents_Req_Flag = false;

  _Eof = false;

  // Open the file previously specified in call to IPersistFile::Load

  if (0 != FileName)
  {
    if (INVALID_HANDLE_VALUE != FileHandle)
```

```
    {
      CloseHandle (FileHandle);
      FileHandle = INVALID_HANDLE_VALUE;
    }

    FileHandle = CreateFile
      (
        (LPCWSTR)FileName,
        GENERIC_READ,
        FILE_SHARE_READ | FILE_SHARE_DELETE,
        0,
        OPEN_EXISTING,
        FILE_ATTRIBUTE_NORMAL,
        0
      );

    if (FileHandle == INVALID_HANDLE_VALUE)
      return FILTER_E_ACCESS;
  }
  else
    return E_FAIL;

  // Enumerate OLE properties, since any NTFS file can have them

  *pFlags = IFILTER_FLAGS_OLE_PROPERTIES;

  // Re-initialize

  ChunkID = 1;
  return S_OK;
}
```

The CTeXFilter::GetChunk method retrieves the source data in chunks of 10,000 bytes. Each chunk is read into a chunk buffer in turn. After a chunk is read into the buffer, it's converted to wide-character (Unicode) form using the current ANSI code page. The support function ConvertCP2Wide provides this conversion functionality. After the buffer conversion all subsequent manipulations are performed, and results are returned, in Unicode.

SQL Server automatically calls the filter's GetChunk method when you indicate that all text has been returned from the current chunk. When all chunks have been processed, the GetChunk method returns the FILTER_E_END_OF_CHUNKS status. If a chunk has been successfully retrieved, GetChunk returns S_OK. Listing 10-12 shows the CTeXFilter::GetChunk method.

Listing 10-12. *CTeXFilter::GetChunk Method*

```
SCODE STDMETHODCALLTYPE CTeXFilter::GetChunk
(
  STAT_CHUNK * pStat
)
```

```
{
  if (FileHandle == INVALID_HANDLE_VALUE)
    return FILTER_E_ACCESS;

  // Read characters from single-byte file

  char InBuffer[TEXT_FILTER_CHUNK_SIZE];

  if (!ReadFile
    (
      FileHandle,
      InBuffer,
      TEXT_FILTER_CHUNK_SIZE,
      &Chunk_Length,
      NULL
    )
  )
    return FILTER_E_ACCESS;
  else if (Chunk_Length == 0)
    _Eof = true;

  if (!Contents_Req_Flag || _Eof)
    return FILTER_E_END_OF_CHUNKS;

  ConvertCP2Wide(InBuffer, CodePage, Chunk_Length);

  // Set chunk description

  pStat->idChunk    = ChunkID;
  pStat->breakType = CHUNK_NO_BREAK;
  pStat->flags      = CHUNK_TEXT;
  pStat->locale     = GetSystemDefaultLCID();
  pStat->attribute.guidPropSet        = guidStorage;
  pStat->attribute.psProperty.ulKind = PRSPEC_PROPID;
  pStat->attribute.psProperty.propid = PID_STG_CONTENTS;
  pStat->idChunkSource  = ChunkID;
  pStat->cwcStartSource = 0;
  pStat->cwcLenSource   = 0;

  ChunkID++;
  Chunk_Read_Pos = 0;
  CurrentChar = Chunk_Buffer;
  return S_OK;
}
```

Once the source buffer has been populated and converted to Unicode, it's time to start reading the text from the buffer line by line. The CTeXFilter::GetText method provides this functionality. Once the buffer has been filled with GetChunk, SQL Server calls the GetText method continuously until the buffer has been depleted. It's within the GetText method that we perform special processing, such as recognizing comments, markup tags, and special characters. During processing, we also process end-of-line and end-of-buffer conditions. Listing 10-13 shows the GetText method.

Listing 10-13. *CTeXFilter::GetText Method*

```
SCODE STDMETHODCALLTYPE CTeXFilter::GetText
(
  ULONG * GetText_Buffer_Length,
  WCHAR * GetText_Buffer
)
{
  if (Chunk_Buffer == NULL)   // If buffer is empty, return no more text status
    return FILTER_E_NO_MORE_TEXT;

  // Initialize variables
  ULONG GetText_Write_Pos = 0;
  ULONG Output_Buffer_Length = *(GetText_Buffer_Length);
  bool Done_Flag = false;

  // Grab the first char, and continue grabbing chars until
  // end of buffer, output buffer full, or other done indicator
  WCHAR Wch = GetChar();
  while (
    (GetText_Write_Pos < Output_Buffer_Length) &&
    (!Eob()) &&
    (!Done_Flag)
  )
  {
    if (!In_Comment_Flag)    // If not in a comment then check these
    {
      if (Wch == '\\')       // Look for a markup tag leading backslash
      {
        Markup_Tag = L"";
        GetMarkup();         // Get the markup tag
        Wch = ' ';
      }
      if (In_Markup_Flag)    // If in a markup tag already, continue
                             // getting markup
      {
        GetMarkup();
        Wch = ' ';
      }
      if (Wch == '%')        // If a comment start, set in comment flag
```

```
      {
        *(GetText_Buffer + GetText_Write_Pos) = ' ';
        In_Comment_Flag = true;
      }
      else if (Eol())          // If at end of line then done flag
      {
        *(GetText_Buffer + GetText_Write_Pos) = Wch;
        In_Comment_Flag = false;
        Done_Flag = true;
      }
      else                     // Otherwise just output the char to the buffer
      {
        *(GetText_Buffer + GetText_Write_Pos) = Wch;
      }
      GetText_Write_Pos++;     // Increment output buffer pointer
    }
    else
    {
      if (Eol())               // If at end of line then done
      {
        In_Comment_Flag = false;
        Done_Flag = true;
        *(GetText_Buffer + GetText_Write_Pos) = Wch;
        GetText_Write_Pos++;
      }
    }
    Wch = GetChar();           // Get next character
  }

  // Set the output text buffer length
  *GetText_Buffer_Length = GetText_Write_Pos;

  // If the output buffer length is 0, delete the buffer
  if (GetText_Write_Pos == 0)
  {
    delete Chunk_Buffer;
    Chunk_Buffer = NULL;
    return FILTER_E_NO_MORE_TEXT;
  }

  return S_OK;
}
```

The GetText method depends on several private functions, including the following:

- GetChar, which retrieves the text from the buffer one character at a time

- UngetChar, which puts a single character back on the buffer

- GetMarkup, which reads and subsequently processes markup tags

As each line of the buffer is read and processed, it's written back to the output buffer. The output buffer and the number of characters in the output buffer are both returned when a call to GetText completes. The text returned by GetText is subsequently fed into word breakers to complete the indexing process.

CHUNKING AND EFFICIENCY

Data is read in chunks for efficiency reasons. If you had to read an entire 50, 100, or 500 MB file into memory all at once in order to index it, you'd tie up a lot of server resources, including CPU and memory, for an extended period of time. Multiply that by 10, 100, or 1,000 files of that size and you could cause a serious drain on your server until indexing completes. By reading the data in small chunks of well-defined size, you get the benefit of being able to amortize the resource cost of indexing over a longer period of time, ensuring that filtering and indexing documents doesn't bring your server to its knees. Chunking does introduce some complexities, however, which we'll describe later in this section.

While the design for the GetText routine is relatively simple, it's complicated by the fact that you're retrieving the text from the file in chunks. You essentially have to maintain some state information between calls to GetText. For instance, if GetText is in the middle of a comment in the buffer when the method ends due to an end of buffer condition, and you haven't reached the end of line yet, GetText needs to resume reading the comment once the buffer has been refreshed with a new chunk.

To keep this example simple, we decided to simply retrieve the data a single line at a time with GetText; however, more complex design patterns are possible. For instance, it's possible to populate an internal memory structure, such as a linked list or b-tree, with the contents of structured source data in the index. Subsequent calls to GetText could be used to traverse the in-memory structure and return elements from memory.

The balance of the remaining filter code represents support functions, such as EatLine and EatBraces, which grab characters from the input buffer in response to calls from the DoMarkup routine. The DoMarkup routine itself handles LaTeX markup tags.

Compiling and Installing the Filter

There are four steps required to compile and install a filter for SQL Server 2008 iFTS:

1. Compile the source code.

2. Copy the DLL to the Windows\System32 directory.

3. Register the DLL on the server and create appropriate registry entries.

4. Configure SQL Server to load unsigned system resources.

We'll cover all of these steps in this section. To perform the first step, filter compilation, simply load the TeXFilt solution into Visual Studio and choose Build ➤ Compile from the menu, as illustrated in Figure 10-6.

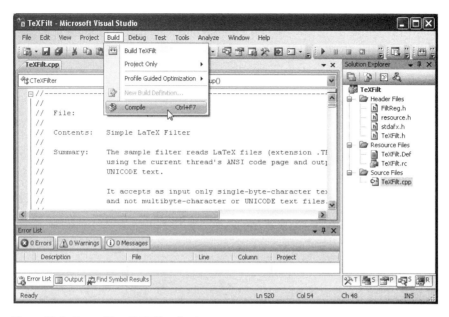

Figure 10-6. *Compiling TeXFilt solution*

The result of compiling the solution is a DLL called `TeXFilt.dll`. To perform the second and third steps, copy the filter file to the `Windows\System32` directory and run `regsvr32` on it, as shown in Figure 10-7.

Figure 10-7. *Copying the DLL to the System32 directory and registering it*

Filter DLL registration for SQL Server also requires that additional registry entries be created. Although these additional registry entries are often included in the registration methods of the DLL, we've decided to separate them out into a separate TeXFilt.reg file because it's easier to read. After copying the DLL and running regsvr32, double-click the TeXFilt.reg file to install the appropriate registry entries. The registry entries are shown in Listing 10-14.

Listing 10-14. *TeXFilt.reg Filter Registry Entries*

```
Windows Registry Editor Version 5.00

[HKEY_CLASSES_ROOT\.tex]
@="LaTeX.Document"

[HKEY_CLASSES_ROOT\.tex\PersistentHandler]
@="{51BFBAD1-09B0-4BD4-9509-FD09E26FF32A}"

[HKEY_LOCAL_MACHINE\SOFTWARE\Classes\LaTeX.Document]
@="Class for LaTeX Documents"

[HKEY_LOCAL_MACHINE\SOFTWARE\Classes\LaTeX.Document\CLSID]
@="{098f2470-bae0-11cd-b579-08002b30bfeb}"

[HKEY_LOCAL_MACHINE\SOFTWARE\Classes\CLSID\{098f2470-bae0-11cd-b579-➥
08002b30bfeb}]
@="LaTeX Document Files"

[HKEY_LOCAL_MACHINE\SOFTWARE\Classes\CLSID\{098f2470-bae0-11cd-b579-➥
08002b30bfeb}\CLSID]
@="{51BFBAD1-09B0-4BD4-9509-FD09E26FF32A}"

[HKEY_LOCAL_MACHINE\SOFTWARE\Classes\CLSID\{51BFBAD1-09B0-4BD4-9509-➥
FD09E26FF32A}]
@="LaTeX Document Persistent Handler"

[HKEY_LOCAL_MACHINE\SOFTWARE\Classes\CLSID\{51BFBAD1-09B0-4BD4-9509-➥
FD09E26FF32A}\PersistentAddinsRegistered\{89bcb740-6119-101a-bcb7-00dd010655af}]
@="{6fc40ad8-8657-4429-a816-abef6974b763}"

[HKEY_LOCAL_MACHINE\SOFTWARE\Classes\CLSID\{6fc40ad8-8657-4429-a816-➥
abef6974b763}]
@="LaTeX Document Filter"

[HKEY_LOCAL_MACHINE\SOFTWARE\Classes\CLSID\{6fc40ad8-8657-4429-a816-➥
abef6974b763}\InprocServer32]
@="c:\\windows\\system32\\TeXFilt.dll"
```

When SQL Server needs to index a document, it traverses the registry to match the document type with the appropriate filter. Figure 10-8 shows a simplified version of how SQL Server uses the registry to connect the file extension .tex to the TeXFilt.dll filter.

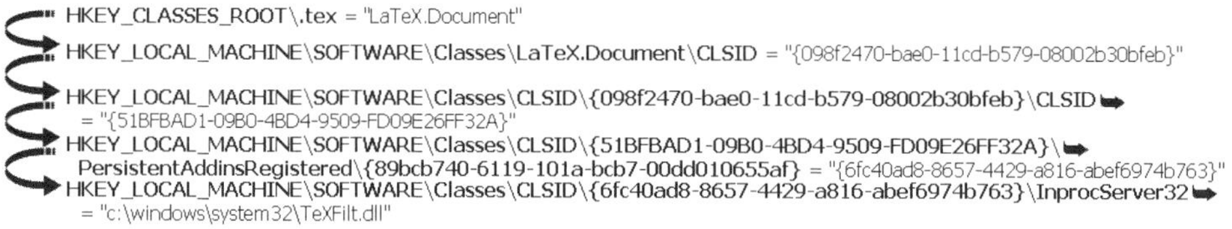

HKEY_CLASSES_ROOT\.tex = "LaTeX.Document"
HKEY_LOCAL_MACHINE\SOFTWARE\Classes\LaTeX.Document\CLSID = "{098f2470-bae0-11cd-b579-08002b30bfeb}"
HKEY_LOCAL_MACHINE\SOFTWARE\Classes\CLSID\{098f2470-bae0-11cd-b579-08002b30bfeb}\CLSID
  = "{51BFBAD1-09B0-4BD4-9509-FD09E26FF32A}"
HKEY_LOCAL_MACHINE\SOFTWARE\Classes\CLSID\{51BFBAD1-09B0-4BD4-9509-FD09E26FF32A}\
  PersistentAddinsRegistered\{89bcb740-6119-101a-bcb7-00dd010655af} = "{6fc40ad8-8657-4429-a816-abef6974b763}"
HKEY_LOCAL_MACHINE\SOFTWARE\Classes\CLSID\{6fc40ad8-8657-4429-a816-abef6974b763}\InprocServer32
  = "c:\windows\system32\TeXFilt.dll"

Figure 10-8. *Traversing the registry to relate a file extension to the appropriate filter DLL*

On the SQL Server side, you need to tell SQL Server to load OS resources and turn off signature verifications for iFTS components. Listing 10-15 shows a script that will do this for you.

Listing 10-15. *Configuring SQL Server to Load Unsigned Filters*

```
EXEC sys.sp_fulltext_service N'load_os_resources', 1;
GO


EXEC sys.sp_fulltext_service N'verify_signature', 0;
GO


EXEC sys.sp_fulltext_service N'update_languages', NULL;
GO
```

Testing the Filter

You can use the utilities provided in the Platform SDK to test your custom filters. The Platform SDK provides three tools for testing your filters, all located in the Platform SDK bin subdirectory. The first tool is filtreg.exe. Running this tool at the command line shows you a list of all registered filters on the computer, as shown in Figure 10-9. This is useful for determining whether your filter is installed correctly. The LaTeX filter is shown highlighted in the figure.

■**Tip** Microsoft supplies several tools, utilities, and code samples in the Windows Platform SDK. The Platform SDK can be downloaded for free from www.microsoft.com/downloads. We highly recommend downloading and installing the Platform SDK if you're developing custom filters and other iFTS components.

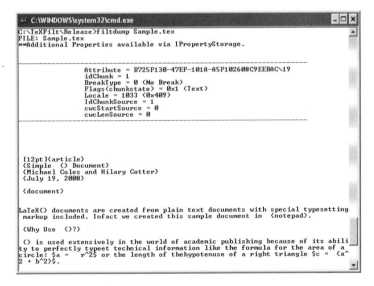

```
.sym --> Null filter (query.dll)
.sys --> Null filter (query.dll)
.sy_ --> Null filter (query.dll)
.tar --> Null filter (query.dll)
.tex --> TeX Filter (TeXFilt.dll)
.tgz --> Null filter (query.dll)
.tif --> MODI Document Filter class (C:\PROGRA~1\COMMON~1\MICROS~1\MODI\11.0\MSP
FILT.DLL)
.tiff --> MODI Document Filter class (C:\PROGRA~1\COMMON~1\MICROS~1\MODI\11.0\MS
PFILT.DLL)
.tlb --> Null filter (query.dll)
.tsp --> Null filter (query.dll)
.ttc --> Null filter (query.dll)
.ttf --> Null filter (query.dll)
.txt --> Plain Text filter (query.dll)
.URL --> Plain Text filter (query.dll)
.vbs --> Plain Text filter (query.dll)
.vbx --> Null filter (query.dll)
.vdx --> Microsoft Office Visio IFilter (C:\Program Files\Common Files\Microsoft
 Shared\Visio Shared\VISFILT.DLL)
.vsd --> Microsoft Office Visio IFilter (C:\Program Files\Common Files\Microsoft
 Shared\Visio Shared\VISFILT.DLL)
.vss --> Microsoft Office Visio IFilter (C:\Program Files\Common Files\Microsoft
 Shared\Visio Shared\VISFILT.DLL)
.vst --> Microsoft Office Visio IFilter (C:\Program Files\Common Files\Microsoft
 Shared\Visio Shared\VISFILT.DLL)
.vsx --> Microsoft Office Visio IFilter (C:\Program Files\Common Files\Microsoft
 Shared\Visio Shared\VISFILT.DLL)
.vtx --> Microsoft Office Visio IFilter (C:\Program Files\Common Files\Microsoft
 Shared\Visio Shared\VISFILT.DLL)
.vxd --> Null filter (query.dll)
.wav --> Null filter (query.dll)
.wax --> Null filter (query.dll)
.wll --> Null filter (query.dll)
.wlt --> Null filter (query.dll)
.wm --> Null filter (query.dll)
.wma --> Null filter (query.dll)
.wmf --> Null filter (query.dll)
```

Figure 10-9. *Filtreg.exe registered filter list*

The second tool is filtdump.exe. This tool takes the name of a document as a parameter. It automatically loads the correct filter based on the file extension and filters the document contents. The result is that you see exactly the type of output SQL Server iFTS gets when it invokes the filter on documents of the same type. This is particularly useful for troubleshooting the GetChunk and GetText methods. Figure 10-10 shows the output of filtdump.exe on the Sample.tex document.

```
C:\TeXFilt\Release>filtdump Sample.tex
FILE: Sample.tex
**Additional Properties available via IPropertyStorage.

---------------------------------------------------------
          Attribute = B725F130-47EF-101A-A5F102608C9EEBAC\19
          idChunk = 1
          BreakType = 0 (No Break)
          Flags(chunkstate) = 0x1 (Text)
          Locale = 1033 (0x409)
          IdChunkSource = 1
          cwcStartSource = 0
          cwcLenSource = 0
---------------------------------------------------------




[12pt](article)
(Simple  () Document)
(Michael Coles and Hilary Cotter)
(July 19, 2008)

(document)


LaTeX() documents are created from plain text documents with special typesetting
 markup included. Infact we created this sample document in  (notepad).

(Why Use  ()?)

() is used extensively in the world of academic publishing because of its abili
ty to perfectly typeet technical information like the formula for the area of a
circle: $a =   r^2$ or the length of thehypotenuse of a right triangle $c = (a^
2 + b^2)$.
```

Figure 10-10. *Results of filtdump.exe*

The `ifilttst.exe` filter test utility is located in the `bin\winnt` subdirectory of the Platform SDK. This tool accepts command-line switches such as `/i` to specify an input file name, `/d` to specify a file dump, and `/l` to specify logging to a file. The following command line shows how to run ifilttst.exe on the `Sample.tex` file:

```
ifilttst /i Sample.tex /d /l
```

The results are output to the following files:

- `Sample.tex.dmp`: a dump file that contains the output of the filter produced by `ifilttst.exe`

- `Sample.tex.log`: a log file that shows the result of all the calls to the filter methods that `ifilttst.exe` tests

Figure 10-11 shows a portion of the `Sample.tex.log` file generated by `ifilttst.exe`.

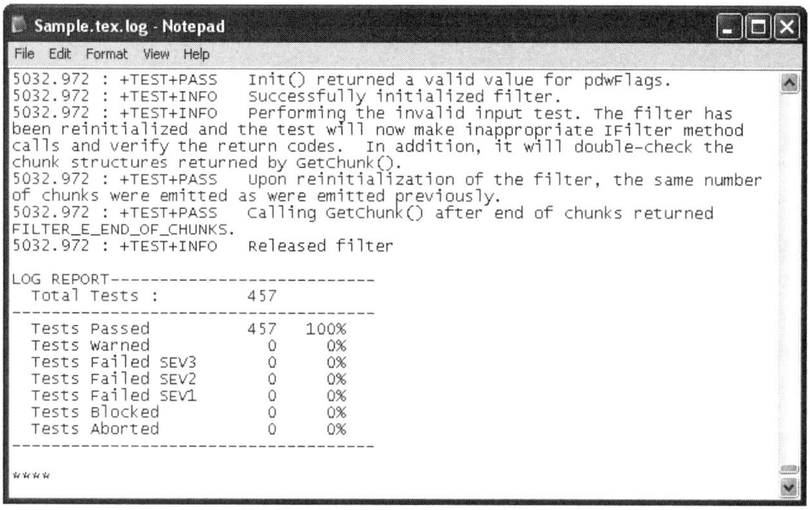

Figure 10-11. *Results of ifilttst.exe*

In addition to the tools that come free with the Platform SDK, there's a tool called IFilter Explorer, available from Citeknet at `www.citeknet.com`. This tool lets you view all of the filters installed on your computer, for all applications that use them. Figure 10-12 shows the IFilter Explorer in action.

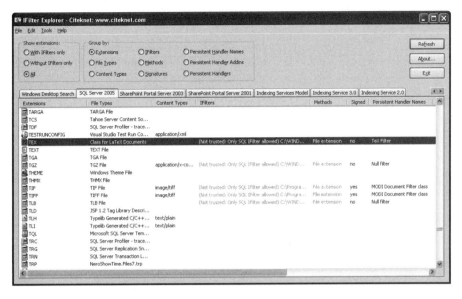

Figure 10-12. *Citeknet IFilter Explorer*

Gatherer and Protocol Handler

The gatherer and protocol handler are two closely related components. The protocol handler is a data source–specific component that feeds the gatherer during full-text crawl operations. The protocol handler component supplied with SQL Server is specific to SQL Server, and provides connectivity and communication capabilities between SQL Server and iFTS. Because of its data source–specific functionality, it's unlikely that you'll need to create a custom protocol handler for SQL Server; generally the need for custom protocol handlers is based on a requirement to use Indexing Service to index data in a custom data source.

The gatherer component is responsible for scheduling and driving full-text index population. The gatherer works in conjunction with the full-text crawl threads, in turn launching the filter daemon process that manages filters.

Word Breakers and Stemmers

Word breakers are language-specific components that literally break up the text returned by the IFilter::GetText method into individual words. The rules that define exactly what consti-tutes a word vary depending on the language. Consider the following two sys.dm_fts_parser queries:

```
-- Parse 'data-base' in English
SELECT *
FROM sys.dm_fts_parser('data-base', 1033, 0, 0);

-- Parse 'data-base' in German
SELECT *
FROM sys.dm_fts_parser('data-base', 1031, 0, 0);
```

The English and German word breakers in this instance treat the hyphen differently. The English word breaker breaks the word into three pieces: *data*, *base*, and *database*. The German word breaker enforces a more strict interpretation of the hyphen, returning only *data* and *base*.

The word breaker feeds its words into the stemmer to retrieve stemmed versions of the words. The stemmer takes your words and returns variants, including verb conjugations and pluralized nouns, based on a language-specific dictionary lookup. For instance, the stemmer is responsible for returning the search terms *goes*, *going*, *gone*, and *went* when you specify a search for the inflectional forms of the word *go*. We discuss inflectional word forms in detail in Chapter 3.

The word breaker and stemmer are so closely interrelated that they're implemented within the same DLL. Like filters, word breakers and stemmers are COM-based. Word breakers implement the IWordBreaker interface, while stemmers implement the IStemmer interface.

■**Note** Both of these interfaces are documented at Microsoft's MSDN web site: http://msdn.microsoft.com.

The Platform SDK includes a simple example of a word breaker and stemmer combination DLL, referred to as the *language resource sample* (or *lrsample* for short). The lrsample shows how to create a simple word breaker that recognizes word-breaking characters and tokenizes words from input. It also includes a simple stemmer that performs a dictionary lookup to return inflectional forms of a small set of words.

■**Tip** It's unlikely that you'll encounter a need to create custom word breakers and stemmers. The excep-tions are if you decide to implement support for a language that's currently not supported by iFTS, or if your business is a third-party provider of such tools.

Summary

In this chapter, we discussed the details of full-text search components including filters, word breakers, and stemmers. We talked about the built-in iFTS filters, as well as additional filters available from Microsoft and third parties, and then demonstrated the creation of your own COM-based filters. We detailed the COM implementation including the interfaces you must implement in order to create a custom filter.

We also discussed word breakers and stemmers, which are language-specific. Generally speaking, the only time you'll need to install or create a custom word breaker or stemmer is for specialized applications, such as implementing support for a language that's not supported by default.

CHAPTER 11

Advanced Search Techniques

A computer will do what you tell it to do, but that may be much different from what you had in mind.

—Joseph Weizenbaum

The focus of this book has been on full-text search, specifically the SQL Server 2008 iFTS implementation. Full-text search falls into a class of search technologies known as *fuzzy search*. The main idea behind fuzzy search is that the computer should accept user requests and return what the user actually wants, which as we all know is not necessarily the same as what was asked for. While iFTS is a highly optimized and proven technology for performing fuzzy searches on documents and large blocks of textual information stored in the database, it's not ideal for other types of searches. We'll explore some of these additional search requirements in this chapter and provide sample code to fulfill these needs.

Spelling Suggestion and Correction

A common user request is for a means of taking user input and suggesting spelling corrections for misspelled words. If your user inputs *cw*, for instance, you might want to suggest possible corrections such as *cow* and *caw*. Many proposed solutions for this problem introduce inefficiencies, because they involve prefix and mid-string wildcard searches that don't work well with most indexing structures.

Though not natively supported by SQL Server, there is a data structure that provides an excellent facility for this type of fuzzy matching. The *ternary search tree* has the efficiency of a string prefix tree (or *trie*, which is a "digital tree") with the space efficiency of a binary tree. Unlike binary trees, in which each node has two child nodes, each node in a ternary search tree has three child nodes: a low child node, a high child node, and a middle child node. Figure 11-1 shows the structure of a small ternary search tree. This ternary search tree contains five short words: *cash, caw, cow, dog,* and *fish*. Note that although each node logically has three child nodes, we've eliminated all empty child nodes from the diagram to keep the representation simple.

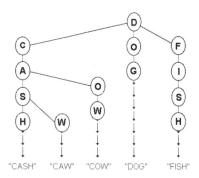

Figure 11-1. *Ternary search tree structure*

The ternary search tree has some interesting properties that we can take advantage of to implement spelling suggestion and spell checking functionality, including the following:

- Each node of the tree stores a single character for comparison, making searches of the tree extremely efficient.

- Ternary search trees can quickly retrieve words containing single-character wildcards.

- Words that are similar tend to group together within the tree structure. It's this last property, known as a *near neighbors*, that we'll exploit to create a SQL Server–based spelling suggestion feature.

Hamming Distance

When you search for word suggestions based on a given input string, how do you measure the similarity of dictionary words against the input string? The answer is *Hamming distance*. The Hamming distance of two strings (strings of characters or strings of bits, in fact) of equal length is the number of differences between them. Another way of thinking about Hamming distance is the number of actions required to convert one string to another. Converting the word *cow* to *dog*, for instance, requires two changes: replacing the initial *c* with the letter *d* and replacing the final *w* with the letter *g*. Therefore, the Hamming distance (or *edit distance*) between these two words is 2.

Note The *edit distance* between two strings is the difference between them, as measured by the number of deletions, insertions, replacements (and in some algorithms, two-character transpositions) required to convert one string into another. Edit distance is actually a generalization of Hamming distance, though the terms can be used nearly interchangeably for our purposes.

Spelling Suggestion Implementation

We decided to implement a ternary search tree–based spelling suggestion feature for SQL CLR in C#. We used the excellent C# ternary search tree implementation by Jonathan de Halleux, with only a few minor modifications, as the basis for our SQL CLR assembly. We won't dive deeply into the ternary search tree implementation, but Jonathan's source code is available for download at http://www.codeproject.com/KB/recipes/tst.aspx if you want to get into the details.

The iFTS_Books database contains a table called dbo.Dictionary. This dictionary contains more than 43,000 words from the "alternate unofficial" *12Dicts* dictionary, compiled by Kevin Atkinson. The *12Dicts* dictionary and other dictionaries are available for download at ftp://ftp.gnu.org/gnu/aspell/dict/0index.html. The assembly we've created for spelling suggestion, called SpellCheck, has four public methods that are exposed as SQL CLR stored procedures:

- The ReloadDictionary procedure loads the dictionary from the dbo.Dictionary table into the internal ternary search tree structure. Populating the tree involves opening a context connection to the database and querying the dbo.Dictionary table to get all the dictionary entries.

- The GetDictionary procedure lists all of the dictionary entries stored in the internal ternary search tree structure. This is useful for debugging purposes, since the recomposed ternary search tree contents should match the contents of the dbo.Dictionary table.

- The GetSuggestions procedure accepts two parameters: an input string and an edit distance. This procedure traverses the ternary search tree and returns all entries that are within the specified edit distance of the input string. The procedure also returns a column containing the actual calculated edit distance, so you can see exactly how far apart the dictionary entries are from your input string.

- The GetMatch procedure is a bonus procedure we've included to demonstrate the ternary search tree's wildcard searching ability. The procedure accepts a single parameter, an input string, which can contain *?* wildcard characters. The wildcard characters match a single character in the string, so that *c?w* will match the dictionary words *cow* and *caw*.

SQL CLR SHARED STATE

In order to make the code as efficient as possible, the SQL CLR assembly stores a static ternary search tree in memory. This introduces the practical issue of maintaining shared state within the assembly, something that SQL CLR takes very seriously. One issue with shared state is maintaining integrity when multiple users are simultaneously updating and accessing the shared state. Based on our design, updating the static ternary search tree is an all-at-once operation. Dealing with simultaneous updates isn't as big an issue as it would otherwise be.

The other issue is that SQL Server can unload an AppDomain completely at any point if an error occurs or if memory pressure demands it. Because of this, we perform a check every time you run the GetSuggestions or GetMatch procedure to see if the ternary search tree is populated. If not, the assembly kicks off the method that populates the tree.

When you run the `GetSuggestions` procedure as in Listing 11-1, it returns results like those shown in Figure 11-2.

Listing 11-1. *Getting Suggestions for the String "cow"*

```
EXEC dbo.GetSuggestions 'cow', 2;
```

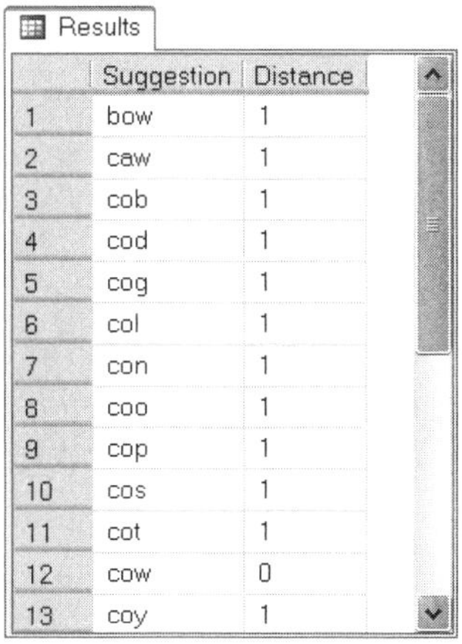

	Suggestion	Distance
1	bow	1
2	caw	1
3	cob	1
4	cod	1
5	cog	1
6	col	1
7	con	1
8	coo	1
9	cop	1
10	cos	1
11	cot	1
12	cow	0
13	coy	1

Figure 11-2. *Suggestions within an edit distance of two for the word "cow"*

For this example, the procedure returns 23 suggestions. Note that the suggestions returned are all less than the edit distance specified in the query. A distance of 0 represents an exact match. You can use the `Distance` column to sort results in client applications based on relevance. If you expand the search by increasing the edit distance, you'll get significantly larger numbers of results. As a rule, we'd recommend using an edit distance of 2 or 3 in most instances to keep the result set manageable.

We've also included a C# Windows forms spell check client in the download code. When you run this sample client in Visual Studio, it automatically retrieves word suggestions from SQL Server as you type. You can also change the sensitivity level, which adjusts edit distance specified in the stored procedure calls. This type of utility is easily adaptable to Web 2.0–style applications, where this type of functionality is demanded by sophisticated users. Figure 11-3 shows a sample of the client application in action.

The bonus procedure we've included, `GetMatch`, demonstrates simple wildcard searching with the ternary search tree. Listing 11-2 calls this procedure to return all words from the dictionary that are five characters long, begin with the letter *c*, and contain the letter *d* in the third position. The second, fourth, and fifth characters are unknown, as represented by the wildcard *?* character. The results are shown in Figure 11-4.

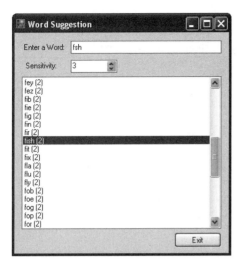

Figure 11-3. *Word suggestions for the word "fsh" in a client application*

Listing 11-2. *Wildcard Search in the Ternary Search Tree*

```
EXEC dbo.GetMatch 'c?d??';
```

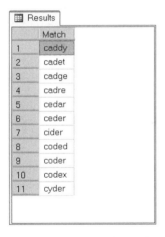

Figure 11-4. *Wildcard search against the ternary search tree*

Name Searching

Another area in which fuzzy search techniques are often needed, but where full-text search doesn't necessarily help, is name-based searching. Searching for customer or other information in a database by name is a common scenario. Unfortunately, there are many factors at play, not the least of which is the countless number of ways to pronounce different words with similar spellings. This is particularly bad with surnames, which are often derived from other languages with different (often regional) pronunciation rules from English.

Another problem, particularly with the English language, is the dizzying array of exceptions to every rule in the language. George Bernard Shaw used the made-up word *ghoti* as an example to demonstrate some of the strange rules of English. Ghoti is an imagined alternate spelling for the word *fish*. This alternate spelling applies the following rules of English:

- *gh* is pronounced *f* as in *cough*.

- *o* is pronounced *i* as in *women*.

- *ti* is pronounced *sh* as in *nation*.

Although ghoti is a contrived example, it encapsulates many of the problems involved in name-based searching. The fact of the matter is that someone searching for a name pronounced "jeer-a-dell-ee" might have to search for several variations including *Jeradelli, Jaerardeli, Ghiradelli, Jheradeli*, and possibly many others. Wouldn't it be great if you could enter a search string that approximated the sound of a name and still locate the necessary customer (or other) records? One answer to this problem is *phonetic search*.

Phonetic Search

Phonetic search includes methods of encoding words as their phonetic equivalents. It's implemented by algorithms that attempt to approximate the pronunciation of words. Back in the early 20th century, Robert Russell and Margaret O'Dell patented a sound-based indexing system known as Soundex. The Soundex system was designed for indexing U.S. Census Bureau records from the late 19th century. Many modern phonetic algorithms are based, to some degree, on Soundex.

Of course, Soundex has many shortcomings, not the least of which is its simplicity, which was actually its prime asset before the age of computers. Soundex encoding was designed so that it could be performed by clerks with varying levels of education. The rules had to be formulaic in their simplicity, easy to memorize, and capable of being implemented with the most rudimentary of tools (for example, with pencil, paper, and an occasional preprinted template). This simplicity doesn't work well these days, due in large part to a great increase in surnames of non–Western European origin.

Fortunately for us, several people have developed more advanced Soundex replacements, all of which improve upon the algorithm in some areas but inherit some of Soundex's limitations in other areas. In this section, we'll discuss some of these phonetic search algorithms.

Soundex

SQL Server includes a version of the Soundex algorithm natively via the SOUNDEX function. When you pass a string to the SOUNDEX function, it returns a four-character phonetic encoding. Soundex codes consist of an alphabetic character followed by three numbers, each representing a grouping of letters that are pronounced similarly. For instance, the letters *B*, *F*, *P*, and *V* are all grouped together and converted to a numeric code of 1.

SQL Server also provides Soundex match scoring via the DIFFERENCE function. The DIFFERENCE function accepts two strings, Soundex-encodes them, and then compares the encoded values. DIFFERENCE returns values between 0 (worst match) and 4 (best match). Listing 11-3 uses the

DIFFERENCE and SOUNDEX functions to retrieve surnames from the dbo.Surnames table that have a Soundex code close to the code for *Johnson*. Partial results are shown in Figure 11-5.

Listing 11-3. *Using SQL Server's SOUNDEX and DIFFERENCE Functions*

```
SELECT
  Id,
  Surname,
  SOUNDEX(Surname) AS Surname_Soundex,
  DIFFERENCE(Surname, N'Johnson') AS Soundex_Difference
FROM dbo.Surnames
WHERE DIFFERENCE(Surname, N'Johnson') >= 3;
```

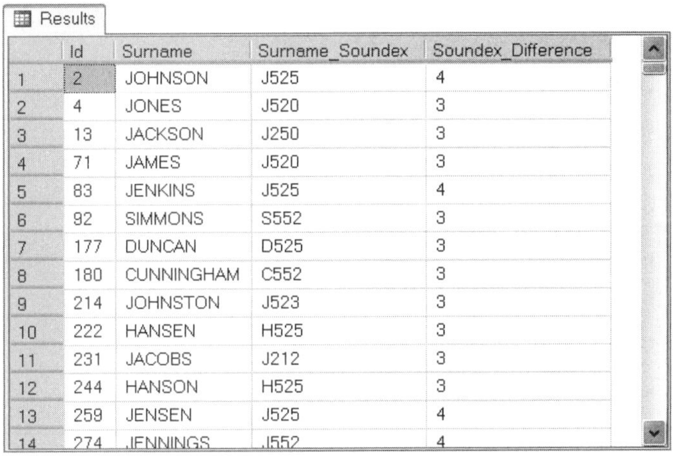

	Id	Surname	Surname_Soundex	Soundex_Difference
1	2	JOHNSON	J525	4
2	4	JONES	J520	3
3	13	JACKSON	J250	3
4	71	JAMES	J520	3
5	83	JENKINS	J525	4
6	92	SIMMONS	S552	3
7	177	DUNCAN	D525	3
8	180	CUNNINGHAM	C552	3
9	214	JOHNSTON	J523	3
10	222	HANSEN	H525	3
11	231	JACOBS	J212	3
12	244	HANSON	H525	3
13	259	JENSEN	J525	4
14	274	JENNINGS	J552	4

Figure 11-5. *Surnames matched for closeness by Soundex*

As you can see from the matches that Soundex returns—most people wouldn't tell you that *James* sounds like *Cunningham*—Soundex is not the most accurate algorithm available. In fact, Soundex is infamous for returning a lot of false positives and poor matches. There are other algorithms available including improvements to Soundex, such as the NYSIIS algorithm we'll cover in the next section.

NYSIIS

The *New York State Identification and Intelligence System (NYSIIS)* was created as a Soundex replacement in 1970. NYSIIS performs a function similar to Soundex; namely, it creates a phonetic version of an input name. The phonetic version is a rough representation of the way a name is pronounced. Consider Table 11-1, which contrasts the phonetic encodings generated by both the NYSIIS and Soundex algorithms for the same surnames.

Table 11-1. *Comparison of NYSIIS and Soundex Sample Phonetic Encodings*

Surname	NYSIIS	Soundex
BARRIOS	BAR	B620
BURROWS	BAR	B620
BARRAZ	BAR	B620
CALE	CAL	C400
COLAS	CAL	C420
COLES	CAL	C420
KOHLES	CAL	K420
DUNN	DAN	D500
DEAN	DAN	D500
DENNIS	DAN	D520
DOWNS	DAN	D520
PILON	PALAN	P450
PULLINS	PALAN	P452
PULLIN	PALAN	P450
PALIN	PALAN	P450
SIMS	SAN	S520
SIMMS	SAN	S520
SAMS	SAN	S520

Even though NYSIIS is based on Soundex, the differences in encoding rules used result in quite different encodings in many instances. For one thing, NYSIIS preserves the relative positioning of vowels within a phonetic encoding (it replaces vowels with *A*). Name prefixes are also encoded using different rules. For instance, NYSIIS replaces the letter *K* with *C*, while Soundex always preserves the first letter. Suffix handling is different as well, since NYSIIS strips trailing *S* characters and trailing vowels.

We've implemented the NYSIIS algorithm within a SQL CLR user-defined function called `dbo.NYSIIS` in the `iFTS_Books` sample database. For testing purposes, we've included the `dbo.Surnames` table, which contains the most common 88,000 surnames in the United States as reported by the U.S. Census Bureau. This table contains both a `Surname` column with plain-text surnames and a `Surname_NYSIIS` column with the NYSIIS-encoded versions. Listing 11-4 demonstrates a simple search against this table for names that sound like *Rambo*, courtesy of the `dbo.NYSIIS` function. Results are shown in Figure 11-6.

Listing 11-4. *Searching for Names That Sound Like "Rambo"*

```
SELECT
  Surname,
  Surname_NYSIIS
FROM dbo.Surnames
WHERE Surname_NYSIIS = dbo.NYSIIS(N'Rambo');
```

	Surname	Surname_NYSIIS
1	RAMBO	RANB
2	RUMBO	RANB
3	RAINBOW	RANB
4	ROMBS	RANB
5	RAMBUS	RANB
6	RAMBEAU	RANB

Figure 11-6. *Names that sound like "Rambo"*

As you can see from the results in Figure 11-6, NYSIIS returns better-quality results than Soundex.

String Similarity Metrics

String similarity calculations are another tool that can be used to perform fuzzy searches. *String similarity* is based on similarities between the spelling of two words, rather than pronunciation. String similarity is useful for narrowing down results returned by phonetic search algorithms, or for other situations where you need to calculate the difference between strings.

Longest Common Subsequence

The *longest common subsequence* or *LCS* algorithm is used to calculate the similarity between two strings. LCS compares two strings and retrieves the character subsets they share in common, while maintaining the order of characters. As an example, the LCS for the strings *Joseph* and *Joel* is calculated as shown in Figure 11-7.

The two strings are compared character by character using LCS, and all characters that appear in both strings (in order, though not necessarily contiguous) are combined to create the LCS. Note that, even though the word *Joseph* has an *S* between the *O* and the *E*, the *E* is still considered part of the LCS. The LCS gives you a good approximate calculation of the difference between two strings and provides a good scoring mechanism for calculating a numeric similarity score. LCS and LCS variants are commonly used in a wide variety of applications and utilities (such as diff) that compare files and report their differences.

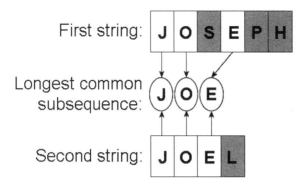

Figure 11-7. *LCS for Joseph and Joel*

▓**Note** Longest common subsequence is not the same as *longest common substring*, though they are easily confused. Longest common substring is actually a specialized application of the longest common subsequence algorithm. Longest common substring requires all characters matched to be contiguous (with no intervening characters in the sequence).

We've implemented the LCS algorithm as a SQL CLR user-defined function named dbo.LCS. The function accepts two strings and returns their LCS. In addition, we've included a function called dbo.ScoreLCS that calculates the LCS for two strings and returns a similarity score. The similarity score is between 0.0 and 1.0, representing the range between no match and a perfect match. This score is calculated by dividing the length of the LCS by the length of the longer input string. Listing 11-5 calculates the LCS and an LCS score for the words *Joseph* and *Joel*. The results are shown in Figure 11-8.

Listing 11-5. *Calculating LCS and Score for Two Strings*

```
SELECT
  dbo.LCS
  (
    N'Joel',
    N'Joseph'
  ) AS LCS,
  dbo.ScoreLCS
  (
    N'Joel',
    N'Joseph'
  ) AS Score;
```

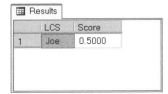

Figure 11-8. *LCS and score for the words Joel and Joseph*

LCS is useful for calculating a similarity metric between two strings; however, it's a rather inefficient algorithm of complexity O(mn), where m and n are the lengths of the two input strings. This algorithm literally builds a matrix with dimensions [m, n], and populates the matrix as it calculates the similarity between the two strings. Because of this complexity, we recommend using another method to narrow down your result set before applying a string similarity algorithm such as LCS to further narrow down your results.

Edit Distance

Another algorithm, closely related to LCS, is edit distance. As we mentioned previously in this chapter, edit distance is a generalized form of Hamming distance. Like Hamming distance and LCS, edit distance is a measure of the similarity (or difference) between two strings.

We've implemented an edit distance algorithm known as the Damerau-Levenshtein Edit Distance as a SQL CLR function. This algorithm acts on two input strings in a manner similar to LCS, by building a matrix. Unlike LCS, Damerau-Levenshtein counts the number of operations required to convert one input string into another. The algorithm accounts for four types of operations:

- *Insertions:* An insertion is a single character that must be inserted into one string to turn it into the other string. For instance, the word *you* needs to have the letter *r* inserted to turn it into the word *your.*

- *Deletions:* A deletion is a single character that must be deleted from one string to turn it into the other string. As an example, the word *places* needs to have the letter *s* deleted to turn it into the word *place.*

- *Replacements:* A replacement is a single character that must be replaced in one string to turn it into the other string. The letter *u* must be replaced with *a* in the word *mush* to turn it into the word *mash,* for instance.

- *Transpositions:* A transposition is a side-by-side swap of two characters in one string to turn it into the other string. Consider the word *cast,* which requires a transposition of the letters *s* and *t* to turn it into the word *cats.*

The Damerau-Levenshtein Edit Distance algorithm is implemented as the function dbo.DamLev. You can call this function with two strings to calculate the edit distance between them. Listing 11-6 calculates the edit distance between the words *lastly* and *listen.* The results are shown in Figure 11-9.

Listing 11-6. *Calculating Damerau-Levenshtein Edit Distance Between the Words "lastly" and "listen"*

```
SELECT dbo.DamLev
(
  N'lastly',
  N'listen'
);
```

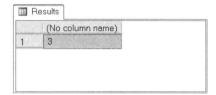

Figure 11-9. *Edit distance between "lastly" and "listen"*

Like the LCS algorithm, Damerau-Levenshtein has a complexity of O(mn), where m and n are the lengths of the two input strings. Because of this, we recommend narrowing down your result set using another method before calculating the edit distance between results.

N-Grams

The complexity of the edit distance and LCS algorithms is generally O(mn), where m and n are the lengths of the two input strings being compared. These algorithms are computationally intensive and aren't efficient for on-the-fly calculations on large data sets. Another algorithm for string comparison that's much more flexible and efficient in T-SQL set-based programming is the *n-gram* algorithm.

The n-gram algorithm requires preprocessing of the strings to be compared. All strings are divided into sequences of contiguous letters of length *n* (generally a length of 3 or 4, *trigrams* and *quadgrams*, are used). By preprocessing the search strings and storing the n-grams in the database, you can use T-SQL's set-based operators to efficiently locate matching approximate strings. Consider Figure 11-10, which shows the trigrams for the surname *Richardson*.

The dbo.GetNGrams SQL CLR function divides a word into n-grams. This function accepts two parameters: a string to process and the length of the n-grams to produce. The result is a table of n-grams, each with an ID number starting with 0 for the first n-gram and increasing from left to right. Listing 11-7 uses the dbo.GetNGrams function to retrieve trigrams for the surname Richardson. Results are shown in Figure 11-11.

Listing 11-7. *Retrieving N-Grams for the Surname Richardson*

```
SELECT *
FROM dbo.GetNGrams
(
  3,
  N'Richardson'
);
```

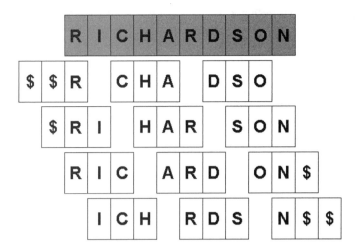

Figure 11-10. *The surname Richardson divided into a set of trigrams*

	Id	nGram
1	0	$$R
2	1	$Ri
3	2	Ric
4	3	ich
5	4	cha
6	5	har
7	6	ard
8	7	rds
9	8	dso
10	9	son
11	10	on$
12	11	n$$

Figure 11-11. *Trigrams produced by dbo.GetNGrams for the surname Richardson*

Once the words are divided into n-grams, you can store them in a table and use simple and efficient T-SQL inner joins to find approximate matches for given strings. The trade-off for n-gram efficiency is increased preprocessing and storage requirements, but the results tend to be both fast and accurate.

The dbo.GetTriGramMatches function performs exactly this type of join against the dbo.Surnames_TriGrams table to retrieve approximate matches for an input surname. The procedure accepts a surname to match and a minimum quality score. The results are returned as a table with the ID for matching surname, the surname itself, and the quality score. The procedure calculates Dice's coefficient to determine the quality of matches. Only matches that have a quality greater than, or equal to, the minimum specified quality score are returned.

The dbo.GetTriGramMatches function is designed as a T-SQL table-valued function and begins with the following function header and results table definitions:

```
CREATE FUNCTION dbo.GetTrigramMatches
(
  @Surname nvarchar(128),
  @Quality decimal(10, 4)
)
RETURNS @r TABLE
(
  Id int PRIMARY KEY NOT NULL,
  Surname nvarchar(128),
  Quality decimal(10, 4)
)
```

The body of the function begins by retrieving the count of trigrams produced by the surname that was passed in as a parameter:

```
DECLARE @i decimal(10, 4);

SELECT @i = COUNT(*)
FROM dbo.GetNGrams(3, @Surname);
```

The function then declares a CTE that performs the bulk of the work, joining the trigrams of the name passed in as a parameter to the dbo.SurnameTriGrams table. The CTE returns three columns: an ID for each surname matched, the matching surname, and Dice's coefficient for matching surnames as a quality metric:

```
WITH NGramCTE
(
  Id,
  Surname,
  Quality
)
AS
(
  SELECT
    t.Surname_Id AS Id,
    s.Surname AS Surname,
    COUNT(t.Surname_Id) * 2.0 / (@i +
      (
        SELECT COUNT(*)
        FROM SurnameTriGrams s1
        WHERE s1.Surname_Id = t.Surname_Id
      )) AS Quality
```

```
FROM SurnameTriGrams t
INNER JOIN Surnames s
  ON t.Surname_ID = s.Id
WHERE EXISTS
(
  SELECT 1
  FROM dbo.GetNGrams(3, @Surname) g
  WHERE g.NGram = t.NGram
)
GROUP BY
  t.Surname_Id,
  s.Surname
)
```

Finally, the function inserts the results of the CTE into the results table, but only where the quality metric is greater than, or equal to, the minimum quality value passed in as a parameter:

```
INSERT INTO @r
 (
  Id,
  Surname,
  Quality
 )
SELECT
  Id,
  Surname,
  Quality
FROM NGramCTE
WHERE Quality >= @Quality;
```

Listing 11-8 shows how to use the dbo.GetTriGramMatches function to retrieve a list of trigram matches for the surname *Smith* with quality of at least 0.6. Results are shown in Figure 11-12.

Listing 11-8. *Retrieving Trigram Matches for the Surname Smith with Quality of at Least 0.6*

```
SELECT *
FROM dbo.GetTriGramMatches
(
  N'Smith',
  0.6
);
```

	Id	Surname	Quality
1	1	SMITH	1.0000
2	4388	NESMITH	0.6250
3	10423	SMITHER	0.6250
4	11153	SMITHEY	0.6250
5	12725	SMIT	0.6154
6	21887	SILVERSMITH	0.6000
7	25498	HYSMITH	0.6250
8	34689	SMITHEE	0.6250
9	34778	SCHMITH	0.6250
10	36802	SMSITH	0.6667
11	39189	SMITHJ	0.6667
12	40940	DESMITH	0.6250
13	41996	STALLSMITH	0.6316
14	45395	SITH	0.6154
15	61796	MITH	0.6154
16	67742	SMITHEN	0.6250
17	78005	SMITHE	0.6667
18	78079	SIXSMITH	0.7059
19	83753	HISMITH	0.6250

Figure 11-12. *Results of trigram matches for surname Smith*

Because the dbo.GetTriGramMatches function uses set-based processing, order is considered unimportant. However, you can increase the accuracy of your results by using positional information in your queries. The dbo.GetTriGramMatches_Distance function performs the same function as dbo.GetTriGramMatches, but it further narrows the results by accepting a distance parameter. The distance calculation enforces another rule on the comparison: matching trigrams must fall within similar relative positions in both strings. The dbo.GetTriGramMatches_Distance function is similar to dbo.GetTriGramMatches, but it includes a BETWEEN predicate in the CTE to limit matching trigrams to those that fall within a specific distance:

```
SELECT
   t.Surname_ID AS Id,
   s.Surname AS Surname,
   COUNT(t.Surname_Id) * 2.0 / (@i +
    (
      SELECT COUNT(*)
      FROM dbo.SurnameTriGrams s1
      WHERE s1.Surname_Id = t.Surname_Id
    )) AS Quality
FROM SurnameTriGrams t
INNER JOIN Surnames s
   ON t.Surname_Id = s.Id
WHERE EXISTS
```

```
  (
  SELECT 1
  FROM dbo.GetNGrams(3, @Surname) g
  WHERE g.NGram = t.NGram
  AND g.Id BETWEEN t.NGram_Id - @Distance AND t.NGram_Id + @Distance
  )
  GROUP BY
    t.Surname_Id,
    s.Surname
```

Listing 11-9 refines the example in Listing 11-8 by specifying a distance of 1, which means that equal trigrams must fall within the range of -1 to +1 positions of each other in both strings to be counted as a match. The results of Listing 11-9 are shown in Figure 11-13. Note that the results have been reduced significantly by narrowing the n-gram relative distances.

Listing 11-9. *Retrieving Trigram Matches with a Distance Indicator*

```
SELECT *
FROM GetTriGramMatches_Distance
(
  N'Smith',
  0.6,
  1
);
```

	Id	Surname	Quality
1	1	SMITH	1.0000
2	10423	SMITHER	0.6250
3	11153	SMITHEY	0.6250
4	12725	SMIT	0.6154
5	34689	SMITHEE	0.6250
6	36802	SMSITH	0.6667
7	39189	SMITHJ	0.6667
8	45395	SITH	0.6154
9	61796	MITH	0.6154
10	67742	SMITHEN	0.6250
11	78005	SMITHE	0.6667

Figure 11-13. *Results of n-gram matches for the surname Smith with additional distance restriction*

N-gram matches are a particularly useful method for finding similarity between strings. When n-grams are treated as sets, their implementation can be quite efficient in T-SQL.

Summary

While full-text search, and SQL Server 2008's iFTS implementation, is great for fuzzy searching of textual data and documents, it's not necessarily the right tool for name-based fuzzy searching. The particular requirements of name-based searching are entirely different from the requirements for document-based searching, so different technology is needed.

In this chapter, we looked at a variety of approximate search technologies that go beyond what full-text search offers. First, we looked at using ternary search trees for spelling suggestion and correction applications. While SQL Server doesn't expose built-in support for ternary search trees, SQL CLR allows us to extend our SQL Server database to support this capability via .NET code.

We also considered simple phonetic matching with SQL Server's built-in SOUNDEX and DIFFERENCE functions. Then we looked at achieving better quality phonetic matches with the more modern NYSIIS phonetic algorithm.

String similarity metrics provide yet another method of fuzzy string matching. We looked at several string similarity algorithms, including the longest common subsequence algorithm, Damerau-Levenshtein Edit Distance, and n-gram matching. We also provided SQL CLR and T-SQL code to implement the wide variety of fuzzy searching algorithms we covered in this chapter.

The authors would like to thank Jonathan de Halleux for providing the base .NET ternary search tree implementation, and Kevin Atkinson for providing the unofficial *12Dicts* dictionary; both of which were used in the spelling suggestion application example.

Glossary

If you wish to converse with me, define your terms.

—Voltaire

During our journey through the functionality in SQL Server 2008 iFTS, we've encountered several terms that may not be familiar and widespread in use. Part of this has to do with the fact that, until this release of SQL Server, full-text search was something of a black art. Only a select few were expert enough at it to take full advantage of the power it provided. In addition, iFTS has removed some terms from the Microsoft full-text lexicon and added new words—some replacements, others brand new. In this appendix, we'll provide definitions for a selection of iFTS-related and other terms that we've used throughout this book.

BLOB
BLOB is an acronym for *binary large object data*. BLOB data can consist of binary documents, graphic images, and other binary data. See also *LOB, CLOB, NCLOB*.

Catalog Views
Catalog views are system views that return information about database objects and catalog metadata. Some of this information isn't accessible through any other means. SQL Server 2008 supports some iFTS-specific catalog views.

CLOB
CLOB is an acronym for *character large object data*. CLOB data consists of large text documents. See also *LOB, BLOB, NCLOB*.

CONTAINS Predicate
SQL Server 2008 supports the CONTAINS predicate, which allows the use of several advanced full-text search options such as inflectional form generation, weighted searches, thesaurus expansions and replacements, phrase searches, and proximity searches. See also *FREETEXT predicate, CONTAINSTABLE function*.

CONTAINSTABLE Function

The CONTAINSTABLE function supports full-text searching with the same options as the CONTAINS predicate, but it returns a table of IDs and rank values for the results. See also *CONTAINS predicate*.

Crawl

See *population*.

Damerau-Levenshtein Edit Distance

The Damerau-Levenshtein Edit Distance algorithm is used to calculate the difference between two strings. Damerau-Levenshtein calculates the number of operations needed to convert one string to another string. The operations counted include deletions, insertions, single-character replacements, and two-character transpositions.

Diacritics Sensitivity

Full-text catalogs (and the indexes they contain) and thesauruses can be made sensitive or insensitive to diacritical marks through the diacritics sensitivity setting. Diacritical marks include grave and acute accent marks, cedilla, and other distinguishing marks.

Dice's Coefficient

Dice's Coefficient is a similarity measure that can be calculated using the following formula:

$$\frac{2 \cdot |x|}{|s| + |t|}$$

where $|x|$ is the number of matching n-grams of two given strings, and $|s|$ and $|t|$ are the number of n-grams in each of the two strings. Dice's Coefficient always falls between 0.0 and 1.0, with 1.0 representing the best match possible.

DocId

The DocId, or Document ID, is an integer surrogate key used by SQL Server to map a table's primary key to the data stored in the full-text index. If you use an integer primary key on your table, SQL Server can eliminate the extra DocId mapping for better performance.

Document

Documents are textual or binary entities indexed and returned by full-text searches.

Dynamic Management Views and Functions

Dynamic Management Views (DMVs) and Dynamic Management Functions (DMFs) return server state information that you can use to retrieve server state information. SQL Server 2008 supports some iFTS-specific DMVs and DMFs.

Edit Distance

Edit distance is a more sophisticated generalization of Hamming distance. Edit distance is calculated by determining the number of operations required to convert one character string into another character string. See also *Hamming distance, Damerau-Levenshtein Edit Distance.*

Expansion Set

A thesaurus expansion set recognizes a word or token and expands the search to include additional words or terms. See also *replacement set.*

Filestream

SQL Server 2008 supports filestream, which is a mechanism for storing BLOB data in the NTFS file system but accessing and managing the data via T-SQL statements and the OpenSqlFileStream API. See also *BLOB.*

Filter

Filters are content-type–specific components that are designed to extract useful data from text-based or binary data. Filters are designed to ignore binary or textual content that is unimportant for purposes of full-text search. Filters invoke language-specific word breakers to tokenize content deemed important for full-text search purposes. See also *word breaker.*

Filter Daemon Host Process

The filter daemon host process (fdhost.exe) is external to the SQL Server process. For security and stability of the SQL Server process, the filter daemon is used to load external filter components.

FREETEXT Predicate

SQL Server 2008 supports the FREETEXT predicate, which performs a full-text search with automatic inflectional form generation and thesaurus expansions and replacements. See also *CONTAINS predicate, FREETEXTTABLE function.*

FREETEXTTABLE Function

The FREETEXTTABLE function supports full-text searching with the same options as the FREETEXT predicate, but it returns a table of IDs and rank values for the results. See also *FREETEXT predicate.*

Full-Text Catalog

In SQL Server 2008, the full-text catalog is simply a logical grouping of one or more full-text indexes. The full-text catalog also defines the diacritics sensitivity settings for the full-text indexes it contains. See also *full-text index, diacritics sensitivity.*

Full-Text Index

A full-text index is an inverted index of one or more documents. SQL Server may store a full-text index entirely in memory or in disk storage. See also *full-text catalog, inverted index.*

Full-Text Search

Full-text search encompasses a variety of techniques used to search textual data and documents. SQL Server 2008 implements full-text search technology in the form of iFTS. See also *Integrated Full-Text Search*.

Fuzzy Search

Fuzzy search encompasses a variety of techniques for searching textual data for approximate matches. Fuzzy search encompasses such technologies as full-text search, phonetic search, substring matching, wildcard searching, n-gram matching, and other approximate or inexact search techniques.

Gatherer

The gatherer component retrieves textual and binary data from database tables, streaming the content to filters for indexing.

Generational Searches

Generational searches are searches that generate inflectional forms of search terms. See also *inflectional forms*.

Hamming Distance

Hamming distance is a measure of the difference between two strings of characters or bits. Hamming distance is determined by calculating the number of operations to turn one string into another string. See also *edit distance*.

IFilter

IFilter is the COM-based interface used by iFTS filter components. Sometimes filters are referred to as IFilters. See also *filter*.

Inflectional Forms

Inflectional forms of words include plural nouns, verb conjugations, and other word forms. SQL Server iFTS can generate inflectional forms of words during searches. See also *generation*.

Integrated Full-Text Search

Integrated Full-Text Search, or iFTS, is the newest version of full-text search functionality available in SQL Server. This version is available beginning with SQL Server 2008 and sports several improvements, including in-database index and stoplist storage, new DMVs and DMFs, and additional functionality not available in prior releases of SQL Server.

Inverted Index

An index structure that stores mapping information from content, such as tokens in documents or text, to their locations. In terms of iFTS, the full-text index is stored as an inverted index that stores mappings from tokens to the rows that contain them. See also *full-text index*.

Jaccard Coefficient

The Jaccard Coefficient is used to calculate rankings for weighted CONTAINS searches in iFTS. See also *CONTAINS predicate, weighted search.*

LOB

LOB is an acronym for large object data. SQL Server can store and manage large object data (such as documents and images) up to 2.1GB in size. LOB data can be further divided into BLOB, CLOB, or NCLOB data. See also *BLOB, CLOB, NCLOB.*

Longest Common Substring

The longest common substring (LCS) algorithm is a fuzzy search algorithm that returns all characters that two strings have in common, where order is preserved. The substrings can have intermediate characters that aren't part of the common substrings.

N-Gram

The n-gram string matching algorithm is an approximate search algorithm. The n-gram algorithm divides given words into sequences of characters of equal length known as n-grams. It then tries to determine the number of exact n-grams that the words have in common. An n-gram can be of any length, but they're generally of length 3 or 4 (trigrams and quadgrams).

NCLOB

NCLOB is an acronym for *national character large object data.* NCLOB data consists of large national character (Unicode) text documents. See also *LOB, BLOB, CLOB.*

Noise Words

Noise words were used in previous versions of SQL Server to eliminate extraneous, unhelpful words from full-text searches. Stopwords replace noise words in SQL Server 2008. See also *stopwords.*

NYSIIS

NYSIIS, the New York State Identification and Intelligence System, was introduced in 1970 as an improved version of the Soundex phonetic algorithm. See also *Soundex.*

Occurrence

SQL Server's full-text indexes store the relative offsets of instances of words. The first occurrence of a given word in a document is occurrence 1, the next is occurrence 2, and so on.

Okapi BM25

The Okapi BM25 method is an alternate search results ranking method used by iFTS to rank FREETEXT searches. See also *FREETEXT predicate.*

Phonetic Search

Phonetic search is a method of searching for words that sound similar to one another.

Phrase Search

Phrases are multiword tokens that are considered as a single atomic unit for purposes of search.

Population

Population is the process of tokenizing documents and textual data and filling full-text indexes with words returned by the word breaker component. See also *word breaker*.

Prefix Search

A prefix search is one in which a word has the wildcard * character at the end. Prefix searches will locate words that begin with the given prefix.

Protocol Handler

The protocol handler is an application-specific component that pulls data from memory using the gatherer and coordinates full-text index filtering and population.

Proximity Search

Proximity searching is the process of searching for words that are close to one another, or within a specified number of words or characters from one another. The SQL Server CONTAINS predicate supports proximity searching. See also *CONTAINS predicate*.

Replacement Set

Replacement sets are defined in iFTS thesaurus files to perform wholesale replacement of specific search terms with other words or terms. See also *expansion set*.

Simple Term

A simple term is a simple word or phrase to be used in full-text search.

Soundex

Soundex is a 90-year-old algorithm for indexing names by sound. In Soundex, a name is converted to a four-character code that begins with an alphabetic character and includes three additional numeric digits. See also *NYSIIS*.

SQL Server Process

The SQL Server process (sqlserver.exe) is the process that hosts the SQL Server query engine and the full-text query engine. Note that in versions of SQL Server prior to SQL Server 2008, the full-text query engine was separated from the SQL Server process.

Stoplists

Stoplists are lists of stopwords stored in SQL Server. Stoplists can be associated with full-text indexes in SQL Server. See also *stopwords*.

Stopwords

Stopwords are tokens that are specifically considered useless for terms of full-text search. Stopwords are generally words that occur frequently in a given language and don't add value during a search of textual data. SQL Server includes several default system-defined stopwords including *and, the,* and *an,* among others. See also *stoplists, noise words.*

Ternary Search Tree

The ternary search tree is a three-way data structure that combines the speed and efficiency of digital search tries and binary search trees. Ternary search trees are useful for performing near neighbor approximate searches.

Thesaurus

SQL Server iFTS supports an XML thesaurus containing replacement and expansion sets to increase the breadth of full-text searches for specified words. See also *expansion sets, replacement sets.*

Token

Tokens are the atomic sequences of characters returned by the word breaker component as it applies language-specific word-breaking rules to textual data. See also *word breaker.*

Type Column

To index BLOB data, iFTS requires that you specify a type column containing a document extension that indicates the type of content contained in the binary data. A type column might include entries such as .doc for a Word document or .xml for an XML document. The value in the type column determines which filter iFTS uses to index the given document. See also *BLOB.*

Weighted Search

A weighted search is one in which some search terms are assigned greater importance than others. In iFTS, you can perform weighted searches with the CONTAINS predicate. See also *CONTAINS predicate.*

Word

See *token.*

Word Breaker

SQL Server uses components known as word breakers to tokenize textual data based on language-specific rules. See also *word stemmer.*

Word Stemmer

SQL Server uses word stemmer components to generate inflectional forms of the words tokenized by word breakers. See also *word breaker.*

APPENDIX B

■■■

iFTS_Books Database

The key, the whole key, and nothing but the key, so help me Codd.

—Mnemonic Summary of Codd's First Three Normal Forms (Anonymous)

While this book was still in the early planning stages, the authors set about investigating how we could best deliver meaningful and easy-to-use code samples. We found out pretty quickly that the official Microsoft AdventureWorks 2008 sample database wasn't up to the task. While AdventureWorks has been completely redesigned for the 2008 release, it doesn't have enough variety and quantity of information to really show off the power and improved functionality of iFTS.

Instead of making extensive modifications to the AdventureWorks database, we decided to create a sample database that would better suit our needs and show off the full range of iFTS functionality. We decided to model only a couple of logical entities in this database—namely, books and book contributors (authors, editors, illustrators, and so on). The normalized physical model of the iFTS_Books sample database is shown in Figure B-1.

The database itself is populated with data from a variety of sources, including public domain books in various forms and information about authors and related topics from Wikipedia (available under terms of the GNU Free Documentation License). This raw data provided us with a widely varied multilingual set of texts to index and query using iFTS.

In addition, we've included sample data to demonstrate non-iFTS functionality, such as the phonetic search functions in Chapter 11. This data comes in the form of common surnames from the U.S. Census Bureau's 1990 census data and the "unofficial" *12Dicts* dictionary. These additional samples are installed separately as described in the "Installing the Phonetic Samples" section of this chapter.

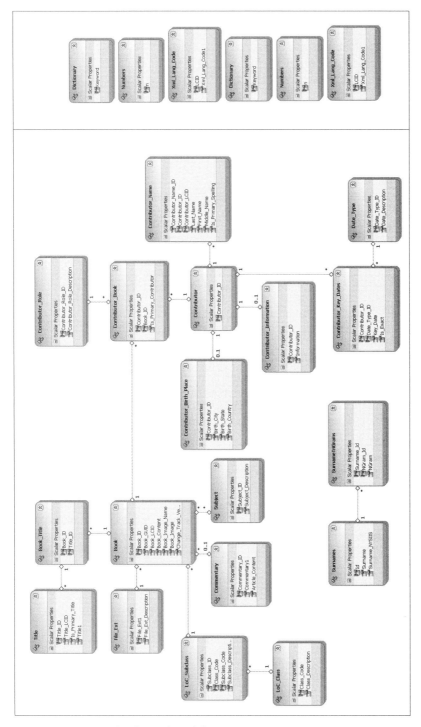

Figure B-1. *iFTS_Books physical model*

Installing the Sample Database

We've attempted to make the installation of the iFTS_Books sample database as simple as possible. To keep the download size manageable, we decided to utilize T-SQL installation scripts to perform the installation. All sample code and iFTS_Books installation scripts are available as a single Zip file download from www.apress.com/book/sourcecode. The installation scripts are located in the \Sample Database subdirectory of the Zip file. To install the iFTS_Books sample database, follow these steps:

1. Download the sample code for this book from the www.apress.com web site.

2. Unzip the contents to your local hard drive.

3. Open the Command Prompt window and change the current directory to the \Sample Database subdirectory. As an example, if you unzip the file to the C:\Sample Code directory on your hard drive, you would change to the C:\Sample Code\Sample Database subdirectory in this step.

4. Run the setup.bat batch file from the command prompt. This batch file takes one or three parameters. The first parameter is the server name. If you're using Windows Integrated security to connect to your SQL Server, this is all that's necessary. If, however, you're using SQL Authentication, you'll need to add two more parameters—a user name and password to log into SQL Server. Figure B-2 shows how to call setup.bat with (local) specified as the server name to install on the local server.

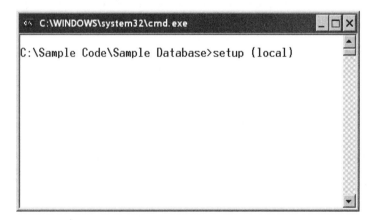

Figure B-2. *Installing the iFTS_Books sample database to the local instance of SQL Server*

5. The setup.bat batch file looks for a folder on your hard drive named C:\iFTS_Books. If the directory doesn't exist, it is created (you can manually modify the scripts to change the installation location if you choose).

6. Setup.bat calls the sqlcmd command-line utility to execute T-SQL scripts that create the iFTS_Books sample database, create and populate tables, define and populate full-text indexes, and create other database objects.

Once the sample database has been installed, you can execute the sample code we've included in this book.

Installing the Phonetic Samples

The iFTS_Books sample database also comes with the non-iFTS phonetic algorithm samples that we described in this book. These are implemented using a combination of SQL CLR assemblies and T-SQL functions. Assuming you've already downloaded and unzipped the sample code files to your hard drive, follow these steps to install the phonetic algorithm samples:

1. Install the iFTS_Books database as discussed in the previous section.

2. Open the Command Prompt window and change the current directory to the \Phonetics subdirectory. For example, if you unzipped to the C:\Sample Code directory, you would change the current directory to C:\Sample Code\Phonetics.

3. Run the setup.bat batch file from the command prompt. This batch file also accepts one parameter (server name) for Windows Integrated security and three parameters (server name, user name, password) for SQL Authentication.

4. The setup.bat batch file uses the sqlcmd command-line utility to execute the appropriate T-SQL installation scripts. These scripts create and load tables, register SQL CLR assemblies, and create T-SQL and SQL CLR user-defined functions.

After the phonetic samples are installed, you can execute the phonetic code samples from Chapter 11.

Sample Code

In addition to the sample databases, we've included sample utilities throughout the book that can utilize the iFTS_Books sample database and the phonetic algorithms demonstrated. This source code is primarily written in T-SQL and .NET using C#.

There are some examples, however, that we created in other languages where appropriate. For instance, the iFTS filter sample from Chapter 10 was written in unmanaged C++, per Microsoft's recommendations. All non-SQL code samples provided were created as Visual Studio 2008 solutions. You can open, compile, and execute the sample code using Visual Studio 2008.

■■■■

Vector-Space Searches

Space is big. You just won't believe how vastly, hugely, mind-bogglingly big it is. I mean,
you may think it's a long way down the road to the drug store, but that's just peanuts to
space.

—Douglas Adams, *The Hitchhiker's Guide to the Galaxy*

Vector-space is an algebraic algorithm for representing text documents as vectors. Vector-space
is used by iFTS to perform weighted searches using the ISABOUT operator. We describe weighted
searches in Chapter 3. In this appendix, we'll describe vector-space and how iFTS utilizes it.
This information is more detailed and technical, dealing with the inner workings of vector-space
search systems, which is why we decided to separate it from the general discussion of weighted
vector-space searches in iFTS.

Documents As Vectors

As we described in previous chapters, when a document is indexed by iFTS, each word is stored
in an inverted index. The index contains the document ID, word, and relative position in the
document where the word occurs. Consider a document containing the following quote from
the Roman poet Virgil:

Fortune favors the bold.

The word breaker and filter generate the token stream and remove stopwords, resulting in
the tokens shown in Figure C-1.

Tokens
fortune
favors
bold

Figure C-1. *Word breaker–generated token stream for Virgil quote*

If we then indexed a second document containing the following Francis Bacon quote, removing stopwords, we would get the tokens shown in Figure C-2:

Behind every great fortune there is a crime.

Tokens
behind
every
great
fortune
crime

Figure C-2. *Word breaker–generated token stream for Francis Bacon quote*

Now that we've tokenized the source documents, the user can apply a search phrase. In this case, we'll use the simple search phrase *bold fortune*. After tokenization, the documents and search phrase are assigned a value of 1 for each token from the stream that they contain, and a value of 0 for each token that they don't contain, as shown in Figure C-3.

Tokens	Virgil Quote	Bacon Quote	Search Phase
behind	0	1	0
bold	1	0	1
crime	0	1	0
every	0	1	0
fortune	1	1	1
favors	1	0	0
great	0	1	0

Figure C-3. *Tokens after ID assignment*

By assigning zeroes and ones to the tokens in the documents and search phrase, we're now representing the text as single-row matrices, or vectors. The vectors are represented as follows:

Fortune favors the bold. ➤ [0 1 0 0 1 1 0]

Behind every great fortune there is a crime. ➤ [1 0 1 1 1 0 1]

bold fortune ➤ [0 1 0 0 1 0 0]

Once the documents and search phrase are converted to their vector equivalents, the differences between the documents can be calculated using the cosines between the vectors, or another calculation of distance between vectors. The cosine distance between vectors can be easily calculated using a simple dot product calculation. The formula is shown in Figure C-4.

$$\cos\theta = \frac{\vec{V_1} \cdot \vec{V_2}}{|V_1|\,|V_2|}$$

Figure C-4. *Dot product calculation*

The mechanics of the dot product calculation are described in the "Dot Product Calculation" sidebar in this section, and more specifics on matrix math and dot product calculations are available at `http://en.wikipedia.org/wiki/Dot_product`. The essential point to take away is that the cosine derived via the dot product calculation gives you a distance measure between your two documents.

By calculating the dot product of the matrices, you're essentially converting them to Euclidean space, and you can plot them in two or three dimensions. Figure C-5 is a representation of vectors plotted in three-dimensional Euclidean space. The black arrows represent the document and search phrase vectors, and the curved white arrows represent the distance between vectors.

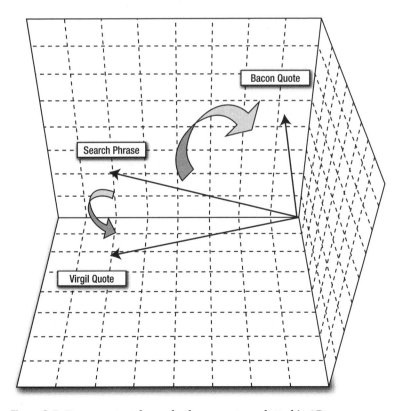

Figure C-5. *Document and search phrase vectors plotted in 3D space*

DOT PRODUCT CALCULATION

The dot product is defined by the relationship between the length and angle of two matrices. Using the formula shown previously in Figure C-4, you can easily calculate the cosine of the angle between two documents that have been converted to matrix representations. This gives you a basic measure of the difference, or distance, between the two documents. The dot product formula begins with a simple matrix multiplication. Assuming V_1 is the matrix that represents the text *Fortune favors the bold*, and V_2 is the matrix for the search phrase *bold fortune*, the formula begins by calculating the divisor, $\vec{V_1} \cdot \vec{V_2}$, as shown:

$$[0\ 1\ 0\ 0\ 1\ 1\ 0] \begin{bmatrix} 0 \\ 1 \\ 0 \\ 0 \\ 1 \\ 0 \\ 0 \end{bmatrix} = 2$$

The bottom dividend consists of the magnitude of V_1 multiplied by the magnitude of V_2, represented as $|V_1|\ |V_2|$. The magnitude of each matrix is calculated by taking the square root of the sum of all the elements in the matrix squared. The following are the magnitude calculations for the previously multiplied vectors:

$$\sqrt{0^2 + 1^2 + 0^2 + 0^2 + 1^2 + 1^2 + 0^2} = \sqrt{3}$$

$$\sqrt{0^2 + 1^2 + 0^2 + 0^2 + 1^2 + 0^2 + 0^2} = \sqrt{2}$$

In the final calculation, you simply divide the result of the matrix multiplication by the product of the two magnitudes. This gives you the cosine between the two matrices. Plugging the values we calculated earlier into the dot product formula, we get the following final result:

$$\cos\theta = \frac{2}{\sqrt{2}\ \sqrt{3}} = 0.816496580927726$$

The final result is the cosine between the two text matrices. By calculating the cosine between other document matrices and the search phrase matrix, you can determine the relative similarity of the documents to the search phrase. Of course, you don't have to perform these types of calculations in vector space, as SQL Server does this for you under the covers. SQL Server actually uses other more modernized calculations that have been shown to give better results than these simple dot product calculations, but the basic idea is the same.

As Figure C-5 indicates, the Virgil quote is closer to the search phrase than the Bacon quote. In the example, the search phrase shares two words in common with the Virgil quote, and has only one word in common with the Bacon quote.

Essentially you can measure the length of the shadow cast by the document vector on the search vector, taking the point of reference as your search vector. This is the functional equivalent of doing a dot product (or inner product) on the search argument, a document collection matrix.

In SQL Server, the older cosine method has been updated to use modern calculations, since the cosine method doesn't consider several factors, such as the frequency of word occurrence in the document. Information retrieval scientists have determined that accounting for additional factors, such as the ratio of the frequency of each term in the document versus the frequency of the term in the entire document collection and document length, results in better quality results when calculating the similarity of document vectors,. For instance, a word that is rare in a document collection but common in a given document should be weighted higher than words that occur frequently throughout the document collection. Additionally, the normalized length of documents should be considered when calculating similarity.

Once you have a document vector representation of a given document, it's relatively easy to compare this document vector to other document vectors with similar distributions of words. For instance, a document vector for an essay on Eastern Canadian agriculture would look nothing like a document vector for a white paper on SQL Server installation procedures. This is because they would use completely different sets of words. However, a document vector for a white paper on upgrading SQL Server 7 to SQL 2000 would have a lot in common with the document vector for a white paper on installation procedures for SQL Server 2005. They would use a lot of the same words and would result in a much closer match than the documents in the previous example.

Informational retrieval researchers have realized this and are doing research into grouping document vectors with similar word distributions together. They know that if your search vector is close to another document vector (in other words, the search vector's pattern word distribution is similar to the document vector's pattern), other document vectors that group closely to a matching document vector probably contain subject matter that the searcher is interested in. This topic is called *latent semantic indexing*, and such groups of document vectors or document collections are one strategy for solving the problem of polysemy and synonymy, which we discussed in Chapter 1. This is based on the fact that there will be similarities in the semantics used in documents pertaining to the same subjects. In other words, documents that are similar will have latent semantic similarities to them. (*Semantics* is the study of meaning in language.)

While vector-space search functionality is often used, it does come under criticism from some corners. The vector-space model has no formal basis in scientific theory, and is instead based on informal observations and experience. While there are other formalized search models based on probability theory, they don't yield significantly better results than the vector-space model.

Index

You Need the Companion eBook

Your purchase of this book entitles you to buy the companion PDF-version eBook for only $10. Take the weightless companion with you anywhere.

We believe this Apress title will prove so indispensable that you'll want to carry it with you everywhere, which is why we are offering the companion eBook (in PDF format) for $10 to customers who purchase this book now. Convenient and fully searchable, the PDF version of any content-rich, page-heavy Apress book makes a valuable addition to your programming library. You can easily find and copy code — or perform examples by quickly toggling between instructions and the application. Even simultaneously tackling a donut, diet soda, and complex code becomes simplified with hands-free eBooks!

Once you purchase your book, getting the $10 companion eBook is simple:

❶ Visit **www.apress.com/promo/tendollars/**.

❷ Complete a basic registration form to receive a randomly generated question about this title.

❸ Answer the question correctly in 60 seconds, and you will receive a promotional code to redeem for the $10.00 eBook.

THE EXPERT'S VOICE™

2855 TELEGRAPH AVENUE | SUITE 600 | BERKELEY, CA 94705

Offer valid through 06/08/09.